HOLLYWOOD'S ANCIENT WORLDS

Hollywood's Ancient Worlds

Jeffrey Richards

continuum

Continuum UK, The Tower Building, 11 York Road, London SE1 7NX
Continuum US, 80 Maiden Lane, Suite 704, New York, NY 10038

www.continuumbooks.com

First published 2008

British Library Cataloguing-in-Publication Data
A catalogue record for this book is available from the British Library.

ISBN 978 1 84725 007 0

Typeset by Pindar NZ (Egan Reid), Auckland, New Zealand
Printed and bound by MPG Books Ltd, Cornwall, Great Britain

Contents

Illustrations

For
James Chapman
Mark Glancy
Sue Harper

Foreword

In this book I have sought to demonstrate the continuity between the painting and drama of the nineteenth century both in Britain and the United States and the emergence and development of the Ancient World epic in Hollywood. To this end, I have charted the production and reception by audience and critics of the great epics. I have also argued that Ancient World epics tell us as much about the preoccupations and values of the period in which they were made as about the period in which they were set. In pursuit of these themes, I have examined every major epic from *Intolerance* (1916) to *Rome* (2005–6). I have omitted the comedies such as *Roman Scandals, A Funny Thing Happened on the Way to the Forum, Carry on Cleo, The Life of Brian* and *Up Pompeii*. This is partly to accommodate a strictly limited word count, but also partly because as someone who is temperamentally melancholic, I respond more productively to tragedy than to comedy.

I have incurred many debts in the writing of this book and I would like to thank the following for help and advice of various kinds: Stephen Wildman, David Shotter, Peter Yeandle, Anselm Heinrich, Kate Newey, Allen Eyles, Mark Glancy, Martin Shephard, Joel Hockey, Bernard Hrusa Marlow and Sir Christopher Frayling. I am permanently indebted to the admirable and ever-helpful staff of the British Film Institute Library, the British Library and Lancaster University Library. I am grateful for the word-processing skills of Linda Persson and June Rye. The stills reproduced in this book are included for the purposes of critical analysis. The book is dedicated to three of Britain's finest film historians, James Chapman, Mark Glancy and Sue Harper, in token of many years of valued friendship, encouragement and support. Stills appear by courtesy of the Kobal collection and the author's own collection. I am grateful to Dave Cradduck for compiling the index.

Jeffrey Richards

The Ancient World: the Nineteenth-Century Context

The astonishing worldwide success of Ridley Scott's Roman epic *Gladiator* in 2000 single-handedly revived a cinematic genre that had been moribund for 35 years. It sent film producers scampering back to the stories that had inspired the previous cycle of Ancient World epics in the 1950s and early 1960s and new versions of the tales of Troy, Thermopylae, Alexander the Great and Julius Caesar duly appeared.

The very last thing that *Gladiator* was about was actual Roman history. Finding all her protests about inaccuracy ignored, historical adviser Kathleen Coleman, Professor of Latin at Harvard University, asked for her name to be removed from the credits.[1] Firstly, *Gladiator* was about Hollywood and secondly, it was about contemporary America. It triumphantly revived the epic film genre by a process of splicing together the narratives of one of the most successful entries in the earlier Hollywood Ancient World cycle (*Spartacus*) and one of the least successful (*The Fall of the Roman Empire*). It highlighted the action, spectacle and romance that had been features of the successful epics. But at the same time the film gave the events a contemporary resonance by constructing them as an explicit commentary on Clintonian America. For, as Gore Vidal has never tired of reminding his countrymen, America is now an empire and beset by the problems all empires face. So what better way of flagging up these problems than a revival of that most imperial of film genres: the Roman epic.

It is a truism that historical films are always about the time in which they are made and never about the time in which they are set. They cannot represent history accurately as they invariably play fast and loose with characters and events to meet the constraints of time, the demands of drama and the expectations of audiences. This is perhaps why all epic film-makers lay such great stress on the visual authenticity of costumes, props and settings and put so much effort and expense into background research. The visual authenticity is seen to make up for the factual inaccuracies. However, P.M. Pasinetti, hired as technical adviser on the 1953 film *Julius Caesar*, remained unconvinced:

Why are experts hired? One version is that the producers want to feel 'protected': that the historical allusion, the armament detail, the duellist's motion, or whatever, will bear the stamp of specialized approval. This attitude is largely fictitious, unrelated to actuality; for the producer knows very well that his historical reconstruction is not going to be exact and 'scholarly' and, which is more important, there is no reason why it should be so. A film is being made, not a contribution to a journal; the requirements are those of the film as a coherent artistic whole. Therefore also, in order to be of any use at all, the technical adviser should keep thinking that he is, in however minor, indirect, and peripheral a way, contributing to the making of a film.[2]

Historical adviser Robin Lane-Fox defended Oliver Stone's *Alexander* (2004) in similar terms:

Epic films about history have been much discussed for showing a 'Past Imperfect', but this neat label is the wrong one to apply. 'Perfect history' does not exist, nor was it ever Oliver's aim. His aim was an intense film-drama, not a documentary, and one source of this intensity is historical reference wherever he felt it appropriate [...] As a result, history is the film-drama's springboard and gives it force. But fiction is built into it too because characters have to speak lines for which there is no evidence [...] So, a script-writer has to invent, and Oliver's script is a historical fiction. But it is a fiction exceptionally rooted in history, with strong interpretations of the person whom it represents.[3]

J. Lesley Fitton of the British Museum who advised the production of *Troy* on details of life in the Ancient World recorded:

I believed that the film was worthy of support by historians and archaeologists because it aimed to bring the story of Troy to new audiences around the world. Moreover, it rapidly became clear that Wolfgang Petersen and his team were taking an extremely thoughtful view of the subject matter [...] Certainly reservations can be expressed about the liberties taken with the story toward the end of the film, when the fates of certain characters were radically different from what the ancient tradition tells us. Of course one could argue that the ancient world knew variants of traditional stories, but these were not motivated by what seemed in the film to be a very Hollywood need for the evil to be punished and the good to prosper.[4]

But *Gladiator* and the new epic cycle it initiated did not exist in a vacuum. Visually and dramatically it had deep roots and these stretched back to the nineteenth century, where painting and the stage together created a vision of the Ancient World that was handed on intact to the new medium of cinema.

Both Britain and the United States were obsessed with the Ancient World in the nineteenth century. For Victorians on both sides of the Atlantic history held the key to understanding the present and the eternal truths about human nature. The Ancient World could be used to represent an escape from an increasingly urbanized and industrialized present to an idealized golden age. It could constitute a vehicle to critique the present. It fulfilled a continuing nineteenth-century taste for the exotic, for spectacle and for education. It could be used to explore the roots of national, communal, individual and gender identity. As William Vance has written:

> From Thomas Jefferson and John Adams down through [...] Henry James and Henry Adams, ancient Rome [...] was for Americans a place of unrivalled cultural significance. The heroes of the Roman Republic – Cincinnatus, Cicero, Cato the Younger – were American heroes because they were champions of liberty, and liberty was the meaning of America. But in the century following (William Dean) Howells' first visit (in 1864), his deafness to the 'vocal glory' of Roman ruins [...] became typical. Instead of being the historical and inspirational source of liberty and law, ancient Rome became at best a setting for costume pageantry and didactic Christian melodrama in novels and films.[5]

The American Founding Fathers consciously saw themselves as the successors of the heroes of the Republic and modelled their institutions, their buildings and their rhetoric on those of Ancient Rome. American statesmen such as Washington, Jackson and Calhoun were depicted wearing togas. One of the most popular plays on the early American stage was the Englishman Joseph Addison's play *Cato* (1713) which eulogized one of the greatest heroes of the Republic. Plays by American authors adopted Addison's approach and attitude. Republican heroes inspired, for instance, John Howard Payne's *Brutus or the Fall of Tarquin* (1818), and Jonas B. Phillips' *Camillus or the Self-Exiled Patriot* (1833). But the most celebrated nineteenth-century Ancient World drama was Robert Montgomery Bird's *The Gladiator* (1831), which retained its popularity in America for 70 years. It told the story of the rebel gladiator Spartacus and his revolt against Rome. In this context, Rome was seen as the analogue of the British Empire, and Spartacus the counterpart of the American colonists whose rebellion ended imperial rule. The role became particularly associated with the American actor Edwin Forrest and when he played it at Drury Lane in 1836, *John Bull* (20 November 1836) reported: 'his fine manly form, great physical force and exceeding energy, were in admirable keeping with our preconceived notions of a Gladiator [...] At times we forgot the actor and fancied that one of the glorious statues of ancient Greece had been suddenly called into life and summoned to the arena'.

The classical myths, suitably sanitized, were retold for American children by writers such as Nathaniel Hawthorne (*The Wonder Book*, 1851; *Tanglewood Tales*, 1853) and Thomas Bulfinch (*The Age of Fable*, 1855). They provided inspiration for painters and sculptors. Henry Peters Gray painted *Proserpine and Bacchus*, *The Judgement of Paris* and *Cupid Begging His Arrows* and William Page painted *Cupid and Psyche* and *Venus guiding Aeneas and the Trojans to the Latin Shore*. William Wetmore Story wrote a series of dramatic monologues as delivered by Phidias, Praxiteles, Marcus Aurelius, Cleopatra, Mark Antony and Cassandra, a play, *Nero*, and sculptures of Cleopatra, Medea, Salome, Helen, Alcestis, Clytemnestra, Judith, Electra and Semiramis.

The two ancient cultures which appealed most to Victorian Britain were Greece and Rome. Antiquity, particularly Ancient Greece, with its classical architecture characterized by rational, balanced and geometric designs, the invention of democracy, a philosophy based on ethics and reason and an aesthetic that celebrated perfect beauty, inspired the apostles and exponents of the eighteenth-century Enlightenment.

The cult of Hellenism was central to the intellectual life of Victorian Britain. Writers and thinkers selected from the Greek heritage those elements which most closely conformed to the preoccupations of the age, essentially celebrating the Ancient Greeks as proto-Victorians. What the Victorians highlighted was the Greeks' development of democracy and the rule of law, at a time when democracy was being extended in Britain, and the Greek appreciation of beauty and celebration of heroism as a contrast to the philistinism and Nonconformist Puritanism associated with the bourgeoisie. They rejoiced in the philosophical humanism which they derived from a study of Plato, Aristotle and Socrates and from which they derived intellectual justification for collective social responsibility, individual self-sacrifice, devotion to duty and enlightened paternalism which was seen as a corrective to the materialism and selfishness associated with industrial capitalism. Ancient Greece, in particular Periclean Athens, was idealized and held up as a model of dignity, decency, restraint, moderation, harmony, balance, reason and purity. Homer was studied as a secular equivalent of the Bible. The *Iliad* and the *Odyssey* were seen in particular as teaching chivalry, nobility, patriotism, and moral and physical strength as characteristics for which to strive. So the language, literature, history and ideas of the Ancient Greeks were taught to the British elite at school and at university to fit them to cope with the modern world.[6]

If Ancient Greece appealed to the intellectuals and artists of Victorian Britain, Ancient Rome appealed to its administrators and empire-builders. For Britain in the second half of the nineteenth century, already master of the mightiest empire the world had ever seen, the reference point for comparison, for guidance, for lessons was the Roman Empire. Anthony Trollope observed in 1870 that Rome and the Roman Empire were part of modern history and modern political life in a way that Greece could never be.[7] Where Rome had the *Pax Romana*, Britain had the *Pax Britannica* with much the same remit. Britain referred to its imperial viceroys as proconsuls. The architecture of the Empire tended to favour the classical style in its public buildings. The utterances of Britain's imperial statesmen were steeped in classical allusion, most famously when in a debate about the manhandling of a British subject Don Pacifico, Lord Palmerston proclaimed as a fundamental of British policy, the protection at all costs of British subjects with the ringing statement 'Civis Romanus sum'. Disraeli, defining his policy, declared it to be *imperium et libertas*, Empire and Freedom. The British admired the Romans for their stoicism, their courage, their administration and their legal system, their concept of citizenship, their straight roads, bridges and aqueducts, their common currency and common language. In Britain Hadrian's Wall, the Roman roads, and the archaeological remains at Bath, Colchester and St Albans were a permanent reminder of Roman architectural achievements. The regular comparisons between the British and Roman Empires culminated in detailed comparative studies: Lord Cromer's *Ancient and Modern Imperialism* (1910) – significantly Cromer was both Britain's proconsul in Egypt and later President of the Classical Association – Sir Charles Lucas' *Greater Rome and Greater Britain* (1912) and Sir James Bryce's *The Ancient Roman Empire and the British Empire in India* (1914). Just as the prospective elite of the Empire were taught Greek, they were also taught Latin and provided with inspiring examples of dedication, duty and service from Roman history, notably in Lord Macaulay's *Lays of Ancient Rome* (1842), a popular poetic retelling of four episodes from Roman history, regularly learned by heart by Victorian schoolboys of all classes. The Roman poets Lucretius, Catullus, Virgil and Horace were as much a part of nineteenth-century culture as were the Greek poets and philosophers.[8]

However, Britain did not just look to Rome for laudatory parallels; it looked to Rome also for lessons about what destroys empires and this was a source of much reflection, thought and argument. A classic example of this is to be found in *The Roman and the Teuton*, a series of inaugural lectures given by the Reverend Charles Kingsley on his appointment as Regius Professor of Modern History at Cambridge and published in 1864. He begins by painting a lurid picture of the Roman Empire in the later fourth century, an empire under the absolute rule of an emperor, whose palace is 'a sink of corruption', where the Senate only exists to carry out the orders of the tyrant, where the free middle classes have either disappeared or linger on, 'too proud to labour, fed on government bounty, and amused by government spectacles', where the arts and science have died, where everything is done by an army of slaves supplied by a cruel and degrading slave trade and where the normal condition of the Empire is one of 'revolt, civil war, invasion'. 'And yet', says Kingsley, 'they called themselves Christians – to whom it has been said "Be not deceived, God is not mocked. For these things cometh the wrath of God on the children of disobedience"'. The wrath did come and the Empire fell. So the absence of true spirituality, of real Christianity, is the root cause of the fall of the Roman Empire. This picture, he warned, could be repeated in the British Empire 'if we are not careful'.[9]

For Kingsley the key factors in Rome's decline, and the ones to be avoided by the British Empire if it was to escape the same fate, were the absence of parliamentary democracy and a responsible aristocracy, the existence of slavery, the decay of public spirit, civic virtue and morality, the dominance of sensuality, the employment of mercenaries, the decline of racial purity, and the absence of genuine Christianity. For Kingsley, as for many other commentators (from Ruskin to Kipling), the last of these was the most significant. In the nineteenth century, which saw a major revival in Britain of both Evangelicalism and Catholicism, the role of Christianity in the Roman Empire became a major subject of debate.

Major religious polemicists took to the novel to work out their debates about the nature of the faith and, writing as they were during the heyday of the British Empire, they often set their debates during the Roman Empire. Of whatever persuasion, they were as one in the belief that the most potent force to deploy against the paganism, slavery, unrestrained sensuality and political despotism of the Empire was Christianity.

The fashion for Roman novels essentially began with Bulwer-Lytton's *The Last Days of Pompeii* (1834) and climaxed with General Lew Wallace's *Ben-Hur* (1880) and Henryk Sienkiewicz's *Quo Vadis* (1896), novels by an Englishman, an American and a Pole respectively, but all hugely popular bestsellers worldwide, endlessly reprinted, translated and adapted for and performed on the stage and, during the twentieth century, in the cinema. An estimated 200 novels on Roman life were written by British and American authors between the 1820s and the First World War.[10] They were characterized by that mixture of 'costume pageantry and didactic Christian melodrama' identified by William Vance. In most of these novels, Christianity was seen as the answer to the tyranny and corruption of a pagan empire. In general terms, it was possible to argue that without a genuinely felt and practised Christianity, empire will fail. For Christianity is seen here to be synonymous with democracy, humanity and public virtue. But it was on the question of what kind of Christianity – Catholic or Protestant – that the nineteenth-century novelists crossed swords. Charles Kingsley published his novel *Hypatia* in 1853. It recounted the religious clashes in fifth-century Alexandria, highlighting the theological disputes and divisions weakening the Empire. Kingsley lays the blame on hysterical, celibate, neurotic and fanatical monks, who are his analogue of the Catholics, and of scheming politico bishops in a theocratic state – and his Bishop Cyril of Alexandria is a thinly disguised picture of Cardinal Wiseman, leader of the English Catholics. His heroes, the monk Philammon and the Jew Raphael Aben-Ezra, are converted to his preferred model of Christianity, a simple proto-Protestant Christianity, which Kingsley calls 'the only real democratic creed'. Kingsley was one of the pioneers of 'muscular Christianity', was strongly opposed to priestly elitism, celibacy and popery and an enthusiastic advocate of marriage. As a direct response to Kingsley's novel both Cardinal Wiseman and John Henry Newman, later himself a Cardinal, also wrote extremely influential novels. Wiseman's *Fabiola* was published in 1854 and Newman's *Callista* in 1855. The former, set in Rome in 302 and the latter in North Africa in 250, commemorate the Christian martyrs of the Roman persecutions of those periods, but in particular write up, celebrate and affirm Catholic beliefs and practices, such as the cult of the saints and the Papal hierarchy. Kingsley,

Newman and Wiseman all see the Roman Empire as synonymous with decay, despotism and sensuality and see Christianity as its salvation, but as the cure for sensuality, Newman and Wiseman prescribe celibacy and Kingsley monogamous marriage. Where Newman and Wiseman prescribe a strong hierarchical Catholic church, Kingsley argues for proto-Protestant individualism. These are only three of a torrent of novels dealing with the conflict of Christianity and Empire in ancient Rome. This conflict and its working out in Christianity's favour made these novels as appealing to the American audience as to the British.[11]

Then towards the end of the century other concerns arose to parallel the debate about spirituality in the Empire. There was anxiety about manpower shortage and the degeneration of the race when the Boer War revealed a third of all recruits to be physically unfit to serve, and there was panic about the decadent movement and in particular the celebrity of Oscar Wilde and Wildeanism. This inspired disapproving descriptions of sensuality in the novels of the time linked to the gospel of Wildeanism and visually half-horrified, half-fascinated paintings such as Alma-Tadema's *The Roses of Heliogabalus* (1888) in which the debauched emperor Heliogabalus and his decadent companions watch with world-weary amusement while his dinner guests are smothered to death beneath a torrent of rose petals released from a canopy above them.

There was a widespread sense of crisis in intellectual and elite circles, a crisis which produced such works as Elliot Mills' bestselling work of 'future history', *The Decline and Fall of the British Empire* (1905) which attributed the decline to 'town life, demoralizing luxury, physical inertia, gradual decline in physique and health and lack of confidence in the imperial mission'.[12] Sir Robert Baden-Powell founded the Boy Scouts partly to prevent the British Empire suffering the same decline as the Roman, a decline he attributed in *Scouting for Boys* (1908) to the abandonment of soldiering, manliness and patriotism.

The characteristics of the Ancient World novel were essentially set by its progenitor, Edward Bulwer-Lytton, later the first Lord Lytton, novelist, poet and statesman, in his phenomenally successful *The Last Days of Pompeii*, which was the product of visits to the ruined city in 1832–3. Pompeii, an otherwise unremarkable Roman provincial town, was made immortal by its destruction along with neighbouring Herculaneum in AD 79 by an eruption of Mount Vesuvius and its rediscovery by archaeologists seventeen centuries later.

It was the chance discovery in 1711 of stone fragments by a peasant digging a well that led to systematic excavations on the site of Herculaneum by the kings of the Two Sicilies. The much richer neighbouring site of Pompeii was only identified in 1763 and it was not until 1863 that systematic, scientific excavation began there with the appointment of trained archaeologist Giuseppe Fiorelli as Director of the Museum and Excavations. But long before this the ruins of Pompeii and Herculaneum had become a regular port of call for travellers on the

Grand Tour. Goethe, Dickens, Dumas and Mark Twain visited them. But the most productive visit was that of Bulwer-Lytton; for it directly inspired his best-selling novel *The Last Days of Pompeii*.

Lytton's fictional plot centred on Glaucus, an Athenian resident of Pompeii, and his love for the beautiful Ione. But Ione is also loved by her guardian, Arbaces, the High Priest of Isis. Arbaces murders Ione's brother, Apaecides, a priest of Isis who has converted to Christianity, and frames Glaucus for the murder. Glaucus is condemned to the arena but as he is facing the lions, another priest Calenus reveals that he witnessed the murder and Glaucus is innocent. At this point, Vesuvius erupts. Various characters, among them Arbaces and Calenus, are killed. But Glaucus and Ione are saved by the blind slave girl Nydia, who loves Glaucus. She leads them safely through the smoke and the darkness to a ship which carries them to safety. Having selflessly united the lovers, Nydia drowns herself in the sea. Glaucus and Ione marry and settle in Athens.

The action of the novel takes place amid precisely described locations, uncovered by archaeologists: the Pompeian amphitheatre, the villa of the tragic poet, the villa of Diomedes, and the temple of Isis. Declaring himself with regard to prose fiction 'thoroughly aware of its power in teaching as well as amusing', Lytton sought to give a faithful picture of the customs, costume and superstitions of the age, in accurate topography of his setting but also 'a just representation of the human passions and the human heart, whose elements in all ages are the same'.[13] Together with his detailed historical research and his exploration of the secrets of the human heart there was another powerful inspiration – painting. While he was in Italy, Lytton visited a collection of pictures in the Brera Gallery in Milan and wrote in his journal that one picture in particular was making a 'considerable sensation'. The painting *The Last Days of Pompeii* was by the Russian artist Karl Pavlovich Bryulov (1799–1852) which set a series of 'human interest' stories against an apocalyptic background.[14] The impression this picture made upon Bulwer-Lytton was reinforced by another. One of John Martin's epic canvases, exhibited at the Egyptian Hall, Piccadilly in 1822, was *The Destruction of Pompeii and Herculaneum*. Lytton knew and admired Martin's work, calling him in 1833 'the greatest, the most lofty, the most permanent, the most original genius of his age. I see in him [...] the presence of a [...] great soul lapped in majestic and unearthly dreams'.[15]

In its turn the novel inspired painters. An estimated thirty-five paintings based on episodes in the novel are recorded in the sixty years after its appearance, among them Paul Falconer Poole's *The destruction of Pompeii* (c. 1835) and *The escape of Glaucus and Ione, with the blind girl Nydia from Pompeii* (1861) and Joseph Severn's *The Witches' Cavern: Glaucus and Ione* (1840). The American sculptor Randolph Rogers sculpted *Nydia the Blind Girl of Pompeii*.[16] The paintings, like the novel, embodied the characteristics which were to become identified with the

Ancient World genre: archaeological authenticity, emotional truth, visual power and a desire to educate as well as to entertain. The same characterizations were to be carried over into stage adaptations of the major novels.

The nineteenth century was the century when archaeology emerged as a science – the word only came into common currency in 1851 – and the recovery of the Ancient World proceeded apace in Italy, Greece, Egypt and the Near East. The Elgin Marbles had been sent from Athens to London between 1801 and 1811, creating a sensation. But it was not until the 1860s that digging began at Olympia and Samothrace to recover the remains of Ancient Greece. In 1879 the British School of Archaeology in Athens was established and in 1885 Oxford University established a chair of Classical Archaeology. It was, however, the German, Heinrich Schliemann, who had made the most sensational discoveries in Greece. Schliemann, fantasist, romantic, self-publicist and pioneering archaeologist, in the twenty years following 1870 astonished the world with his finds at Troy, Mycenae and Tiryns which appeared to confirm the literal truth of the events related by Homer and the Ancient Greek playwrights.

The siege of Troy is one of the great epics of European culture, with its parade of heroes (Hector, Achilles, Odysseus, Ajax, Aeneas and Paris) and its succession of mythic events (the Judgement of Paris, the abduction of Helen, the sacrifice of Iphigenia, the Wooden Horse). It has inspired great writers and artists down the years from Homer, Aeschylus and Virgil through Chaucer and Shakespeare to Berlioz and Yeats. Caesar and Alexander both visited the putative site of Troy. Fugitive Trojans were said to have founded Rome, France and even Britain. But did the Trojan War actually ever happen? Some of the greatest classical scholars have doubted it. George Grote, premier historian of Ancient Greece in the nineteenth century, dismissed it as a legend in 1846. This view is still held by some today. But the search for Troy is one of the great romances of modern archaeology. It was an Englishman, Frank Calvert, who decisively identified Hisarlik in modern Turkey as the site of Ancient Troy and suggested it to Schliemann. Between 1870 and his death in 1890, Schliemann returned regularly to Troy, proving beyond doubt the existence of a city of Troy. It was in 1873 that he uncovered what he dubbed 'the treasure of Priam' and 'the jewels of Helen'. But before his death it had become clear that there was not one Troy but seven successive cities built on the same site and his discoveries came from Troy II, whose remains dated from a thousand years before the putative date of Homer's Trojan War. Schliemann's assistant Wilhelm Dorpfeld, who continued the excavations after Schliemann's death, thought that Troy VI was probably Homeric Troy, an identification which still holds true today. Supplementary evidence for a Trojan War emerged later not from Greek sources but from the discovery and decipherment of the diplomatic archive of the Hittite Empire, where documents suggest that Troy may have been a vassal state of the Hittites, and an attack on it in the thirteenth century BC by the Greeks as part of a wider clash of empires over dominance on the coast of Asia Minor is therefore entirely plausible.[17]

It was Schliemann who also excavated Mycenae, a uniquely preserved example of a Bronze Age fortress city. The walls, the tombs, the Lion Gate and the so-called Treasury of Atreus were all known sites and regularly visited by curious travellers from the eighteenth century onwards when interest in pagan antiquities revived. In 1876 Schliemann uncovered five graves, full of treasures, including gold face masks, one of which Schliemann confidently proclaimed to be the mask of Agamemnon. Later this was dated to the sixteenth century BC, long before the age of Agamemnon. The building identified as Agamemnon's Palace turned out not to be and the Treasury of Atreus was actually a beehive-shaped tomb. Although Mycenae did not yield evidence relating to Troy, Schliemann's discoveries and his published accounts in the books *Mycenae*, *Ilios* and *Tiryns* enthralled a generation. It was such discoveries that inspired writers with a passion for accurate descriptions of the places, customs, costume and artefacts of the Ancient World. They provided equal inspiration for painters, whose work came first to fix the image of the Ancient World in the popular mind.

John Martin was the master of 'the apocalyptic sublime'. His huge canvases which combined immensity of scale, intricacy of detail and an overpowering atmosphere appealed powerfully to the nineteenth-century sensibility, a sensibility shaped by the world-changing experiences of the French Revolution and the Industrial Revolution. He painted visions of cosmic catastrophe drawn both from the Ancient World and the Bible. Among them were *The Fall of Babylon* (1819), *Belshazzar's Feast* (1821), *The Destruction of Pompeii and Herculaneum* (1822), *The Seventh Plague of Egypt* (1824), *The Fall of Nineveh* (1829), *The Destruction of Pharaoh's Host* (1833), *The Deluge* (1834) and *The Destruction of Sodom and Gomorrah* (1852). They were to influence the great epic film-makers of the twentieth century, D.W. Griffith and Cecil B. De Mille. But Martin was not alone. Similar pictures were painted by J.M.W. Turner, David Roberts, Samuel Colman, Francis Danby, George Miller and Thomas Cole. Martin's influence was at its height in the early 1830s, coinciding exactly with the vogue for Lytton's *The Last Days of Pompeii*. As Martin's biographer William Feaver puts it:

Martin's special contribution was to popularize and make immediate vanished civilizations. While offering little or nothing in terms of original research, he turned literary references into visual reality [...] he concentrated on architectural heroics – the immense promenades, viaducts, canals, and sewers which had been commonplace, it appeared, in the ancient Egyptian and Babylonian empires [...] There were few precedents in fine art for this brand of panoramic epic painting [...] he made no serious attempt to represent these cities as they had actually appeared, but showed them instead as sublimely inauthentic permanent stage sets [...] the neo-classical taste for accurate reconstruction of an exemplary, awe-inspiring past [...] was propagated by way of theatre design, panoramas, and architecture. These are the frames of reference within which Martin's epic 'machines' truly belong – not among the conventional history paintings of the academy.[18]

When Martin was painting, Babylon and Nineveh had yet to be excavated and when excavations revealed Martin's views to be essentially fanciful, he fell out of popularity, following his death in 1854. Accuracy became the watchword for history painting.

Typical of the new school of painters of the Ancient World is Jean-Léon Gérôme (1824–1904). Gérôme was a leading figure in the group, dubbed by contemporaries *Néo-Grecs*. Inspired by archaeological excavations at Pompeii and elsewhere, the *Néo-Grecs* were animated by enthusiasm for depicting scenes of everyday life in accurate antique settings furnished with authentic artefacts. Two of Gérôme's most enduring and influential pictures were his paintings of the arena, *Ave Caesar, Morituri te Salutant* (1859) showing a group of gladiators saluting the Emperor, and *Pollice Verso* (1872) showing a gladiator straddling a fallen opponent and waiting for the thumbs up or thumbs down sign from the crowd. Feeling that some of the archaeological detail in *Ave Caesar* was incorrect, he studied costumes on Trajan's column and had moulds made from gladiators' helmets, greaves and buckles from Naples. He made several bronze statues of gladiators in 1875 and 1878. Other canvases included *Cleopatra before Caesar* (1866), *Julius Caesar and his staff* (1863) and *Death of Caesar* (1867), showing Caesar dead beneath Pompey's statue and the senators fleeing. Later in the century he painted *Circus Maximus* (1876) showing chariots racing round a central spina and *The Christian Martyrs' Last Prayer* (1883) with a huddled group of Christians in the circus as lions emerge from an underground tunnel. Both were commissioned by wealthy Americans and displayed in America. They look to have directly influenced the visuals in the films *Ben-Hur* and *The Sign of the Cross*. Gérôme's ancient world scenes were familiar through the mass reproduction in engravings both in Britain and America.[19]

In Britain a classical revival in painting, celebrating the civilizations and values of Greece and Rome, lasted from the 1860s to 1914. According to Christopher Wood in his authoritative *Olympian Dreamers*, Victorian classicism is not easy to define. 'Inevitably it meant different things to different people; it was an influence rather than a coherent body of opinion; a catalyst rather than a clearly defined artistic movement.' In support of this view, he differentiates the characteristics of the leading classical painters: 'the lofty aspirations of Leighton, the antiquarianism of Alma-Tadema, the aesthetic classicism of Moore and Burne-Jones, the decadence of Simeon Solomon and Aubrey Beardsley, and the high romanticism of Waterhouse'.[20] Sir Frederic Leighton painted idealized pictures of a Greek World that was a vision of beauty, order and human perfection. His biographer Mrs Barrington said: 'Probably no Englishman ever approached the Greek of the Periclean period so nearly as did Leighton'.[21]

The Olympians mostly steered clear of the Roman Empire, preferring the abstract purity and marmoreal perfection of Ancient Greece. But Sir Lawrence Alma-Tadema, 'best known and best paid of all Victorian classical painters', was celebrated for the fidelity of his genre paintings of everyday life in the Ancient World, particularly Rome. His desire, as he put it in an 1899 interview, was 'to express in my pictures that the old Romans were flesh and blood like ourselves, moved by the same passions and emotions'.[22] The secret of his success was to portray the rituals, practices and mores of wealthy Romans – their dinner parties, their courtship rites, their shopping expeditions, their visits to the Baths – so that they appeared to spectators, as one commentator put it like 'Victorians in togas'. At the same time he drew on archaeology to create as accurate a picture as possible for buildings, furniture and clothing, so that spectators felt they were learning while viewing. Alma-Tadema said: 'If I am to revive ancient life, if I am to make it relive on canvas, I can do so only by transporting my mind into the far off ages, which deeply interest me, but I must do it with the aid of archaeology. I must not only create a *mise-en-scène* that is possible but probable'.[23] It was his archaeological accuracy and sense of dramatic composition that led to Alma-Tadema becoming the established painter most often employed by the leading actor-managers of the Victorian stage.

Besides Greece and Rome, popular interest in the empires of the Near East (Egypt, Assyria, Babylonia) was also stimulated by archaeological discovery. It was Napoleon Bonaparte's expedition to Egypt in 1798 that initiated a new interest in that country and its ancient past. The expedition was accompanied by 151 scientists and artists, charged with documenting all aspects of the country, including its ancient monuments. One of the discoveries during the expedition was the Rosetta Stone which contained an inscription written in both Egyptian and Greek. This enabled Jean-François Champollion to decipher the hitherto incomprehensible Egyptian hieroglyphs, a discovery made public in 1822. This began the process of allowing scholars to read the records of Egyptian history.

The first half of the nineteenth century saw a scramble for antiquities to supply the demands of European museums and private collectors. The Muslim rulers of Egypt, incurious about the country's pre-Islamic past and uninterested in pagan relics and monuments, were perfectly happy to grant concessions to Europeans to investigate, excavate and collect. During this period, Giovanni Batista Belzoni (1778–1823), conducted pioneering excavations at Gizeh, Thebes and Abu Simbel. Systematic archaeological investigations only began after 1850, dominated initially by the French archaeologist Auguste Mariette, who created the first

Museum of Egyptian Antiquities in 1863. Major discoveries were subsequently made by Sir Gaston Maspero and Sir Flinders Petrie, under whom the science of Egyptology developed. In 1866 the British Museum established a separate department of Egyptian and Oriental Antiquities. The Egyptian Exploration Fund was established in 1882 to finance archaeological digs. Academic posts for the study of Egyptology were established at the universities of London (1892), Oxford (1901), Liverpool (1906) and Manchester (1913).

The discoveries, the archaeological activities and the work of painters in recording both the ruins and imaginative reconstructions of ancient Egyptian life sparked a craze for all things Egyptian, dubbed Egyptomania and lasting throughout the nineteenth century. It received a new stimulus with the opening of the Suez Canal on 17 November 1869 and the premiere soon after at the Cairo Opera House of Verdi's opera *Aida* from a story provided by Auguste Mariette. It was given another major boost when Howard Carter discovered the tomb of Tutankhamun, which was opened in 1923 to reveal a fabulous array of treasures and artefacts. It created a worldwide sensation dubbed Tutmania. Its impact was enhanced and perpetuated by the legend of the curse of the Pharaohs, given substance by the death of the expedition's backer, Lord Carnarvon, less than five months after the opening of the tomb. This inspired a series of 'Mummy' films, featuring murderous Egyptian mummies and flashbacks to the ancient kingdom. The contents of the tomb inspired fashionable new lines in clothing, jewellery, hats, furniture and cosmetics.[24]

What accounts for this obsession with Egypt rather than other ancient Near Eastern empires like Assyria and Babylon, which were also excavated? It was partly a byproduct of Romanticism, with its preoccupation with the past and with the occult. The monumental physical remains (pyramids, obelisks, sarcophagi, the Sphinx) appealed to the cult of the picturesque, which included a fondness for ruins. The customs and practices recorded in such works as Sir Gardner Wilkinson's *Manners and Customs of the Ancient Egyptians* (1836), which has been called 'the most influential book on Ancient Egypt to appear in English during the nineteenth century',[25] catered to a taste for the exotic which represented an escape from the drabness and conformity of modern industrial society (mummification, the animal-headed gods and goddesses, the brother/ sister marriage of the monarchs). Ancient Egyptian beliefs and lore informed various esoteric cults such as Theosophy and Freemasonry.

There was also an ideological significance in Egyptomania. The nineteenth century was an age of empires. Egypt had been an empire and had lessons to offer on the rise and fall of imperial powers. Professor Fekri Hassan has plausibly argued that the acquisition and transportation of Egyptian monuments, particularly obelisks, recognized as symbols of cosmic power, was a decisive bid to legitimize the rule of modern empires 'by cannibalizing other civilizations in order to assume a superior position in the order of the world'.[26] This practice dated back at least to the Roman Empire which began the process of removing obelisks from Egypt to Rome partly as victory trophies but also partly as symbols of the process by which a new and thriving empire in the West was replacing an old, worn-out, decadent empire in the East.

For Britain, there was an additional stimulus to interest. Egypt featured significantly in two of the most important cultural icons of the Victorian Age – the Bible and Shakespeare. The Bible included the story of Moses and the exodus of the Jews from their captivity in Egypt to the creation of a new kingdom in the Holy Land. Shakespeare dramatized the story of Antony and Cleopatra with its clash of empires, temperaments and civilizations.

Egyptomania had a vast range of cultural expressions. As early as 1812 the showman William Bullock created the Egyptian Hall in Piccadilly, nominally inspired by the temple of Hathor at Dendera, complete with statues of Isis and Osiris, sphinxes, hieroglyphs and lotus columns. The Hall contained galleries furnished with Egyptian décor and a representation of the tomb of Pharaoh Seti I, complete with imitation murals and an original sarcophagus. Among the many exhibitions staged there one of the most successful was a display of the artefacts collected by Belzoni in 1821. The Hall survived until 1904, though latterly used for musical and magical shows.[27]

But the Egyptian Hall was not the only manifestation of the craze. The British Museum opened an Egyptian gallery. The Crystal Palace at Sydenham featured an Egyptian court which from 1854 until it burned down in 1936 combined spectacle and education. The Egyptian architectural style appeared across the globe applied to such diverse buildings as zoos, factories, cinemas, amusement parks, department stores, suspension bridges and war memorials, symbolizing monumental solidity and permanence but also suggesting promise of romance, mystery and adventure.[28]

Besides buildings and exhibitions, the public became familiar with the visual imagery of Egypt, its people, its history and its customs from paintings, plays, operas and latterly films. There was substantial overlap between these forms, with paintings in particular influencing the settings and stagings of the dramatic retellings of Egyptian life. Massive, teeming, atmospheric canvases by John Martin (*The Seventh Plague of Egypt, The Destruction of Pharaoh's Host*), J.M.W. Turner (*The Fifth Plague of Egypt*) and David Roberts (*The Israelites leaving Egypt*) with their hordes of extras, monumental buildings and extreme weather, looked like blueprints for the later Hollywood epics. Other episodes from Egyptian history that captured the imagination of painters were Joseph's sojourn in the country and his role at Pharaoh's court and the death of Cleopatra, which inspired a host of artists to depict her, usually gloriously naked, sprawled amid cushions and draperies.[29]

The Victorians were fascinated by the idea that the ancients were 'people like us' in fancy dress and genre painters responded to this by episodes from everyday life, staged amid carefully researched costumes, artefacts, settings, rituals and pursuits. Alma-Tadema painted twenty-five Egyptian genre scenes without ever having been there. Notable among them were *Pastimes in Ancient Egypt*, *An Egyptian Widow* and *Egyptian Games*. In the same vein were Edwin Long's *The Gods and their Makers*, Edward John Poynter's *Adoration to Ra* and Frederick Bridgman's *Procession of the Sacred Bull Apis*.

Elsewhere in the Near East, the primary stimulus to archaeological activity was the desire to prove the truth of the Bible stories and to discredit the attacks on the Creation by geologist Charles Lyell and evolutionist Charles Darwin. The first permanent archaeological body to be set up was the Palestine Exploration Society in 1865, 'for the purpose of investigating the archaeology, geography, geology and natural history of the Holy Land'.[30] These excavations identified towns and cities, battles and foreign conquerors mentioned in the Bible.

There were spectacular discoveries relating to those powerful empires which regularly reached out to swallow up Israel. In the 1840s Paul Emile Botta excavated Khorsabad, uncovering exquisite bas-reliefs which detailed everyday life in Ancient Assyria. Austen Henry Layard excavated Nimrud (the Biblical Calah) and Nineveh. His 1849 book *Nineveh and its Remains* became a bestseller, running through four editions immediately. Henry Creswick Rawlinson deciphered cuneiform writing, making the texts discovered by the archaeologist accessible. Layard had discovered the King's Library at Nineveh with thousands of cuneiform tablets recording the history, mythology, magic, diplomacy, medicine and science of Assyria. In 1853 at Nineveh the palace of King Assurbanipal (known to the Greeks as Sardanapalus) was discovered by Hormuzd Rassam, previously Layard's assistant. In the 1870s interest turned from the Assyrians to the Sumerians and Babylonians. But in 1872 George Smith identified and deciphered a fragmentary Chaldean account of the Deluge, which appeared to confirm the story of Noah's flood. In 1880 Rassam made the first major find in Babylonia, the site of the biblical Sepharvaim, which contained 50,000 inscribed cylinders and tablets. Sumerian Telloh was excavated by the French who found the Stela of the Vultures with its army of Sumerian warriors advancing in phalanx. In 1887 an American expedition excavated Nippur, finding 30,000 Sumerian tablets. It was a German expedition under Robert Koldewey that excavated Babylon in the period 1899–1913. The Ishtar Gate, with its glazed brickwork, dragons and bulls in relief, was reconstructed in Berlin. In the 1920s Sir Leonard Woolley excavated Ur of the Chaldees. As a result of these excavations, much was discovered about the history, religion, life and work of the peoples of Sumeria, Assyria and Babylonia.[31]

Despite the dominance of religion in nineteenth-century life, the Bible was not for the most part on the agenda of contemporary painters. There were comparatively few new Biblical paintings. The Royal Academy catalogues indicate that only an average of 2.5 per cent of the paintings on show annually between 1825 and 1870 had religious subjects.[32] Although the Bible was a favoured theme of the Old Masters, their art was deemed to be inherently Catholic in outlook. There was in Britain no established Protestant pictorial tradition. The Protestant Church did not commission art and painters necessarily catered to the tastes of their patrons and the wider public. Articles in the periodical press regularly called for religious painting to be used as a vehicle to elevate the taste and moral values of the public. Critics such as Mrs Anna Jameson in *Sacred and Legendary Art* (1848) and John Ruskin in *Modern Painters*, Volume 2 (1846) advocated the study of the techniques and approach of early art and combining this with up-to-date realism and the creative use of symbolism and typology to create a truly Protestant art.

It was the Pre-Raphaelite Brotherhood that put this recommendation into effect. A recognizable informality and domesticity characterized works like Ford Madox Brown's *Our Lady of Good Children* (1848), which showed Mary washing the fingers of the Baby Jesus, Brown's *Jesus Washing Peter's Feet* (1852–6) and Millais' *Christ in the House of his Parents* (1849–50). But it was Holman Hunt who became known as 'The Painter of Christ'. As Michaela Giebelhausen puts it: 'Rigorously Protestant in outlook, his work combined an understanding of contemporary Biblical scholarship with naturalist and Orientalist modes of representation. It presented a successful interpretation of scripture that spoke to the age.'[33]

The mid-nineteenth century was the time when Biblical scholarship focused on the historicity of Jesus, a trend which produced such influential works as David Friedrich Strauss's *Das Leben Jesu* (1835, revised 1864), Ernest Renan's *Vie de Jésus* (1863) and John Seeley's *Ecce Homo* (1865). The historicity of Jesus the man was combined with the demand for authenticity in settings and trappings, which sent Holman Hunt travelling in the Holy Land and researching the props in his paintings. This combination of historicization, Orientalization and spiritual uplift through the application of symbolism and typology made Holman Hunt's Jesus pictures, *The Light of the World* (1851–3), *The Finding of the Saviour in the Temple* (1854–60) and *The Shadow of Death* (1870–3) among the most influential and recognizable of nineteenth-century paintings.

There was another and equally influential source of Biblical illustration and this was the pictorial Bible, which became a fixture in many Victorian homes, shaping the popular perception of the Bible stories. Charles Knight, the great advocate of popular education and the diffusion of useful knowledge, trans-formed the established format of the illustrated Bible with his *Pictorial Bible* (1836–8) in which, alongside engravings of the Old Masters' paintings, included new engravings showing the flora and fauna, architecture, customs, dress and landscape of the Bible. During the 1840s the work of contemporary artists began to be included in illustrated Bibles. For the third edition of his *Pictorial Bible* (1847–8) Knight eliminated the Old Masters' pictures because of their inaccuracies of manners and costume and replaced them by modern, archaeologically accurate pictures. *The Illustrated Family Bible* (1859–63), published by John Cassell, adopted the same approach as Knight.[34]

But it was the work of two contemporary French painters, Gustave Doré and James Tissot, which had the most long-lasting influence on the popular imagination of the Victorian public and upon the visuals of stage and screen. The 228 illustrations that Doré provided for an edition of the Bible published in 1866 in London and Paris became his most popular work. Doré's biographer Joanna Richardson thought the Bible peculiarly suited to his powers:

> It offered him an almost endless series of intensely dramatic events. His visions of the looming tower of Babel, the plague of darkness in Egypt, the death of Samson, Isaiah's vision of the destruction of Babylon; these vast, forbidding scenes, heavy with doom, remind one of the visions of John Martin. They also reveal many elements by now familiar in Doré's work: the mountain scenes, the lurid skies, the complicated battles, the almost unremitting brutality. Doré's illustrations of the Old Testament remind us, above all, of the God of Wrath: of massacres and murders, decapitations and avenging angels. There is, too, a period element: the angels are Victorian angels, full of sentiment; the women are, again, keepsake women, the children are Victorian children: sentimental or wise beyond their years.[35]

In England, Doré was sometimes called 'the preacher-painter'. Sermons were preached on his work and Cassell reproduced his Bible illustrations in their *Daily Devotion for the Household*. As Richardson puts it: 'The Victorians delighted in Doré's sentimentality, and in his drama. They were touched, too, by his religious leanings'.[36]

Tissot, painter of fashionable society ladies and their luxurious lifestyle, underwent a religious conversion in 1885 when he claimed to have had a vision of Christ during mass at the church of St Sulpice in Paris, which he had attended to gather atmosphere for his proposed picture 'The Choir Singer'. He was inspired to embark on an illustrated version of the New Testament. The so-called Tissot Bible coincided exactly with a Catholic revival in France, underway from the 1880s onwards, which was mystical, visionary and anti-rationalist. In preparation for his work, he visited the Holy Land in 1886–7 and 1889 sketching and photographing dress, faces, architecture and topography. He studied archaeological and theological literature. The result was *The Life of Our Saviour Jesus Christ: 365 compositions from the four gospels with notes and explanatory drawings*, in which everything was documented and theological doctrine explained. The pictures were shown first in Paris in 1894 and London in 1896 and then on tour in the United States in 1898. Everywhere they were a remarkable success. The pictures were published with the Bible text in a luxury edition in 1896–7, earning Tissot a million francs. The 1897 English edition was dedicated to Mr Gladstone. Tissot's biographer Michael Wentworth explains the popularity of the Tissot Bible thus: 'In its blend of discursive erudition, documentary reportage and carefully delineated "inspiration", the Tissot Bible is a mirror image of the literal-minded faith prevalent at the end of the century.'[37] The Bible proved equally acceptable to Catholics and Protestants and became familiar throughout the Anglo-Saxon world. The success of his New Testament inspired Tissot to turn next to the Old Testament. There was a further trip to the Holy Land in 1896. But Tissot died in 1902 with the project uncompleted. Only 200 of the projected 396 pictures had been completed. Other artists finished the project from Tissot's sketches and they were published in a two-volume edition in 1904. Like Doré's illustrations Tissot's were to provide the most familiar visual illustrations of the Old and New Testaments for several decades.

Just as in paintings, so too in the Victorian theatre history was a staple subject. As theatre historian Richard Schoch has written: 'Performance was a powerful agent of historical consciousness in the nineteenth century [...] greater than that of literature, painting or even photography.'[38] The visual imagery of these historical plays was often directly inspired by famous paintings and plays were staged, framed and lit like paintings. Performance and visual imagery combined to create a popular memory of history, but one which often looked to romance, myth and melodrama for inspiration rather than to academic research.

But the theatre operated under certain inescapable constraints. One was censorship. From 1737 to 1968 the stage functioned under the oversight of the Lord Chamberlain's office and had to conform to a strict set of regulations designed to preserve moral standards and the political, religious and social status quo. All plays had to be submitted to the Lord Chamberlain's office and could not be performed without his official imprimatur. This effectively meant the exclusion from the stage of explicit discussions of politics, religion and sex.[39]

One particular prohibition in force throughout the century was the ban on the dramatization of Bible stories on the stage which explains why, in marked contrast to twentieth-century Hollywood, Biblical stories were absent from the Victorian stage. As the examiner of plays William Bodham Donne said in 1866: 'both as a matter of morality, and as a matter of taste, I never allow any associations with scripture or theology to be introduced into a play.'[40] Works which fell foul of this ban included Racine's Athalie, Rossini's opera Moses in Egypt and Wilde's Salomé. The first major West End production to receive a licence was Sir Herbert Beerbohm Tree's Joseph and His Brethren in 1913. The Lord Chamberlain's ban was underpinned by the long-running hostility of the church to the stage which began to moderate significantly only in the 1890s. This may explain the relaxation of the censorial ban in 1913, something that was generally welcomed in the press.

A second constraint on theatrical producers was the commercial imperative of the box office. Plays would run only as long as the audiences came. Success in any particular genre inspired imitations. The public by their repeated attendance created a repertoire of much-loved favourite plays from which leading actors departed at their peril. Until 1843, three theatres, Covent Garden, Drury Lane and Haymarket, had a monopoly of spoken drama in London, with the so-called 'minor theatres' able only to perform *burlettas*, or musical entertainments. But the monopoly was ended by the 1843 Theatre Regulation Act.

One popular appeal that was constant throughout the Victorian period was the taste for theatrical spectacle. Spectacle was an integral part of everyday life, from the Great Exhibition at the Crystal Palace through to the Golden and Diamond Jubilees of Queen Victoria. It was a feature of Victorian painting, of public buildings and shows of all kinds.[41] Audiences had a passion both for the visual and for archaeological and historical accuracy and theatres supplied it, happily justifying the expense on the grounds of the educational value, a recurrent refrain from within the theatre world which waged a continuing campaign to raise the social status of the stage. So spectacle and authenticity went hand in hand in the recreation of the Ancient World.

In both Britain and America, plays set in Republican Rome were much more in evidence in the earlier nineteenth century than in the later nineteenth century. This directly reflected the political circumstances of the time. The early nineteenth-century stage was politically much more radical then the later nineteenth-century stage and the sentiments associated with Republican Rome chimed with those aroused by the French and American revolutions and by the British domestic reform movement. Revolutionary France had wholeheartedly taken up the ideas, festivals and even fashions of Republican Rome. Plays and paintings celebrated the great republican heroes, the tribunes of the people, and their destruction of monarchical tyrants. Cato, Brutus and the Gracchi were the ideals, their virtues, incorruptibility, stoicism, civic virtue, love of the people and defence of freedom. The golden age for this era ended with the dictatorship of Julius Caesar. These ideas and images influenced the culture of both America and Britain.

Perhaps the most famous and enduring of the Roman republican dramas was Joseph Addison's *Cato*. First performed at Drury Lane in 1713, this celebration of the stoic Roman statesman who committed suicide rather than submit to the dictatorship of Julius Caesar, held the stage throughout the century and was still being performed as late as 1838 by the radical actor-manager William Charles Macready (1793–1873). Macready also achieved success in two other plays with republican sentiments, Sheridan Knowles' *Virginius* (1820) and Thomas Talfourd's *Ion* (1836). Popular in Britain during the first half of the nineteenth century, they remained enduringly popular in America throughout the century. Shakespeare's two plays set in Republican Rome, *Julius Caesar* and *Coriolanus*, were much performed in the first half of the nineteenth century in Britain before largely disappearing from the repertoire in the second half. Interestingly, they too remained popular in America until the end of the century.

It was the actor-manager Charles Kean (1811–68) in a remarkable series of Shakespearean revivals at the Princess' Theatre in Oxford Street in the 1850s who so successfully married spectacular and archaeological recreation that this mode of production became dominant for the rest of the century. His principal contribution to the staging of the Ancient World was his revival in 1853 of Lord Byron's poetic tragedy *Sardanapalus* about the downfall of the Assyrian philosopher-king. The great feature of this production was an accurate recreation of Nineveh based on the discoveries made by Austen Henry Layard, described in his best selling book *Nineveh and Its Remains* (1849), and on the sculptures and artefacts he had shipped to the British Museum.

Sir Henry Irving who followed in the footsteps of Kean in the combination of spectacle and pictorialism which he applied to his productions, also, like Kean, preferred plays with medieval or Renaissance setting. But when he did venture into the Ancient World he brought his strong visual sense to bear on their staging. In 1881 he produced Lord Tennyson's poetic drama *The Cup* which has been identified as the first of the late nineteenth-century toga play cycle, which had different preoccupations from the earlier republican cycle.[42] *The Cup*, for which Irving had an archaeologically accurate reconstruction of the temple of Diana at Ephesus made, explored some of the themes that dominated the later toga cycle: the proper role for women in society, the denunciation of decadence, and an exploration of the conflict of ethics and political necessity in imperial rule. Critics, entranced by the visual splendour of the production, turned to painting to describe the stage effects, invoking Leighton and Alma-Tadema as the inspiration of the visuals. Irving actually turned to painters to design two later productions, Ford Madox Brown to provide the Romano-British setting of *King Lear* in 1892 and Alma-Tadema to provide the settings for *Cymbeline* in 1896 and *Coriolanus* in 1901.[43]

If Irving was comparatively reluctant to enter the Ancient World, two of his most notable contemporaries as actor-managers were more eager.[44] Wilson Barrett (1846–1904) and Sir Herbert Beerbohm Tree (1853–1917) became masters of the Ancient World epic. Barrett's plays were designed by E.W. Godwin, architect, antiquarian and theatrical *metteur-en-scène*, who believed in both archaeological accuracy and visual harmony. Oscar Wilde called Godwin 'one of the most artistic spirits of this century in England'. The Barrett–Godwin collaborations were widely described as aesthetic triumphs. As Wilde wrote of *Claudian* (1883), the first of them, 'The Ancient World awakes from its sleep and history moves as a pageant before our eyes'.[45] Such notable figures as the critics John Ruskin and Clement Scott and the writer and clergyman Lewis Carroll went to see the play three times and admired its message of Christian repentance and redemption. *Claudian* was set in fourth-century Byzantium and Bithynia, *Brutus* (1885) in Republican Rome and *Clito* (1886) in Athens in 404 BC and each play was hailed as a lesson in stage archaeology.

After Godwin died in 1886, Barrett set plays in Egypt (*Pharaoh*) and Babylon (*The Daughters of Babylon*), but his greatest success came with *The Sign of the Cross*. Set against the background of the persecution of the Christians by the Emperor Nero, the play told how the proud pagan aristocrat Marcus Superbus, put in charge of rounding up the Christians, fell in love with the gentle Christian maid Mercia, converted to her faith and gladly went with her to suffer martyrdom in the arena. It opened in America in 1895 and in London in 1896. It ran initially for 453 performances and had by 1904 been performed an estimated 10,000 times all over the world. Mocked by intellectuals, it was praised by church authorities of every denomination. Sermons were preached on it and Barrett received many letters from people telling him the play had changed their lives.

Tree's first toga play was an adaptation of Charles Kingsley's novel *Hypatia*, produced in 1893. It revolved around the struggle between pagans and Christians for supremacy in early fifth-century Alexandria. It highlighted the need for an empire to have a proper religious faith which is neither fanatical nor pagan. It condemned sexual immorality and mob rule and denounced scheming clerics and politicians who threaten the stability of the empire. It was designed for Tree by Alma-Tadema, whose sets elicited widespread praise. Alma-Tadema was also enlisted to provide sets for Tree's spectacular revival of *Julius Caesar* in 1898. The critics lavished praise on both costumes and sets.

Three of Tree's greatest successes were the poetic dramas, *Herod* (1900), *Ulysses* (1902) and *Nero* (1906), written specifically for him by Stephen Phillips (1864–1915). *Herod*, a study in Oriental tyranny, boasted a palace set, designed and painted by Hawes Craven, which earned an admiring article in the *Architectural Review* for its historical accuracy. *Ulysses* had sets by Professor W.R. Lethaby based on recent archaeological discoveries from the Mycenean Age and costumes by Percy Anderson inspired by the mural decorations at Knossos. *Nero*, another study in tyranny, made it clear that an empire could not be run by a Wildean aesthete who saw art as superior to imperial administration. The 1906 production of *Antony and Cleopatra* contrasted 'the austere grandeur of Rome' with the 'gorgeous splendour of the East' and pointed up the lesson for imperialists about what happened when you put private passion ahead of public duty.

Tree's final two Ancient World plays recreated Pharaonic Egypt. *False Gods* (1909), with the temple of Isis set modelled on the hall of columns in Karnak, dealt with the failed attempt of a religious reformer to destroy the power of the pagan priesthood. *Joseph and his Brethren* (1913) received considerable publicity as it was the first time that the Lord Chamberlain had relaxed his ban on Biblical subjects for a major West End production. While the life of Christ remained taboo, the Old Testament had finally been deemed suitable for dramatization, provided it was reverently treated.

Hypatia was not the only Ancient World novel to be dramatized for the stage. The three most important and long-lasting novels were also. Bulwer-Lytton's *The Last Days of Pompeii* was produced on the London stage in 1834, 1835 and 1872. When Henryk Sienkiewicz's *Quo Vadis* was published in 1896, three separate stage adaptations immediately appeared in the United States. One of them, a version by Stanislaus Stange, transferred to London in 1900 but closed after only four weeks. Wilson Barrett mounted a rival production which received better reviews but since the plot of Sienkiewicz's novel had a virtually identical plot to Barrett's own *The Sign of the Cross*, it inevitably seemed rather second-hand.

Far more successful was the stage version by William Young of General Lew Wallace's *Ben-Hur*. With Christ represented by a beam of light, to avoid offending religious susceptibilities, and the healing of the lepers on the Mount of Olives providing the dramatic climax rather than the crucifixion, the play included both the ramming of the Roman galley by a pirate ship and the chariot race, done with real horses racing on a treadmill as a moving panorama unfolded behind them. It opened in 1899 in New York and was an instant hit, returning again and again and touring the United States for twenty-one years. By the time it finally closed in 1920, it had been performed six thousand times and seen by an estimated twenty million people. The New York production was transported to London and opened at Drury Lane in 1902. It ran initially for 122 performances but was successfully revived in 1912.

The era of the toga play ended with a change in the nature of the audience and a transformation of theatrical taste, both of which occurred at the time of the First World War. The rise of the cinema creamed off the mass working-class audience which now preferred to see realistic versions of its old theatrical favourites on a screen not limited by the three walls of the stage and a proscenium arch. But with the theatre audience shrinking to a largely middle-class constituency, the nature of theatrical fare changed. Melodrama and poetic drama went out of fashion and modernity and sophistication were the order of the day, at least on the West End stage. Sheer economics dictated that few theatres could now afford the lavish stagings with hordes of extras that had been an integral feature of the toga play.

Symptomatic of the change is the sardonic subversion of previously popular genres by that sly old iconoclast George Bernard Shaw. He provided a modern-dress version of *Pygmalion* (1914). The mythic tale of the sculptor whose beloved statue came to life was a staple of the toga stage in a version by W.S. Gilbert. Shaw transposed it to Edwardian England and centred it on a professor of phonetics who converts a cockney guttersnipe into a lady.

He also provided his own versions of toga plays in *Caesar and Cleopatra* (1906) and *Androcles and the Lion* (1913). *Caesar and Cleopatra* was Shaw's response to Shakespeare's Roman plays which were enjoying a new popularity at the high noon of British imperialism. Shaw was disdainful of both *Antony and Cleopatra* ('I have a technical objection to making infatuation a tragic theme. Experience proves that it is only effective in a comic spirit') and *Julius Caesar* ('Shakespear [*sic*] who knew human weakness well, never knew human strength of the Caesarian type. His Caesar is an admitted failure.')[46] Utilizing the recognized ingredients of the toga genre (spectacle, lavish sets and costumes, large casts), he created his own version of the story, deliberately intruding anachronisms, inserting a critique of British imperialism and constructing a Caesar who rather than a ruthless dictator enslaved by a grand passion for Cleopatra emerged as a wise and witty analogue of Shaw himself, an intellectually superior being who undertakes to educate the schoolgirl Queen for rulership.

Shaw delivered the *coup de grâce* to the toga play with *Androcles and the Lion*. It is a precise parody of *The Sign of the Cross* with characters, settings and situations direct analogues of those in Wilson Barrett's play. To add insult to injury, Barrett's erstwhile leading lady Lillah McCarthy played the Christian heroine Lavinia.

The theatrical future lay with Shaw as the toga play disappeared from the stage repertoire. But as a genre it survived, transferred lock, stock and barrel to the cinema where it was destined to scale greater pictorial heights and reach many more millions of spectators than the theatre had ever dreamed possible. Many of the stage hits of the nineteenth century were refurbished for the twentieth-century screen. But there was one significant difference. Where toga plays had flourished equally on the British and American stages in the nineteenth century, the British cinema could never afford the massive investment that Ancient World recreations entailed. So the cinematic future of the Ancient World lay with Hollywood and provided another genre with which it might conquer and colonize the imagination not just of British but of global audiences.

2

The Birth of the Ancient World Epic in the Cinema

When the cinema emerged in the early years of the twentieth century to displace the melodramatic and spectacular stage as the entertainment form of choice for the masses, it turned naturally to the ancient world and scores of short films were produced with pocket versions of the familiar stories from the Bible, ancient history and classical mythology. But the feature-length Ancient World cinematic epic was born in 1908 when *The Last Days of Pompeii* was produced in Italy. It was Italy which took the lead in crafting these early epics, directors drawing on the native tradition of staging grand opera but, by shooting on location, constructing massive sets and deploying thousands of extras, establishing the visual parameters of the new cinematic genre. The choice of the early nineteenth-century British novel by Bulwer-Lytton, already adapted three times for the stage in England, as the basis of the first great epic underlines the continuity with the existing literary and theatrical tradition. Two new film versions of Lytton's novel were produced in Italy in 1913 and they were joined in the cinemas by adaptations of Sienkiewicz's *Quo Vadis* (1912), Gustave Flaubert's *Salammbô* (filmed as *Salambo* (1914)) and Cardinal Wiseman's *Fabiola* (1916).[1]

But the most celebrated and influential of Italy's Ancient World epics was Giovanni Pastrone's *Cabiria* (1914). Two hours long and a triumph of set and costume design, it was artfully put together by Giovanni Pastrone from existing Ancient World texts: the volcanic eruption from *The Last Days of Pompeii*, the strong-man protector of the heroine based on Ursus in *Quo Vadis*, his condemnation to turn the millstone borrowed from *Samson and Delilah*. Other elements look to be drawn from Gustave Flaubert's Carthaginian romance, *Salammbô* (1862) and *Carthage in Flames* (1906), a novel by the prolific Italian historical novelist Emilio Salgari (rescue of the heroine from sacrifice in the temple of Moloch). Historical figures such as Hannibal, Archimedes and Scipio Aemilianus make guest appearances. Also grafted onto the narrative is the historical story of Sophonisba, daughter of a Carthagian general, married to King Syphax of Numidia but loved by Syphax's rival, Massinissa, an ally of Rome. When Sophonisba is captured, Massinissa sends her poison so that she may avoid the humiliation of being paraded in the Roman triumph. The story had already formed the basis of stage tragedies by John Marston, Nathaniel Lee and Pierre

Corneille among others. The floridly poetic intertitles were provided by the poet Gabriele D'Annunzio, giving the film added celebrity value.

It is an epic of the Punic Wars between Rome and Carthage and a celebration of Italy's imperial traditions. The heroine of the film is Cabiria, who for much of the film is a young child. The film opens with the destruction of the Sicilian villa of Cabiria's family by the eruption of Mount Etna. Fleeing, the child is captured by Phoenician pirates and sold into slavery in Carthage. She is rescued from the threat of sacrifice to the god Moloch by the Roman patrician Fulvius Axilla, who is spying on Carthaginian defences for Rome, and is accompanied by his strong man servant Maciste. Fulvius, Maciste and Cabiria are ambushed by Carthagian soldiers, Fulvius escapes but Maciste, after entrusting the infant Cabiria to Sophonisba, is himself captured. Ten years later Fulvius, again reconnoitring Carthage for the Romans, rescues Maciste and escapes with him to the desert, where they are captured and taken to Cirta. But after Cirta surrenders to the Romans and Sophonisba takes poison, she reunites Fulvius with Cabiria, now her handmaiden.

Although the film is rather static, as Pastrone cuts from one medium-shot setup to another with little camera movement and only one close-up, he achieves a powerful narrative drive, dynamic editing, and innovative lighting. He deploys several breath-taking long-shots (Fulvius diving from a clifftop into the sea; a ladder of shields being created by Roman soldiers to let Fulvius scale the walls of Carthage) and the scale and spectacle are enormously impressive (the eruption of Mount Etna; the siege of Syracuse and destruction of the Roman fleet; the siege of Cirta; the human sacrifice in the temple of Moloch). The strong man Maciste became a cult hero and was featured in a succession of subsequent action films. The temple of Moloch with its gaping, fanged mouth entrance was copied directly by Fritz Lang in *Metropolis* (1926) and the siege of Cirta and the Carthagian décor of the film directly influenced D.W. Griffith in his filming of *Intolerance* (1917).[2]

It was a visit to an earlier Italian epic *Quo Vadis*, then showing in New York, that had so inspired Griffith that he deliberately expanded a planned two-reel version of the Biblical story of Judith and Holofernes to four reels, producing a feature film running 55 minutes which had been budgeted at $18,000 but ended up costing twice as much to the annoyance of his employers, Biograph Films. Much of the cost overrun went on building the gigantic walls of Bethulia at Chatsworth in the San Fernando Valley. The row between Griffith and Biograph prompted him to leave and work instead for the more accommodating Mutual.[3]

Often erroneously described as the first American feature film, it is nevertheless a transitional film which marks Griffith's move from short to long films. *Judith of Bethulia* (1913), celebrating a Jewish heroine, was based on the Apocrypha and on a poetic tragedy by the nineteenth-century American playwright Thomas

Bailey Aldrich in which Griffith had performed during his career as an actor. It combined the biblical narrative (Assyrians besiege Bethulia; devout widow Judith goes to their camp, seduces the general Holofernes, gets him drunk and cuts off his head) with a conventional romantic subplot (Naomi loves Nathan; Naomi is captured by the Assyrians; Nathan rescues Naomi). Griffith utilized his stock company of actors (Henry B. Walthall as Holofernes; Blanche Sweet as Judith; Mae Marsh as Naomi; Bobby Harron as Nathan; Lillian Gish as The Young Mother). Walthall, unrecognizable under a massive Assyrian beard, folds his arms and glowers a lot to convey the tyrannical disposition of the Assyrian general. Bobby Harron, sporting an entirely inappropriate Edwardian moustache, plays the dashing hero. Blanche Sweet, favoured by many telling close-ups, gives a passionate performance as Judith, grieving for her suffering fellow countrymen, genuinely attracted to Holofernes and, when torn between love and duty, finally settling for duty and the gratitude of the Bethulians. She is, however, kitted out in the manner of Edwardian haute couture, with an extraordinary peacock feather headdress. Large-scale siege and battle scenes are interspersed with interiors, featuring some rather tame 'Bacchanalian festivities' in Holofernes' tent, the punishment of cowards and the antics of dancing girls and a somewhat camp chief eunuch. Silent film historian Anthony Slide found the battle scenes 'the biggest disappointment. The staging is quite frankly a mess, and there is every sign of a small group of people desperately pretending to be a crowd.'[4] The film as a whole did not impress silent film historian William K. Everson who found it 'confused and protracted' and showing 'far less control and instinctive understanding of the medium in the best of Griffith's Biograph films', putting this down to its expansion from the planned two-reeler. But he sees it as a useful exercise in the handling of a larger-scale subject as Griffith moved to the next phase in his career.[5]

It was D.W. Griffith and Cecil B. De Mille who were the godfathers of the Hollywood Ancient World epic. Both were Victorians steeped in the traditions and conventions of the melodrama stage, both were former actors and playwrights with experience both in dramatic construction and performance, and both were attracted by the possibilities of the new medium. It was Griffith who was to be the pioneer, developing a visual language, making a sophisticated use of the close-up, perfecting a dynamic style of editing and carefully rehearsing his actors to shape the desired emotional performances. All these characteristics were to be found in his American Civil War epic, *The Birth of a Nation*, which electrified critics and audiences in 1915.

Despite the critical and box office success of *Birth of a Nation*, a campaign was mounted against it by the NAACP (National Association for the Advancement of Colored People), backed by leading intellectuals. They called for it to be banned on the grounds of its glorifying the Ku Klux Klan and its demeaning depiction of Negroes. Hurt and angered by the campaign, Griffith put together his own cinematic response in the form of the film *Intolerance*, subtitled 'Love's Struggle through the Ages'. Linked by the recurrent image of a woman (Lillian Gish) rocking a cradle, inspired by Walt Whitman's lines 'out of the cradle endlessly rocking; Uniter of Here and Hereafter', the film tells four stories, cross-cutting between them to underline the parallels, the eternal conflict between love and intolerance and the universal nature of human feelings. Interestingly the examples of intolerance conspicuously failed to include race hatred.

Griffith had already completed a hard-hitting contemporary melodrama with a strong social conscience, *The Mother and the Law*. It centred on the Boy (Bobby Harron), wrongly sentenced to death for the murder of a gangster and the efforts, ultimately successful, of his wife (Mae Marsh) and a friendly policeman to prove his innocence, which they do in the nick of time to prevent the execution. The film contained a powerful attack on ruthless industrialists who use the troops to shoot down strikers; unemployment which leads to crime, prostitution and poverty; and an interfering and do-gooding Reform Party which separates mothers from their children and seeks to ban drinking and dancing, forcing them underground. It is the only story to have a happy ending. The other three historical strands end in tragedy.

There is the St Bartholomew's Day Massacre in 1572 when the Catholics, stirred up by Queen Catherine de Médicis, slaughter the Protestants of France. Included among the Protestant victims is Bright Eyes (Margery Wilson), whose lover is left grieving over her body. There are episodes from the life of Christ (Howard Gaye), designed to show him at odds with hypocritical Pharisees, notably their disapproval of the dancing and revelry at the wedding at Cana where he turns the water into wine and where they encourage the stoning of the woman taken in adultery, provoking Christ's comment: 'Let him who is without sin amongst you cast the first stone'. This episode culminates in the Crucifixion, the ultimate act of intolerance.

The final and most spectacular episode is the siege and capture of Babylon by the Persians in 539 BC. Babylon is portrayed by Griffith as a model of tolerance, justice and love. It is ruled on behalf of his father King Nabonidus by Prince Belshazzar (Alfred Paget), described as 'an apostle of tolerance and religious freedom' and betrothed to the Princess Beloved (Seena Owen). Belshazzar seeks to promote the cult of Ishtar, goddess of love, provoking the jealousy of the High Priest of Bel-Marduk. The Persian Army under Cyrus besieges Babylon but Belshazzar leads a successful defence of the city and, when the Persians retire, stages a celebratory feast. But the priests of Bel betray the city, admit the Persians, and Belshazzar and the Princess Beloved commit suicide to avoid capture. The obligatory romantic subplot has the tomboyish Mountain Girl (Constance Talmadge) loved unrequitedly by the Rhapsode (Elmer Clifton), a warrior-poet. She dies defending Belshazzar at the end. *Intolerance* ends with scenes of fighting armies laying down their weapons, prisons replaced by fields of flowers and angels looking down on a world of peace and brotherhood. It is Griffith's vision for the future after the repeated intolerance of the past.

Along with what is in effect a sermon on the subject of intolerance, the film also embodies a strong commitment to visual and historical education. Griffith's assistant director Joseph Henabery was put in charge of research particularly for the Babylonian sequence but also for the Judean sequence. He recalled assembling a fifteen-foot-long shelf crammed with history books relevant to the periods and he compiled a scrapbook of illustrations both of Victorian paintings and of archaeological finds from Assyria.[6]

The necessity for the infant motion-picture art to draw inspiration from the older art forms was an axiom of early theoretical writing on the cinema. The poet Vachel Lindsay in his influential *The Art of the Moving Picture* (1915) had separate chapters on 'Sculpture – in motion', 'Painting – in motion', and 'Architecture – in motion', signalling the appropriate sources of visual illustration for the film-maker. Early film-makers sought to justify and elevate their fledgling art form by explicitly combining entertainment with moral, historical and visual education in a way that can properly be described as Ruskinian. Audiences would have recognized the paintings providing Griffith with his inspiration as he chose canvases familiar from extensive reproduction in engravings. The layout of Babylon as seen through the window of the palace was an exact reproduction of John Martin's 1819 painting *The Fall of Babylon* and it was a combination of Martin's *Belshazzar's Feast* (1821) and Georges Rochegrosse's *The Fall of Babylon* (1891) which provided the visual inspiration for the sequence of Belshazzar's Feast. One of the most famous of Victorian Ancient World paintings, Edwin Long's *The Babylonian Marriage Market* (1875) was directly reproduced in the sequence in which the Mountain Girl is sent to the Marriage Market. The life of Christ sequences were modelled on James Tissot's famous four-volume set of illustrations of the Bible (1896–7). This was recognized by the critic of *Photoplay* (December 1916): 'Pictorially the greatest filmings are the Judaean scenes, perfect in composition, ideal in lighting, every one in effect a Tissot painting of the time of Christ.'[7]

Anxious throughout to stress the historical authenticity of his imagery, Griffith added explanatory notes to his intertitles about customs, buildings and antique terms used. The treachery of the priests of Bel was attributed to the evidence of recently discovered Babylonian cuneiform cylinders. The marriage at Cana was said to be staged 'according to Sayce, Hastings, Brown and Tissot'. In addition to the French painter, these were James Hastings, author of *The Dictionary of the Bible*, Francis Brown, author of *Assyriology: its use and abuse in Old Testament Study* (1885) and Archibald Henry Sayce, British-born author of *Israel and the Surrounding Nations* (1898) and *Babylonians and Assyrians* (1900). Sayce wrote to Griffith praising the film and his letter was reproduced in the souvenir programme for the film:

> The Babylonian scenes are magnificent, as well as true to facts. I was much impressed by the attention that had been paid to accuracy in detail. The drama is educational in more than one direction, and the interest it must excite in Babylonian history is especially gratifying to the Assyriologist.[8]

Henabery's scrapbook contained archaeological illustrations cut from books such as Georges Perrot and Charles Chipiez, *A History of Art in Chaldaea and Assyria* (1884) and Morris Jastrow Jr, *The Civilization of Babylonia and Assyria* (1915). Like Sayce, Jastrow also wrote to Griffith praising the film's historical authenticity and his letter too appeared in the souvenir programme:

> You have succeeded in conveying to the audience a remarkably vivid picture of the art, architecture, costumes, public and private life of Babylonia. I was amazed to see how carefully you reproduced our knowledge of the enormous walls of the city, with their battlements and gates, the palace, the battle towers, the battering rams and other instruments of ancient warfare.

He singled out for special praise 'the splendid and thrilling scenes' of the attack on Babylon and also the feast of Belshazzar.

Despite these encomia, there were limits to the vaunted historical accuracy. Cyrus, for instance, had not besieged the city prior to being admitted by the priests. The gates of Babylon were actually based on the South-Eastern gates of the Palace at Khorsabad. The wall relief beneath which the Rhapsode sits in one scene actually bears the picture of a lion hunt featuring King Assurnasirpal II from his palace at Nimrud. So at best Griffith's Babylon is an amalgam of Assyrian archaeological sources.

But there was another unacknowledged source of visual inspiration and that was *Cabiria*, which had been shown in New York in 1914. The siege of Cirta in the Italian film looks to have provided direct inspiration for Griffith's siege of Babylon. Griffith insisted on reproducing the rampant elephant statues which Giovanni Pastrone had borrowed from India to decorate his Carthaginian palace in *Cabiria*, even thought there was no historical support for such statues in Babylon. Even individual shots like a Babylonian noble patting a pet leopard had direct analogues in *Cabiria*. Interestingly, Griffith invited Vachel Lindsay, who had praised and analysed both *Judith of Bethulia* and *Cabiria* in *The Art of the Moving Picture*, to the premiere of *Intolerance*.[9]

Even now the film remains an astonishing achievement. As William K. Everson has written: 'In terms of technique … the film is a virtual textbook, containing forerunners of glass shots, an ingenious improvised camera crane which even foreshadowed the effects of the zoom lens in certain shots, the most sophisticated use yet of toning and tinting, coupled with mood lighting, for dramatic effect; some astonishingly "modern" performances from Mae Marsh and Miriam Cooper; and of course a pattern of editing, or montage, which was to be of profound influence on the Soviet films of the twenties.'[10] Different sequences were tinted in different colours (blue for night scenes, red for Babylonian night battles, amber for the French Court) to intensify the emotional impact.[11] The magnificent battle scenes by night and by day, the huge siege engines rumbling into position, the chariots racing up and down, Elmo Lincoln, the future screen Tarzan, as 'the mighty man of valour' slicing off heads in a single blow, remain unforgettable as does the procession through the Great Court of Babylon, a superb set, complete with its rampant elephant statues and its dancing girls gyrating in ecstasy. It was done by using a specially constructed elevator in a tower on wheels and on tracks, allowing the camera to move up and down, backwards and forwards. There was a platform on it large enough to hold Griffith, cameraman Billy Bitzer and Lillian Gish. Lillian Gish described the effect in her autobiography:

> The forerunner of the modern camera crane enabled Mr Griffith to create one of the most fabulous effects ever filmed. Having perfected the close-up and set a standard for crowd scenes, he now fused the two techniques. At the opening of Belshazzar's feast, the camera was a quarter-mile from the end of the great court. It started the move toward the set, then glided slowly down over the heads of the extras and dancing girls, then moved forward again to halt before a miniature chariot drawn by two white doves and holding a white rose – a gift from the King to the Princess Beloved, who sat at the other end of the table. Fantastic in conception, the shot was also a tribute to Billy's skill, for throughout the long swooping ride on the crane, he had managed to keep his camera in perfect focus from the enormous expanses of the entire set to the petals on the rose.[12]

The Babylon sets covered 250 acres, the walls enclosing the court were 200 feet high, and that sequence involved the use of 15,000 extras and 250 chariots. The film as a whole cost $485,000, the cost of 40 ordinary films and originally ran for 8 hours, cut eventually to 3 hours and 15 minutes for its release. Although praised by the critics – *Film Daily* called it 'stupendous, tremendous, revolutionary, intense, thrilling' – perhaps inevitably it failed at the box office. The audiences, used to linear narratives, were bewildered by the cross-cutting between different stories – *Variety* claimed it was difficult to follow – and after the United States entered the First World War in 1917 the national mood was against explicitly pacifist sermons. To recoup some of his losses, Griffith released *The Mother and the Law* and *The Fall of Babylon* as self-contained films in 1919, shooting extra footage to allow them to stand alone. The new material for *The Fall of Babylon* built up the romance between the Mountain Girl and the Rhapsode, introducing a happy ending in which they escaped to a new life in Nineveh.[13]

After the financial failure of *Intolerance*, Griffith made a series of popular and highly praised melodramas (*Broken Blossoms*, *Way Down East* and *True Heart Susie*) but the relative financial failure of later epics (*America*, *Orphans of the Storm*) led to the loss of his independence and a retreat to more conventional studio film-making at Paramount. He became the most spectacular casualty of the conversion to sound, unable to adjust to the new medium and to changing audience tastes and sensibilities. Inactive for sixteen years, he took to drink and died in 1948.

Cecil B. De Mille, who learned much from Griffith, did not suffer the same fate, weathered the transition to sound and crowned his career with a blockbusting success, *The Ten Commandments* in 1956 in which he returned to the subject of one of his earliest triumphs. De Mille had grown up in a devout Episcopalian family, where the Bible was regularly read aloud by his father and he became very familiar with the Gustave Doré illustrations of the Bible, which became one of his continuing sources of inspiration.

In the 1920s De Mille became one of the major exponents of the idea of the Ancient World as a lesson for the Modern. *Male and Female* (1919) was his 'delightful' adaptation of J.M. Barrie's play *The Admirable Crichton*. The central idea was the comic possibilities of the idea of class reversal when, after a shipwreck, the butler becomes king of the desert island and the aristocratic family for whom he works become his servants. De Mille included a flashback based on the story told in W.E. Henley's poem 'Or Ever the Knightly Years' with its once-famous lines: 'I was a King in Babylon/And you were a Christian Slave'. In Ancient Babylon, the King takes a female slave as his mistress and later, in a demonstration of autocratic power, sends her to her death in the lion's den. The final scene was a recreation of the celebrated Victorian painting 'The Lion's Bride' by Gabriel Cornelius Ritter von Max.[14]

Manslaughter (1922) was the story of a jazz-mad girl whose dangerous driving causes the death of a police motorcyclist and earns her a sentence in jail where she learns the error of her ways. The film was marketed with the slogan 'A Drama of the Mad Age! Is the Modern World Racing to Ruin on a Wave of Jazz and Cocktails?' To reinforce his message, De Mille cut from a scene of the excesses of 1920s flappers to a flashback to the decadence of Ancient Rome, characterized by orgies and gladiatorial displays. Although De Mille ensured that the 'details of the food served at Roman banquets, the rules governing gladiatorial combat, the clothing and arms of Roman ministers, and the proper choreography of a Roman ballet' were established by his team of researchers, Kevin Brownlow dismissed the sequence as 'an excruciating combination of cardboard costumes and half-naked extras'.[15]

In *Adam's Rib* (1922) De Mille told parallel tales of a love affair conducted in the present-day Museum of Ancient History (modelled on the Smithsonian

Institution) and an affair conducted in prehistoric times, for which art director Wilfred Buckland constructed a complete redwood forest on the sound stage and the make-up for the prehistoric men and women was based on the dried heads of Jivaro Indians.[16]

In the same year De Mille, publicity conscious as ever, sponsored a competition for story ideas for future films and several of the respondents suggested the story of the Ten Commandments. De Mille decided on a modern story centred on two brothers, one of whom breaks all the commandments and is punished by God when the cathedral he has built with substandard materials collapses killing his mother, he contracts leprosy from his Eurasian mistress and he is killed in a storm at sea. But De Mille prefaced the modern story with a 55-minute prologue, telling the story of the oppression of the Jews by Pharaoh, the plagues sent by God, the exodus from Egypt, the crossing of the Red Sea, the granting to Moses of the Ten Commandments, the worship of the golden calf and God's vengeance on the idolaters. The film was prefaced by opening titles saying that the modern world had dismissed the Ten Commandments as old-fashioned, but following the First World War they were needed more than ever: 'They are not laws – they are The Law'. De Mille spared no expense to get this prologue right. He despatched an agent, Florence Meehan, around the Middle East to collect authentic artefacts. Her shipments 'filled a studio storage room – silks, swords, tiger skins, tapestries, earrings, embossed plates, rubies from the famous mine at Magot, Burma, and a 1,000 year old suit of Persian armour, and numberless gewgaws for dressing the sets'.[17] Taking advantage of the recent discovery of the tomb of Tutankhamun, which had created a worldwide wave of interest in things Egyptian, De Mille had the treasures photographed and described in detail, so that his designer Paul Iribe could produce authentic sketches for detailed reconstruction. Frustrated in his desire to film in Egypt and Palestine, which Paramount vetoed as too expensive, he proceeded to construct the Egyptian city of Per-Rameses and an avenue of sphinxes at Guadalupe, near Santa Maria, California, to which he imported 2,500 extras and 3,000 animals. He insisted on several hundred Orthodox Jews to give visual authenticity to his 'children of Israel' and a thirty-piece orchestra to provide mood music – it was the largo from Dvořák's New World Symphony that accompanied the exodus. There was a major falling-out during shooting. De Mille disliked the lighting by cameraman Alvin Wycoff, which he thought was obscuring the details of Paul Iribe's sets, and replaced him with the young Peverell Marley, after also recruiting Bert Glennon and Archie Stout, experts in outdoor photography.

With intertitles drawn largely from the Book of Exodus, and a spectacular realization of Edward Poynter's famous painting Israel in Egypt, with the Hebrew slaves hauling a giant sphinx past the great gateway of the city, the prologue told the Biblical story of the exodus straightforwardly. In retrospect, it looks like a blueprint for the 1956 remake, in which many of the camera set-ups and camera angles were reproduced exactly from the silent film. Particularly impressive for 1923 were the special effects, notably the parting of the Red Sea.[18] *The Ten Commandments* was shot between 21 May and 16 August 1923 and it was premiered in Hollywood on 4 December 1923. It had been made at a cost of $1,475,863 and eventually grossed $4,169,798.[19] *Photoplay* (February 1924) called it 'the greatest theatrical spectacle in history, and *The New York Times* (22 December 1923) thought it probable that 'no more wonderful spectacle has ever been put before the public'. Several newspapers reported enthusiastic cheers and applause from audiences.[20]

But De Mille had fought constantly with Paramount about the escalating costs and it was not long before he left to set up his own production company, purchasing the Thomas Ince Studios in Culver City, and inaugurating a programme of production with funding provided by the newly created Producers Distributing Corporation (PDC).

The suggestion for a film on the life of Christ and even the title *The King of Kings* seems to have come on 20 May 1926 from screenwriter Denison Clift. De Mille had been planning to make a film on the subject of Noah's Ark, *The Deluge*, but when he learned that Warner Brothers were intending to produce their own version of the story he switched his attention to the life of Christ.[21] De Mille gained the enthusiastic backing of Jeremiah Milbank, the financier behind PDC, who was so committed to the project that he never took a penny of profits from it, but devoted his share to making and distributing copies of the film to churches and missionaries.[22] This continued to be the case up to the 1960s.

The script for the film was written by De Mille's regular scriptwriter Jeanie Macpherson, in consultation with De Mille. She worked a sixteen-hour day during the production.[23] But there was uncredited assistance on the script from Denison Clift, Jack Jungmeyer and Clifford Howard. As always, for De Mille research was essential. Mrs Elizabeth McGaffey and a staff of twelve spent two months studying 2,500 books and 50,000 feet of documentary film, eventually compiling ten volumes of research notes to ensure that costumes, settings, customs and artefacts were authentic. De Mille instructed cameraman Peverell Marley to study biblical paintings in order to get the lighting of the film correct. According to Charles Higham, 298 paintings were 'fully reproduced' during the course of the film, and Marley used seventy-five different camera lenses instead of his usual four and seven different kinds of film stock, to ensure lighting that matched that of the old masters.[24] But as on *The Ten Commandments* there was a major falling-out with a key member of the creative team. Paul Iribe was designing the sets, as he had on *The Ten Commandments*, but De Mille found them 'too plain, too severe, too dull' and wanted greater richness of texture.

Iribe refused to compromise and De Mille sacked him, replacing him with the set-dresser Mitchell Leisen who was to enjoy a major Hollywood career as designer and, later, director. The massive outdoor sets of the Temple, the Nicanor Gate, and the streets of Nazareth and Jerusalem were designed by the architect Pridgeon Smith.[25] De Mille had sketches made for every scene, shot, costume and prop by a team of artists, Dan Groesbeck, Anton Grot, Edward Jewel, Julian Harrison and Harold Miles.[26] De Mille took great care over the casting, settling on H.B. Warner to play Jesus:

> There was only one man, I felt, who could portray the Christ, with all the virility and all the tenderness, with all the authority yet all the restraint, with all the compassion and all the strength, and with the touch of gentle humour and enjoyment of small simple things and human love of friends, and divine love of His enemies, that the Man of Nazareth had. It was literally a superhuman assignment that I gave to [...] H.B. Warner. How perfectly he fulfilled it has never better been told than by a minister who said to him many years later: 'I saw you in *The King of Kings* when I was a child, and now, every time I speak of Jesus, it is your face I see.'[27]

De Mille went further, declaring 'There is not, in fact, a single bad performance in *The King of Kings* ... all the players ... gave to their parts not only finished artistry, but the understanding which made *The King of Kings* for them, as well as for the audience more than a motion picture.'[28] He does not exaggerate. The film does contain a notable display of silent-screen acting in particular from Joseph Schildkraut as Judas, Rudolph Schildkraut as Caiaphas, Victor Varconi as Pilate and Jacqueline Logan as Mary Magdalene. H.B. Warner is impressive as Christ. But although one of De Mille's advisers on the film, Bruce Barton, had written a bestselling life of Christ, *The Man Nobody Knows*, depicting Christ as 'robust, manly, masterful', Warner's Jesus is closer to the Sunday School image of 'gentle Jesus, meek and mild'. He is associated throughout the film with women and children, in one notable scene mending a child's broken toy, a scene that was one of De Mille's favourites and was shot in the garden of his home. What is striking about Warner's performance is how rarely he moves, he is almost a sacred icon, the still, serene centre of the film, with the action swirling about him.

Anxious to avoid offending any religious denomination, De Mille assembled a team of religious advisers, among them not only Bruce Barton but his father, Revd William T. Barton, the Revd George Reid Andrews, Chairman of the Film and Drama Committee of the Federated Churches of Christ in America, and Father Daniel A. Lord SJ. Of Lord, De Mille wrote: 'Father Lord and I did not always see eye to eye on artistic matters, but I never lost my admiration for that devoted, manly, brilliant Jesuit.'[29] Father Lord left his impression of De Mille in his autobiography:

He was a strange and fascinating blend of absolute monarch and charming gentleman, of excellent host and exacting taskmaster, of ruthless drive on the set and a complete letdown the moment that the day's shooting had come to an end; a Renaissance prince who had the instincts of a Barnum and a magnified Belasco; frankly in love with hokum (which he liked to discuss and reduce to terms of understandable basic emotion); a showman who in all his years has had only one failure at the box office; an excellent listener and a voice that spoke with the most compelling possible command; an Episcopalian whose mother (deeply beloved) was, I think, a Jewish convert to Christianity; … a motion-picture director who made even more money in the banking business; extravagant and yet careful to invest money which he borrowed to put on his pictures. He loved to know that that borrowed money ran into millions and that his backers were worried at his extravagance, while at the time he never lost sight of a penny or really wasted a single foot of film.[30]

Acknowledging that his contribution to the filming had been 'singularly slight', he admitted to having been appalled at De Mille's concept of structuring the film around a romantic triangle involving Judas, Jesus and Mary Magdalene (Judas loves Mary but joins Jesus in the hope of advancement; when Jesus converts Mary and she abandons the life of a courtesan, Judas grows to hate Jesus and eventually betrays him). He was relieved when this was trimmed back and dropped after the opening sequences.[31]

Filming began on Catalina Island on 24 August 1926 with an inter-denominational service conducted by Protestant, Catholic, Jewish, Buddhist and Muslim clerics. Throughout filming spiritual music was piped onto the set to maintain a reverential mood – Handel's *Largo*, Stainer's *Crucifixion* and Dykes' *Holy, Holy, Holy* among other pieces.[32] Filming concluded on 10 January 1927. By the time he finished De Mille had shot 1,500,000 feet of film. For its New York premiere at Easter 1927 he had cut it to 14,000 feet, running two hours 40 minutes. After its road-show engagements, and after Pathé had taken over PDC, De Mille cut *The King of Kings* by a further 42 minutes. The scenes removed included Jesus curing a lunatic boy, Peter thrice denying Christ after his arrest and Claudia Procula (Pilate's wife) interceding for Christ. Most of the best scenes of Peter (Ernest Torrence) were lost in the cutting. It was this cut version that was re-issued in 1931 with Hugo Reisenfeld's score, written for the original release, included on a soundtrack together with sound effects. This is the version most frequently shown but the original roadshow version was recently issued on DVD in the United States. The initial release was greeted with laudatory reviews. *Variety* (20 April 1927) called it a film that 'will live forever, on the screen and in the memory', *The New York Times* (20 April 1927) called it 'the most impressive of all motion pictures' and *The Film Spectator* (11 June 1927) said it was 'something that will live for a long, long time and which will gross more money than any other picture ever made'.

The film declares its evangelical intent at the outset when it says that the film has been made in obedience to Jesus' command that his message be spread to 'the uttermost parts of the earth'. But the opening sequences are pure Hollywood and wholly without scriptural warrant. Unlike other lives of Christ which include the Nativity and boyhood of Christ, this starts with Christ already embarked on his ministry. But the film begins in the luxurious villa of high-class courtesan Mary of Magdala, 'an extraordinary masterpiece of design' as Higham correctly describes it.[33] There, amid a supremely sensuous setting of half-naked slaves, scantily clad dancing girls, swans, gauzes, grapes, silks, jewels, and ostrich-feather fans, painted toothless old men and lascivious voluptuaries recline on couches gorging themselves on fine wines and exotic delicacies. Mary presides, stroking the obligatory pet leopard, established cinematic symbol of decadence (cf. *Cabiria*, *Intolerance*). When Mary enquires after her lover Judas and is told he has gone with a Galilean carpenter and his band of ragged followers, she leaps up demanding imperiously: 'Go fetch my richest perfumes – and harness my zebras – gift of the Nubian King'. Then she is off in her zebra-drawn chariot to win back Judas from Jesus. When Father Lord saw this sequence, he records that he winced: 'It was De Mille at his most De-Millish'. But De Mille explained to him 'how essential it was that the Broadway audience of the world be won over; how they could not be introduced to burlap and desert sands, but must have a sense of luxury and beauty, the kind of life they would themselves like to lead. 'If they fall in love with Magdalene, then when she leaps into her chariot and says, "I go to find a Carpenter", they will go along.'[34]

The scene shifts to the house where Jesus is staying. Crowds gather outside, seeking cures for their ailments. The boy Mark emerges cured of his lameness, throwing away his crutch. The intertitle identifies him as the future gospel-writer (another Hollywood invention). It is Mark who leads a blind girl to Jesus. She asks to be able to see and, in a superbly engineered sequence, the screen floods with light and gradually, as the girl's sight returns, the face of Jesus comes into focus, and he is seen by the audience for the first time. Mary Magdalene arrives in her chariot to confront Jesus, who says to her: 'Be thou clean' and in a powerful allegorical scene, the seven deadly sins emerge from her body – lust, greed, pride, gluttony, indolence, envy and anger, leering superimposed figures writhing and clawing around her. They disappear and, now cleansed of her sins and aware of her semi-nakedness, she draws her cloak around her. Thus cleansed, she is saved and thereafter appears with Jesus at the temple, at the trial, at the Crucifixion and the Resurrection.

These invented sequences establish from the outset the conflict of spirituality and sexuality which would be a recurrent theme in De Mille's Ancient World and Biblical epics. Thereafter with a powerful narrative drive and arresting visual compositions the film covers the raising of Lazarus, Jesus driving the moneychangers from the temple, his temptation by Satan, the Last Supper, the arrest in the garden of Gethsemane, the trial, the Crucifixion and the Resurrection. The action gains from the magnificence of the sets, in particular the monumental Temple and Pilate's Praetorium, with the Procurator seated beneath an enormous eagle, symbol of Roman imperial power. Characteristically, De Mille accompanies the crucifixion with thunder and lightning, a hurricane, the veil of the temple rent and burned, and an earthquake, which among others swallows up the body of Judas hanging from a tree overlooking Golgotha. The Easter sequence with the resurrected Christ emerging from the tomb and appearing to the disciples before ascending to heaven is in colour.

With intertitles drawn mainly from the Authorized Version of the Bible, identified by chapter and verse, with imagery strongly influenced by Doré's illustrations to the Bible and a score incorporating a series of much-loved nineteenth-century hymns, this is a full-blooded Victorian version of the life of Christ. For all the study of the Old Masters, and in particular Rubens for the Crucifixion, the film is suffused by Doré, many of the scenes in composition, lighting and design direct reproductions, among them the raising of Lazarus, the garden of Gethsemane, the Last Supper and Simon of Cyrene taking up the cross. H.B. Warner's make-up and hair as Christ were evidently inspired by Holman Hunt's celebrated painting *The Light of the World*. Reisenfeld's score includes along with his original compositions snatches of Wagner and Liszt, the 'Hallelujah' chorus from Handel's *Messiah* and favourite hymns fitted exactly to key scenes: 'Lead Kindly Light' when the blind girl regains her sight, 'Blessed are the pure in heart' for the exorcism of Magdalene, 'Oh, sacred head, sore wounded' for the last supper, 'Nearer, my God, to thee' for the crucifixion, 'Jesus Christ is risen today' for the Resurrection and 'Rock of Ages' for the Ascension.

Stephenson Humphries-Brooks in his study of Jesus in the cinema says: 'The influence of *King of Kings* at the levels of cinematography, film technique, point of view, and most importantly mythmaking, cannot be overestimated. *King of Kings* moves Christ's image out of church control and into the realm of American popular culture as never before. Christ becomes a major player in the media, and neither the church nor Hollywood would be the same after 1927.'[35] It is certainly taking the story into a new dimension but it should not be overlooked that the film is securely based in the existing and strong traditions of Christian music and Christian art. Nevertheless the fact that an estimated 800 million people had seen the film by 1961 means that it established the popular image of Christ and his mission for several generations.[36] There would be no further life of Christ on screen until the 1961 film *King of Kings*. De Mille received many letters from people telling him that the film had changed their lives.[37]

Stephenson Humphries-Brooks identifies the film, with its 'combination of pseudo-historical authority with a modern Protestant desire to convert' as 'a modern fifth gospel' and one that is predominantly Protestant and American. Comparing the film's narrative to the gospel stories, he identifies an absence of parables, commandments and detailed teaching. 'He is not a preacher nor a revealer of divine speech. He performs miracles of healing and raising the dead in naturalistic scenes. He shows himself to be God ... by means of his penetrating gaze.' He concludes:

> Unlike the Gospel stories of Jesus, in the film there is almost no depiction of the truly poor ... Jesus, his disciples and his mother Mary are presented consistently as pious homeowners not unlike the movie's intended audience. The movie avoids any suggestion of the homelessness of Jesus as depicted in the Gospels. He moves from his house to Jerusalem. He carries out no outdoor ministry to the poor. He heals beautiful, clean, children and women, all represented throughout the course of the film as young and Anglo. *King of Kings* establishes within the first 45 minutes the special relationship of healing between Jesus as the Light of the World and these two groups. No lepers and no vilely oppressed or impoverished people appear. Our Savior is one of us, says the movie: white, male, and Protestant.[38]

However, the film was to cause problems with the Jews. Although Rabbi Edgar F. Magnin wired De Mille to say: 'I believe this picture will exercise a spiritual and wholesome effect upon all who will have the privilege of witnessing it', Rabbi Stephen Wise condemned it. The Jewish actors Joseph Schildkraut and his father, the distinguished stage actor Rudolph Schildkraut, had played Judas and Caiaphas in the film – and they were denounced by some Jews as traitors for doing so.[39] Judas was shown as betraying Christ because of thwarted ambition. He sought to make him King of the Jews and to occupy a major position at his court. However, when Christ declares that his kingdom is not of this world, the disappointed Judas sells him out. But the film shows his torment as he witnesses the scourging of Christ and he later hangs himself in remorse. There is no doubt that Caiaphas is played as a familiar stage Jewish stereotype, handrubbing, hooknosed, scheming and greedy. He is told by Jesus that he has turned the temple into a den of thieves. He is instrumental in arranging Jesus' arrest and trial. The film makes it clear that Pilate is guiltless. He examines Jesus, finds no fault in him and wants merely to chastise and release him. But Caiaphas gets his agents to stir up the people to call for his death. When Pilate offers them the choice of Jesus or Barabbas and they choose Barabbas, Pilate formally washes his hands of the matter. It is Caiaphas who suggests crucifying Jesus but adds that the responsibility will be his alone, thus acquitting the Jewish race of Christ-killing. He repeats his claim of sole responsibility after the Crucifixion. But as Humphries-Brooks notes, the fact that Jesus' opponents are visually and ethnically Jewish tends to shift the guilt back from the individual to the race as a whole.[40]

According to Robert Birchard, a committee of Jewish advisers viewed the film and recommended softening some of the intertitles, in particular: 'the High Priest CAIAPHAS – who cared more for Revenue than for Religion – and saw in Jesus a menace to his rich profits from the Temple' and 'The TEMPLE – to the faithful of Israel, the dwelling place of Jehovah. But to the High Priest, Caiaphas, a corrupt and profitable market-place.' But since they remain intact in the print currently available, they were either changed for the original release and changed back in the 1931 version or not changed at all.[41] Either way, the controversy seems not to have affected the film's profitability. Costing $1,265,283 to produce, the film initially made $2,641,687, but almost all the profit was eaten up by the losses of Cecil B. De Mille Pictures. For *The King of Kings* had been virtually the only successful film to be produced by the new outfit, his other 'specials' *The Volga Boatman, The Yankee Clipper* and *The Godless Girl* being spectacular box office failures. De Mille reluctantly agreed to the takeover of his firm by Pathé, but shortly left to try and re-establish his career at MGM.

There was a potential problem for the film in Britain. The British Board of Film Censors, which had come into existence in January 1913, listed among its screen prohibitions the materialized figure of Christ. A previous life of Christ, Sidney Olcott's *From Manger to Cross*, shot partly in the Holy Land, had been released in 1912 before the Board was established. *Intolerance* (1917) which also featured the figure of Christ, was simply not submitted to the BBFC and somehow avoided condemnation, perhaps because the legal powers of the Board were still unclear. *The King of Kings*, being in clear breach of the rules, was also not submitted but since each local authority retained the power to approve or ban individual films, the distributors took the film to the local councils individually.[42] It was passed initially by London County Council and Middlesex County Council for exhibition in the capital (*The Times*, 27 October 1927). By 1931, 153 authorities out of 160 applied to had granted the film a certificate and it had been successfully shown all over the United Kingdom.[43] *The Times* (15 December 1927) was not impressed by the film:

> Go to a bookshelf that belonged to a Victorian child, take down from it a copy of the Bible richly, reverently, and mawkishly illustrated, and you will find in those illustrations a great part of the inspiration of Mr de Mille's version of the life of Jesus [...] Hollywood, with elaborate self-consciousness, is on its best behaviour; the producer has taken elaborate pains that no great mass of people may be offended. And no one, except certain men and women of taste who resent a sentimental debasement of the Gospel narrative, will find offence in his work; these it will greatly offend. The picture, as it is now shown, is not without emotional effect. It could not be, for the story it tells is not only in itself a great story, but is bound up with our earliest memories [...] But as a work of art, above all as a representation of the personality of Christ, the film is contemptible – a soft and flabby thing, without vigour and without spiritual fire, a piece of conventional 'reverence' in the meanest tradition.

The appearance of the film provoked not only a leader in *The Times* (15 December 1927) ('the film can hardly do harm. It might conceivably do good. There is certainly no case for exceptional ban or boycott'), but also a lively correspondence for and against the film. For the film was the Archdeacon of Rochdale, Thomas Sale, who had seen it in New York: 'everything was done most reverently, and [...] the effect on the audience was comparable with that of the Oberammergau Passion Play, which I have also seen'. Against was F.V. Irwin, writing from The Girls' College, Great Malvern: 'The whole atmosphere of a picture theatre is one of artificiality – an artificiality which does not lend itself to the portrayal of sacred characters in the least [...] the cinema production will always remain bold, crude and unconvincing' (*The Times*, 26 November and 12 December 1927). The controversy doubtless helped to boost box-office takings as controversy generally does.

For Fox in 1921, J. Gordon Edwards directed *The Queen of Sheba* which dramatized the encounter of Solomon and Sheba and the rivalry of Solomon and his brother Adonijah for the throne. Betty Blythe and Fritz Leiber played the leading roles and the action included a chariot race, staged by cowboy star Tom Mix. The film is now lost but surviving stills show spectacular sets and costumes and hordes of extras.[44]

The Wanderer (1926), directed by Raoul Walsh, was recalled by Ivan Butler as 'an extravagant retelling of the parable of the Prodigal Son redeemed by the sincerity of William Collier Jr and the beauty of Swedish actress Greta Nissen'.[45] *The Times* (18 March 1926) thought 'some of the spectacles are magnificent, and the destruction of the city by fire from Heaven is well depicted, but otherwise, there is throughout rather more of Hollywood than of Holy Writ'. Walsh makes no mention of it in his autobiography. Both stories were to be remade during the 1950s' Biblical cycle, as *Solomon and Sheba* (1959) and *The Prodigal* (1955) respectively.

Warner Brothers' film of the Deluge, *Noah's Ark* finally appeared in 1928. It was directed by Hungarian director Michael Curtiz who had made himself a reputation in Europe with two spectacular Ancient World epics, shot in Austria, *Sodom and Gomorrah* (1922–3) and *The Slave Queen* (1924), based on Rider Haggard's novel *Moon of Israel*. Both had been heavily influenced by Hollywood epics – *Sodom and Gomorrah* by *Intolerance*, and *The Slave Queen* by *The Ten Commandments*. On the basis of these productions, Curtiz was signed by Warner in 1926 and assigned to the epic *Noah's Ark*. Costing more than $1 million to make, it was Warner's longest and most ambitious film to date. It was begun as a silent film but, overtaken by the coming of sound, ended up as a part-talkie with dialogue scenes added to the initial silent footage. Based on a screen story by Darryl F. Zanuck, it adopted the familiar De Mille formula of parallel stories set in the present and in the Ancient World. The cast played dual roles, with

George O'Brien as the hero, Dolores Costello as the heroine and Noah Beery as the villain in both narratives.

The Biblical story is heavily derivative, borrowing ideas from *Samson and Delilah*, of which Alexander Korda had directed a version in Austria in 1922 (hero blinded and sent to the grist mill) and *The Ten Commandments* (burning bush, pillar of fire, tablets of stone). It has King Nephilim of Akkad establishing the worship of Hadishah and seizing Miriam, the wife of Japheth, as a sacrifice to the god. Japheth, resisting the seizure, is arrested, blinded and imprisoned. Warned by God, Noah builds an ark, despite the mockery of his neighbours. At the ceremony of sacrifice, a storm breaks out and eventually the flood engulfs the temple. Japheth manages to rescue Miriam, has his sight restored by a miracle and joins Noah and the rest of his family in the ark. They and the animals duly survive the flood which destroys the idol-worshipping Akkadians. The flood was the highlight of the film with 500,000 tons of water dumped on the temple set, causing injuries to several extras.

The modern story, naive and heavy with coincidence, included a spectacular wreck of the Orient Express but concentrated on the First World War, with two American friends sent into battle, leading to the death of one of them, and the heroine rescued from the clutches of a Tsarist secret agent. A padre makes an explicit comparison between the Great War and the Deluge, with God using both phenomena to cleanse the world. The film made a small profit in the United States but recouped $900,000 in Europe, giving it a total profit of $1,250,000.

Only a truncated version of the film now exists. The 135-minute full version which premiered in 1928, was cut to 105 minutes for its general release in March 1929. In 1957, at the behest of American anti-war pressure groups, a streamlined 75-minute version with a spoken commentary replacing the intertitles, was re-issued and has subsequently been seen on television.[46] Even in this form, it is possible to appreciate the superb sets and costumes, the staging of the deluge and Curtiz' ability to handle ceremonial and spectacle, of which his later films gave abundant evidence.

Making absolutely no pretensions to archaeological accuracy in sets or costumes or to moral improvement and educational enlightenment was *Salome* (1922), one of the most extraordinary films to come out of silent Hollywood. It was based on Oscar Wilde's play *Salomé*, the quintessence of fin-de-siècle decadence and the culmination of a continuing exotic and erotic interest in the story of Salome which had already found expression in painting, poetry, novels and opera in France: Flaubert (*Hérodias*, 1876), Gustave Moreau (*Salomé Dansant*, 1876), Massenet (*Hérodiade*, 1881), Huysmans (*A Rebours*, 1884) and Mallarmé (*Hérodiade*, 1891).

Written in French and intended as a vehicle for Sarah Bernhardt, it was already in rehearsal in London in 1892 when it was hurriedly banned by the Lord Chamberlain's office for infringing the established ban on biblical subjects on the stage. Wilde defiantly published it in French with a vivid purple cover early in 1893. *The Times* called it 'morbid, bizarre, repulsive and very offensive'. It was published in English translation in 1894 with illustrations by Aubrey Beardsley. The play was produced in Paris in 1896 and in Berlin in 1903. It was turned into an opera in Germany by Richard Strauss in 1905, a version successfully produced in England at the Royal Opera House, Covent Garden in 1910. The original play continued to be denied a licence by the Lord Chamberlain but it was performed privately at the Court Theatre, London, in 1911.[47] The ban on public performance was only lifted in 1931.

In 1922 Alla Nazimova, the Russian actress who had been acclaimed for her stage performances in Ibsen, decided to film Wilde's play as part of her bid to raise the aesthetic level of the cinema. She had formed an artistic partnership with the designer Natacha Rambova (née Winifred Shaughnessy) and it was Rambova's suggestion that the designs be based on the Aubrey Beardsley illustrations. So sets and costumes were designed in an exclusive colour scheme of black, white and gold and recreated Beardsley with all the associated implications of fin-de-siècle decadence. The film was directed by Charles Bryant but the creative decisions were all those of Nazimova, who adapted the play for the screen under the pseudonym of Peter Winters.

The film emerged as a semi-surreal paean to perversity, with actors striking poses and moving in such a stylized fashion that it ended up looking more like a ballet than a film. There were only two sets, the terrace and banqueting hall of Herod's Palace, but they were filled with an atmosphere that was at once exotic and erotic. Herod himself was played as a leering satyr by Mitchell Lewis, his head garlanded with a wreath of blossoms; the Young Syrian who kills himself for love of Salome was played by Earl Schenck, who with his curly wig, painted lips and languid air, seemed rather more interested in the youthful page whose hand he held for much of the action. There were strapping black slaves, clad only in silver lamé loincloths, a forest of ostrich feather fans, clouds of incense, a gaggle of court women who were men in drag; and an orchestra of capering dwarfs. The overpowering air of effeminacy was insisted on by Nazimova to convey the decadence of the court.

At the centre of the action is the 15-year-old Salome played by the 43-year-old Nazimova, first in a vibrating black wig studded with silver bobbles and later a silver wig. From her statements at the time, it is clear that Nazimova saw Salome as something of a feminist heroine. But her bid for independence resolved itself into the attempt to seduce a holy prophet and a culminating act of necrophilia.

Salome vamps John the Baptist, played by Nigel de Brulier, his ascetic features and emaciated pale body a strikingly spiritual contrast to the sensual atmosphere all around him. With intertitles taken directly from Wilde's play, she seeks to caress his body, his hair and his lips as he sternly repels her, calling her 'Daughter of Sodom'. Salome then performs the dance of the seven veils, clad in what looks like a satin bathing suit. Finally having secured the head of John the Baptist, she kisses its lips, exulting in her triumph as soldiers move in to surround her with raised spears, preparing to carry out Herod's order 'Kill that woman'. The popular reaction to the film was summed up by *Photoplay* who called it 'a hot house orchid of decadent passion' adding 'You have our warning; this is bizarre stuff'. Audiences took the warning and stayed away. It was a box office failure and put an end to Nazimova's programme of artistic improvement, though retrospectively it has been dubbed 'America's first art film'. Nigel de Brulier and Mitchell Lewis would see greater success when cast as Simonides and Ilderim in *Ben-Hur*.[48]

The film that best exemplifies the strong continuity between the nineteenth-century stage and the twentieth-century screen is *Ben-Hur* based on the novel by General Lew Wallace. It had already made film history in 1907 when the Kalem Company was sued by Lew Wallace's son and heir Henry Wallace, his publisher Harper Brothers and the producers of the stage version, Klaw and Erlanger, for breach of copyright. Kalem had, without clearing copyright, produced a 15-minute film version of *Ben-Hur*, complete with painted backdrops, costumes borrowed from the Metropolitan Opera, a handful of extras and a chariot race staged at Manhattan Beach. They were ordered to pay $25,000 for infringement of copyright.

The officially sanctioned film version of *Ben-Hur* eventually reached the screen in 1926 after a turbulent production history. Klaw and Erlanger purchased the film rights from Henry Wallace in 1921 and sold them to Frank Godsol of the Goldwyn Company in return for the promise of half of the profits of the film version. Goldwyn's head scenarist June Mathis, the discoverer of Rudolph Valentino and the moving spirit behind the success of *The Four Horsemen of the Apocalypse*, was put in charge of the project. She prepared a script, cast George Walsh, Francis X. Bushman and Gertrude Olmstead as Judah Ben-Hur, Messala and Esther respectively and selected British-born Charles Brabin as director. The production was to be undertaken in Italy and shooting began in 1923 with the sea battle, which was staged off the coast near Anzio. In the meantime Goldwyn had been absorbed in the merger that created Metro-Goldwyn-Mayer and studio head Louis B. Mayer became increasingly dissatisfied with the footage being shot by Brabin. Mayer's daughter Irene recalled the footage as 'terrible'.[49] So Mayer and his fellow executives Irving Thalberg and Harry Rapf decided on a wholesale change of personnel. Brabin was replaced as director by Fred Niblo, who had directed the Douglas Fairbanks swashbuckler *The Three Musketeers* and the Rudolph Valentino vehicle *Blood and Sand*. Francis X. Bushman was retained as Messala but Ramon Novarro replaced George Walsh and May McAvoy replaced Gertrude Olmstead. Novarro makes a more convincingly boyish Ben-Hur than Charlton Heston in the remake, as the character is supposed to be only 17 when the story starts. Bess Meredyth and Carey Wilson were set to rewrite Mathis' script. All Brabin's footage was scrapped and Niblo reshot the sea battle with full-scale triremes off Livorno. After fire destroyed the property warehouse in Rome, Irving Thalberg ordered the production back to Hollywood where new sets were built and the chariot race was staged by second-unit director, B. Reeves 'Breezy' Eason, who later shot the climactic charge in *Charge of the Light Brigade* (1936) and the land rush in *Cimarron* (1931). It used 12 chariots and 48 horses and proved every bit as exciting and impressive as the 1959 remake.[50] The finished film was premiered on 30 December 1925, road-shown in special presentations throughout 1926 and finally went on general release in 1927. It had cost $4 million to make and grossed $9 million, but distribution and promotion costs were so great that, combined with the deal that gave Klaw and Erlanger half the profits, MGM made a million-dollar loss on the production, though this was eventually recouped when an abridged version with synchronized score and sound effects was released in 1931. Mussolini banned the film in Italy for its hostile depiction of the Roman Empire and it was banned in China as Christian propaganda. *Photoplay* (March 1926) said: 'This is a truly great picture. No one, no matter what his age or religion, should miss it.'

The film is structured around the conflict of values between Christianity and Imperial Rome. So it intercuts episodes from the life of Christ (the Nativity, the Sermon on the Mount, the Woman taken in Adultery, Palm Sunday, the Last Supper – composition based on Leonardo's painting – the Trial, the Via Dolorosa, the Crucifixion, the Resurrection (all in Technicolor)) and the story of Ben-Hur and his rivalry with Messala, filmed in black and white and then tinted. The lives of Jesus and Ben-Hur overlap when Jesus gives the parched, whipped and brutalized Ben-Hur water as he is being led to the coast to join the slave galleys, and when Christ cures the leprous mother and sister of Ben-Hur. Christ is not shown but represented only by his hand or his feet.

The opening titles explain that the world is under the iron heel of pagan Rome and the people call for a deliverer. This tyranny is made obvious in the film's opening sequence at the Joppa Gate when Roman soldiers manhandle, rob and abuse the natives. When Ben-Hur's boyhood Roman friend Messala returns to Jerusalem, he has become arrogant and aloof, telling Judah that the stiff-necked Jews must learn to obey their masters. He urges Ben-Hur to forget that he is a Jew: 'To be a Roman is to rule the world – to be a Jew is to crawl in the dust.' When Ben-Hur is condemned to the galleys for an alleged attempt on the life of the new

Governor, and his mother and sister are imprisoned, Ben-Hur swears vengeance on Messala. Freed after saving the life of the tribune Arrius in a battle against the Macedonian pirates, Ben-Hur establishes his reputation as the leading charioteer in Rome, riding in triumph through the streets, showered with petals by bare-breasted maidens. Then he returns to Antioch where he races against Messala, who is beaten, crippled and ruined. Ben-Hur raises an army to install Jesus as King of the Jews but disbands it when he realizes that the Christian message is non-violence ('His sword is truth and his shield is love. He needs no armies'). After Jesus cures his mother and sister, and is crucified and resurrected, Ben-Hur declares: 'He is not dead. He will live forever in the hearts of men', foreshadowing the victory of the Christian message over the tyranny of Rome.

The 1926 version is much more faithful to the book than the 1959 remake. It develops the romance with Esther, daughter of the Hur steward Simonides, more fully, beginning with a charming encounter (not in the book), when Ben-Hur captures a pigeon which Esther has purchased but which has escaped. The film includes the Egyptian temptress Iras, Messala's mistress, who vamps Ben-Hur. Her character was cut from the 1959 version. It also develops the subplot of Simonides who builds up a fortune in Antioch and becomes known as 'the miser of Antioch'. This also is cut in 1959.

The 1926 version is also grimmer and more gruesome in its evocation of Roman tyranny and man's inhumanity to man. Simonides is racked to get information on the whereabouts of the Hur family treasure. On the galley, a slave goes mad, tries to escape and is lashed to death. During the sea battle, the pirates strap a Roman captive to the prow of their ship before ramming the Roman galley and they release poisonous snakes among the Romans. The crucifixion is followed by darkness, earthquake and the collapse of Pilate's palace, symbol of the fall of Roman power.

As in 1959 the action highlights are the sea battle and the chariot race and both stand up remarkably well. The 1926 sea battle, shot at sea with real ships, is actually more convincing than 1959's sea battle, shot with models in the studio tank. The 1926 chariot race around a central spina decorated with crouching giants had clearly been studied by the recreators of the race in 1959, as several of the set-ups are identical and the central spina is clearly modelled on that of 1926. Both remain among cinema's greatest action highlights.

Comparing the two versions, Lew Wallace's biographers the Morsbergers conclude: 'Wyler's is better in human terms and Niblo's in visual cinema ... As 'pure' cinema, the silent film is superior. Its performance may be operatic ... but its visual pageantry compares favourably with the work of D.W. Griffith and Sergei Eisenstein. While the 1959 film lacks any special period distinction, the silent film has both more sense of the ancient world and a flavor of the 1920s.'[51] Kevin Brownlow's verdict on the film remains unarguable:

Undoubtedly one of the best epics ever made, the original has retained its impressive-ness. The performances are remote and theatrical, but their dignity ideally fits the sagaesque quality of the story. The picture, being the achievement of an organization rather than the work of one man, is not consistent. But it is like a great art gallery, in which one or two halls have been emptied for redecoration. You walk through them without complaint, certain of other treasures to come. Passages in *Ben-Hur*, particularly some of the interior dialogue scenes, are unexciting and exist merely to propel the narrative. But such scenes do not impair the effect of the film as a whole; *Ben-Hur* carries almost as powerful an impact today as it did on its release. The chariot race stands out as the finest scene in the picture, followed closely by the galley battle. The worst elements are the vamp scenes, which are dated and ridiculous, and would have seemed foolish in 1926.[52]

After a series of expensive flops at MGM, De Mille returned in 1932 to Paramount and to history to recoup his fortunes. He chose Wilson Barrett's 1895 play *The Sign of the Cross*, which had a long record of popularity on the stage and had already been filmed as a silent movie in 1904 and 1914. Studio head Manny Cohen told him he was on trial with the picture. He was to be kept on a very tight budgetary rein and in the end managed to produce a film that looked both lavish and expensive on a budget of just under $700,000. It would recoup $2,738,993 at the box office and decisively re-establish De Mille as a popular moneymaker.

With the aid of Mitchell Leisen, who was art director and costume designer, De Mille was able to keep to his budget by building only those sections of his sets (the imperial palace, the arena, etc.) which would actually be photographed, deploying artfully constructed miniatures and disguising the artifice by the use of perspective, lighting and back projection. For example, the opening scene of Nero playing the lyre while Rome burns required only the building of a marble balcony for Nero and then beyond it showing a miniature of the city of Rome in flames.[53]

The heart of the film was Barrett's play, its key scenes reproduced more or less intact with only Barrett's consciously archaic dialogue modernized for 1930s' ears. The play was, however, opened out by the inclusion of spectacle that would not have been possible on the stage (notably the opening sequence of Nero singing and playing the lyre while Rome burned in AD 64; Empress Poppaea luxuriating in a bath of asses' milk; the games in the arena). Like the play, the film foregrounds the pursuit of the chaste Christian maid Mercia by the proud pagan Prefect of Rome, Marcus Superbus. This occurs against the background of the persecution of the Christians by the Emperor Nero. When Marcus' attempt to rescue Mercia fails and Nero decrees her death, at the instigation of the jealous Poppaea, Marcus undergoes a last-minute conversion and goes with Mercia to face death in the arena. The clash of the two rival philosophies of Christian spirituality and pagan sensuality is crystallized at Marcus' banquet when Ancaria, 'the most wicked and talented woman in Rome', performs an explicit dance of lesbian desire, 'The

Naked Moon', around the shrinking Mercia. It is interrupted and eventually halted by the singing of hymns by the Christians as they are led to the arena. De Mille sought to justify the exotic excesses in the film by arguing that *The Sign of the Cross* had a moral message. He told *The New York American* (15 June 1932): 'Do you realize the close analogy between conditions in the United States and the Roman Empire prior to the fall? Multitudes in Rome were then oppressed by distressing laws, overtaxed and ruled by a chosen few. Unless America returns to the pure ideals of our legendary forebears, it will pass into oblivion as Rome did.'

The final arena sequence remains one of the most memorable in Ancient World cinema, including as it does recreations of notable Victorian paintings of the games, in particular Simeon Solomon's *Habet* (1865) with its row of bored patrician ladies watching the fighting, and Jean-León Gérôme's *Ave Caesar, morituri te salutant* (1859) with the assembled gladiators saluting the Emperor, and *Pollice Verso* (1872) with a gladiator straddling his fallen opponent and waiting for the thumbs up or thumbs down signal to kill or spare him. De Mille's camera swoops over the crowd, picking out vignettes of audience reaction as, in the arena, we see gladiators fighting, elephants crushing prisoners underfoot, bears being speared, boxers boxing, wrestlers wrestling, pygmies fighting a crowd of barbarian women, alligators menacing a tied up woman and in a particularly disturbing image a huge gorilla lasciviously menacing a half-naked beauty tied to a post.

Visually the film is a sensuous masterpiece – sumptuous images, filled with the sheen and feel of fur, feathers, silks, satins, rose petals, jewels and precious metals, slow dissolves and ritualized movement giving much of it an appropriate atmosphere of luxury. There are brilliant performances from Charles Laughton, in false nose and curled hair, alternating moods of mania and boredom and intoning lines like 'delicious debauchery' with a wicked twinkle in his eye and Claudette Colbert as a feline Empress Poppaea, glorying shamelessly in her immorality. Fredric March makes a fine, virile, flashing-eyed Roman aristocrat, first seen thundering through the streets with a three-horse chariot and then laying about him with a whip. Elissa Landi makes a saintly Mercia. Ian Keith contributes a telling study of thin-lipped, grim-visaged villainy as Tigellinus the Praetorian Prefect and chief Christian-hunter. De Mille saw *The Sign of the Cross* as the completing of a trilogy of linked religious dramas: *The Ten Commandments* as the giving of the Law, *King of Kings* as the interpretation of the Law and *The Sign of the Cross* as the preservation of the Law.[54]

After another failed modern dress drama (*Four Frightened People*), De Mille retreated once again to the Ancient World for *Cleopatra* (1934). As Sir Herbert Beerbohm Tree had cast Constance Collier as Cleopatra after she had played Poppaea for him in *Nero*, so De Mille hired Claudette Colbert to play the Egyptian Queen following her success as Poppaea in *The Sign of the Cross*. With his first choice Fredric March unavailable, De Mille chose a British newcomer to Hollywood, Henry Wilcoxon, to play Antony, and Warren William to play Julius Caesar. The script was written by Vincent Lawrence and Waldemar Young 'from historical material assembled by Bartlett Cormack', though it included sly nods to both Shakespeare and Shaw. The film was shot between 12 March and 2 May 1934 and again De Mille was kept to a tight budget. This time the film came in at $842,908 and eventually grossed $1,929,161, once again vindicating De Mille's approach and appeal. The economy with which he operated can be seen in the montage sequence, created by William Cameron Menzies, to encapsulate the military campaign between Octavian and Antony. It was done with a succession of rapid cuts: trumpets are blown and a forest of moving banners and eagles signals the advance. There are stock-shot battle scenes, footage of charging chariots from *The Ten Commandments* and a fleet of miniatures fighting the battle of Actium, with close-ups of the protagonists superimposed, plus some limited new shooting of Antony in close combat, representing the military action and the whole is bathed in music from Tchaikovsky's suite *Francesca da Rimini*.

Despite De Mille's customary insistence on research and authenticity, the film has an indelible 1930s feel. Travis Banton's elegant costumes and the impressive sets designed by Hans Dreier and Roland Anderson, for all their Egyptian inspiration, are pure art deco. The dialogue is modern colloquial and *Variety* compared Calpurnia's feast in Rome to a present-day bridge party.[55]

Before shooting his own film, De Mille had sent for a copy of Fox's 1917 extravaganza *Cleopatra*, directed by J. Gordon Edwards and starring Theda Bara. The Fox film had boasted a cast of 5,000, 2,000 horses and a budget of $500,000, but Cleopatra had been portrayed as a typical silent screen vamp.[56] The Fox film was subsequently destroyed in a fire in 1937 and no known copy now survives. De Mille would take a different tack.

The film luxuriates in its Orientalism. It opens with a silhouette of pyramids and palm trees, great bronze doors opening, a slave girl raising a smoking censer, and then a statue of the Sphinx, setting the atmosphere from the outset. Cleopatra is kidnapped by Pothinos, chief minister of her brother and royal rival Ptolemy, and dumped in the desert. But after Julius Caesar arrives in Alexandria, she is delivered to him, wrapped in a carpet, and wins his support with her talk of empire. Caesar, first seen examining models of new instruments of war, is attracted to her ('I picked a flower in Britain once the colour of your eyes') and restores her to the throne of Egypt. Later he returns with her to Rome. There is a splendid triumphal entry, beginning with Caesar and his legions with flowers strewn in their path, but then Cleopatra (arrayed as Isis) on a golden palanquin borne by two dozen Nubian slaves, preceded by fan bearers, slave dancers and clouds of incense: the embodiment of the Oriental threat to Rome. Brutus and Cassius plot Caesar's murder at the baths, the décor evoking memories of Alma-Tadema.

Caesar is assassinated and Cleopatra flees back to Egypt. Antony and Octavian divide the empire.

Antony, who swaggers about, accompanied by a brace of wolfhounds on a lead, is an unreconstructed male chauvinist, dismissing women early on: 'They've no place with men! They can't think and they can't fight! They're just playthings for us!' The high point of the film in sheer sensuousness is Cleopatra's seduction and enslavement of Antony. It takes place aboard her royal barge. De Mille had said: 'This entire barge sequence should be the most seductive, erotic, beautiful, rhythmic, sensuous series of scenes ever shown' – and so it was. Antony strides aboard the gleaming barge at Tarsus, slaves waving fans in front of him, as he approaches Cleopatra, seated beneath an awning of feathers. Exotic foods and drinks are served. The erotic dance of Europa and the bull is staged, with the bull, golden-horned and garlanded and Europa strapped to its back. Girls dressed as mermaids are hauled from the sea in a great net and scatter handfuls of jewels among the guests. Girls in tiger skins perform a wild dance, mauling their whip-wielding overseers and somersaulting through flaming hoops. Antony and Cleopatra, drinking heavily, embrace, and at her signal, slaves mask them with silken curtains. Then De Mille pulls his camera back in a long, slow dolly shot through a rain of falling rose petals, clouds of incense, scantily clad dancers writhing sensuously, until Apollodorus raises his arm to signal the oarsmen to row and with the *hortator* beating time, the oars go in and out in regular rhythm, a visual equivalent of the act of sex presumed to be taking place behind the silken curtains.

Back in her palace, Antony, now drinking heavily, and Cleopatra luxuriate in each other's company, amid peacocks and tame leopards. King Herod brings a message to Cleopatra from Octavian. If she poisons Antony, Egypt is guaranteed Rome's friendship. Cleopatra prepares a poisoned rose, tests it on a condemned prisoner and prepares to kill Antony, when news arrives that Octavian has declared war. Antony is galvanized into action and Cleopatra, entranced by the sight, declares: 'I have seen a god come to life. I am no longer a queen. I am a woman.' But Antony is defeated in battle and believing that Cleopatra has deserted him, stabs himself. Cleopatra poisons herself with an asp, and when Octavian and his men break into her mausoleum, they find her dead, arrayed in her full royal regalia, seated on her throne. They stand awed. De Mille holds the shot until Cleopatra comes to seem like some permanent image of Ancient Egypt and then slowly fades.

Claudette Colbert's Cleopatra is a woman who sets out to manipulate men for her own political purposes but ends up falling in love with them. She falls in love with Caesar, though after his death Apollodorus tells her Caesar never really loved her but used her to gain control of Egypt. She falls in love with Antony and when he dies, she does also. This is De Mille's conservative take on the Modern

Woman: her meddling in politics leads to disaster, so she needs to be tamed by love and put in her place. Colbert gives a winningly seductive performance as Cleopatra, ably supported by Warren William as a brusquely calculating Caesar with a sardonic line in humour, Henry Wilcoxon's virile and masterful Antony, Ian Keith's sour, gloweringly vindictive Octavian and Joseph Schildkraut's elegant and slyly scheming Herod. C. Aubrey Smith's bluff, down-to-earth old soldier Ahenobarbus, stripping off his medals when he leaves Antony but giving him a final salute for what he might have been, is moving and actually reduced Wilcoxon to tears during the shooting of the scene.[57]

Director Ernest B. Schoedsack, producer Merian C. Cooper and special effects maestro Willis O'Brien were the team who created the legendary *King Kong* (1933). They regrouped in 1935 to make *The Last Days of Pompeii*. Cooper had visited the ruins of Pompeii on his honeymoon and was inspired to film the disaster of AD 79 which resulted in the city being entombed in ash and lava from Mount Vesuvius. They used only Bulwer-Lytton's title, dispensing with his story entirely, but they added a prologue explaining that they had drawn on Bulwer-Lytton for his descriptions of the city and it had inspired the physical setting of their film.

They replaced the Bulwer-Lytton narrative with a story, scripted by Ruth Rose and Boris Ingster, which was a cross between *Ben-Hur* and *The Sign of the Cross* but also drew on the conventions of three popular 1930s' genres: the disaster film (*San Francisco, The Hurricane, In Old Chicago*); the gangster film (*Little Caesar, Manhattan Melodrama, The Roaring Twenties*) and the father-love film (*Sorrell and Son, My Son, My Son*). The new story responded directly to the plight of the poor in the Depression. Marcus the blacksmith loses both his wife and son after an accident because he cannot afford the doctor's fees and he is evicted from his home for non-payment of tax. As a result, he becomes obsessed with the pursuit of money and power. 'Money is all that matters' he declares and after he gets it, 'Neither God nor Man shall take it from me.' Having at the outset declared himself a man of peace, he is driven to cruel and inhuman pursuits to gain wealth, first as a gladiator killing men in the arena and then as a slave trader, rounding up captives in Africa. Adopting Flavius, the son of an opponent killed in the arena, he finally secures his wealth in Judaea when on behalf of the Governor Pontius Pilate he leads a raid on the Ammonites and returns with a fortune in horses and gold. There are, however, encounters with Christ (who is not actually shown). He cures Flavius after the boy is injured in a fall from a horse and later, as Christ hauls his cross through the crowds to his Crucifixion, Marcus declines to intervene and rescue him.

Back in Pompeii, Marcus becomes the head of the arena. But Flavius turns Christian and secretly helps runaway slaves to hide, planning to transport them all by ship to a free island beyond the reach of Rome. When the fugitives are rounded up and sent to the arena, Marcus begs for his son's life but the Prefect Albus Marcius rejects his pleas. Marcus realizes that all his money cannot save his son's life. At this point Vesuvius erupts; Marcus abandons his gold to rescue survivors – among whom he finds his son. Seeing the survivors safely aboard ship, he holds off the pursuing Prefect and his men until he is mortally wounded. Dying, he has a vision of Christ who blesses him. The moral of the film is that Christian charity is more important than wealth.

Preston Foster, who usually starred in tough contemporary dramas and had made an impact as the condemned gangster in *The Last Mile* (1932), brings a flavour of those roles to Marcus the gladiator. But the film is stolen by Basil Rathbone as the aristocratic Pontius Pilate, tormented by memories of the man he crucified and exiting with the famous line 'What is truth?' There is a nice attention to historical detail (the pouring of libations, the propitiating of the household gods) and some wry topical allusions, as when British prisoners of war are sent by Agricola for the arena and the Prefect sneers: 'Why do we bother with that wretched island. Whatever we do, they will always be barbarians.' But the film is for the most part a character study of a decent man corrupted by the desire for money. The action is mainly kept for the finale. The combat scenes in the arena are effective but quite short and do not measure up to those in *The Sign of the Cross*. The raid on the Ammonites is reported rather than shown. The final disaster, created by Willis O'Brien, is, however, undeniably impressive. Fires rage, buildings topple, lava flows, statues crash and the ground opens up to engulf fleeing people, all to the accompaniment of Max Steiner's *King Kong* music recycled.[58]

The film failed to emulate De Mille's success, losing $237,000. The absence of the De Mille trademarks of vigorous action and sensual atmosphere may have accounted for its lack of success on its initial release. Re-issued in a double bill with *She* in 1949 to capitalize on the renewed interest in the Ancient World it finally recouped its losses.[59]

The failure of *The Last Days of Pompeii*, coinciding with the box-office failure of De Mille's *The Crusades* put an end to the Ancient World cycle. De Mille re-couped his fortunes spectacularly in 1937 with *The Plainsman*, his retelling of the story of Wild Bill Hickok, which sparked off a cycle of epics of American history, including *Wells Fargo* (1937), *Stagecoach* (1939), *Dodge City* (1939), *Northwest Passage* (1939), *Jesse James* (1939), *Drums Along the Mohawk* (1939) and *Santa Fe Trail* (1940), as well as De Mille's *The Buccaneer* (1938), *Union Pacific* (1939) and *Northwest Mounted Police* (1940). With war looming in Europe, cinema looked to teach the essentials of 'Americanism' and the heroic example of American pioneers to its audiences. The Ancient World was shelved for the time being.

3

The 1950s and 1960s:

THE ROMAN EMPIRE

More feature-length films based on the Bible and/or the history of the Roman Empire were made by Hollywood between 1950 and 1965 than in any other period of film history. Why? One obvious reason is the rise of television. Television mounted a major challenge to the cinema during the 1950s, plunging Hollywood into crisis. Between 1951 and 1958 weekly audience figures in the United States fell from 90 million to 42 million; and between 1946 and 1959 the number of cinemas virtually halved from 20,000 to 11,000.[1] In 1953 it was reported that 20th Century-Fox had sacked 500 members of staff and cut its output from 60 films a year to between 12 and 25 and Metro-Goldwyn-Mayer had reduced its work force from 5,000 to 2,700. In Britain, Hollywood's largest overseas market, annual cinema admissions fell from 1,635 million in 1946 to 515 million in 1960. The number of cinemas fell from 4,583 in 1950 to 3,414 in 1959.[2]

Hollywood's reaction was to seek to do things not open to the small flickering black and white box in the corner of the average living room. In terms of films, the early TV channels subsisted chiefly on a diet of old 'B-movie' westerns as the major studios resolved to refuse to release their own back catalogues of classics, a boycott initially breached in 1957 when RKO Radio Pictures closed down, selling its studio to the television company Desilu, and released its past product to television. The opposite extreme was represented by lavish and spectacular recreations of the past, in particular the Ancient World. These subjects were enhanced by technological innovations in colour and screen size. The hitherto monopolistic Technicolor was joined in the 1950s by Eastmancolor, De Luxe color, Warnercolor and Trucolor. The standard screen size was expanded first by Cinemascope but then also by Cinerama, Techniscope, Warnerscope, Panavision and VistaVision. There was also briefly the gimmick of 3D films, until people got fed up with having to wear special glasses and with Indians landing in their laps and tomahawks in their heads. The success of Cinemascope led Darryl F. Zanuck, the head of 20th Century-Fox, to issue a decree (12 March 1953) ordering the abandonment of further work on any project which could not take advantage of the Cinemascope format. In particular intimate comedies and small-scale domestic dramas were to be abandoned for the time being.[3]

Few film genres have been so critically despised and disparaged by film critics as the Ancient World epic. Serious, whole-hearted appreciations of such films in the press have been rare. Ridicule, impatience and disgust tend to permeate the reviews. A typical example is the British critics' reaction to *Quo Vadis*, many of them picking up on the promotional description 'colossal' used in the advertising. 'Three hours of vulgarity, clichés and disgust' said Dilys Powell in the *Sunday Times* (2 February 1952). C.A. Lejeune in the *Observer* (2 February 1952) wrote: 'Good it is not; colossal it undoubtedly is; colossally showy, colossally well-meaning, colossally crowded, conceived in what might be described as colossally poor taste'. Virginia Graham in the *Spectator* (1 February 1952) said: '*Quo Vadis* is certainly colossal; not only as a spectacle but also as a bore [...] The colour is magnificent, the crowd scenes stupendous, the taste poor and the length appalling.' Thomas Spencer in the *Daily Worker* (26 January 1952) agreed: 'the really colossal things about *Quo Vadis* [...] are the vulgarity and the boredom'. Fred Majdalany in the *Daily Mail* (26 January 1952) resorted to sarcasm, saying 'it is epic only in length' and 'the settings are certainly colourful and should be a great source of inspiration to designers of Turkish baths and future Odeons. The arena scenes are on the grand cup-final scale', before moving on to dismiss the acting of Robert Taylor ('sturdily West Point'), Deborah Kerr ('the first Christian martyr to go to the stake in diaphanous blue chiffon') and Peter Ustinov ('ogles his way through Nero rather as if he is Oscar Wilde playing Pantomime Dame').

There were many critics who detested the genre. It was the opposite of the characteristics of quality cinema which emerged in the 1940s, as identified by John Ellis, and dominated critical reaction at least until the 1960s.[4] This critical stance placed the greatest value on documentary realism, literary quality and a middle-class improvement ethic. Several critics openly acknowledged their antipathy to Ancient World epics. The respected *Sunday Times* critic Dilys Powell revealed this when in 1961 she published her 'Scripture Prizes 1932–61':[5]

> *Most Vulgar*: THE SIGN OF THE CROSS
> *Most Nauseating*: QUO VADIS
> *Most Exhausting*: THE TEN COMMANDMENTS
> *Most Nondescript*: THE ROBE
> *Most Luxurious Blood-Baths*: SAMSON AND DELILAH
> *Most Idiotic Additional Dialogue*: THE BIG FISHERMAN
> *Most Genteel Orgy*: SOLOMON AND SHEBA
> *Special Chariot-Race Award*: BEN-HUR

There was self-evidently a middle-class puritan distaste for excess. Michael Wood identified this when he wrote:

The amount of money spent on the film was part of what helped to sell the film – and the principle, presumably, that anything that had cost that much had to be good, and also if it cost that much, we were invited to think, just imagine how much it will make. A projection of fabulous success for the movie becomes part of the movie's story before it even reaches the cinema. To be sure, this was always a Hollywood principle, but the epics consecrated it and interiorized it, so to speak, as if it were the only principle the industry had left [...] Only epics, I think, insist on our thinking so much about money while we are in the cinema. Every gesture, every set piece bespeaks fantastic excess. There is more of everything, and especially there are more extras drawing what we all think of (erroneously) as magnificent daily pay, than even an excessive movie could possibly need. We sit there and brood about (and vaguely exult in) the sheer extravagance of setting up the Exodus from Egypt, say, in this exorbitant way.[6]

This is all in marked contrast to the critical reaction to the Ancient World epics of the 1920s and 1930s.

Rarely has there been such an extreme disjuncture between critics and the public as there has been over the Ancient World epic. For by comparison with the critical dismissal of so many of these films, the public have flocked to see them in their millions. Between 1950 and 1963, Ancient World epics topped the US box office returns in seven out of the thirteen years: *Samson and Delilah* in 1950, *David and Bathsheba* in 1951, *The Robe* in 1953, *The Ten Commandments* in 1957, *Ben-Hur* in 1960, *Spartacus* in 1962, and *Cleopatra* in 1963, while in 1952 *Quo Vadis* came second only to *The Greatest Show on Earth*. The same pattern was repeated internationally.

All these films, apart from *Spartacus* and *Cleopatra*, centred on conflict between on the one hand Christianity or Judaism and on the other hand tyranny. *Spartacus* represented a departure from this religion-based cycle, as we shall see, and signals something of a sea change. The films were made against the background of the two principal political events overshadowing 1950s America: the Cold War and the domestic anti-Communist witch-hunt. It did not take long for America's wartime ally, the Soviet Union, to turn into an enemy. In 1946 Churchill made his famous 'Iron Curtain' speech. The Berlin Blockade followed in 1948. Russia acquired the Atomic Bomb in 1948 and the Korean War broke out in 1950. Thereafter the world was basically divided into two blocs; one supporting the USA and the other supporting the USSR.

The domestic by-product of the Cold War was the rise of anti-Communist paranoia in the USA and the McCarthyite inquisition against not just Communists but also liberals and radicals. This was crystallized in the activities of the House Un-American Activities Committee (HUAC) which began work in 1947. Hollywood became a primary target of their investigations, vulnerable because all the studios had produced pro-Russian pictures during the war. The Hollywood producers took fright and agreed not to employ anyone believed to be a Communist. A blacklist was established which was firmly in place by 1950. In 1947 ten Hollywood writers and directors, called to give evidence, were deemed unfriendly witnesses, convicted of contempt of Congress and sent to prison. Others fled to Europe. For a decade Hollywood operated in the shadow of the blacklist, which was finally broken in 1960.

Films in the 1950s overtly and covertly attacked the Soviet Union. But some also more circumspectly attacked HUAC. Ancient World epics were among the genres used for both purposes. There was another subtler anti-imperialist message encoded in the Ancient World epics and this was what one scholar has called 'the aural paradigm', which dictated that rulers should almost invariably be played by British actors, the precisely enunciated voice recalling the aristocratic Empire from which the United States had emancipated itself in 1776, and about which despite alliance in two world wars it always entertained ambivalent feelings.[7] Thus we saw Peter Ustinov as the Emperor Nero and Leo Genn as Petronius Arbiter in *Quo Vadis*, Ernest Thesiger as the Emperor Tiberius in *The Robe*, Barry Jones as the Emperor Claudius in *Demetrius and the Gladiators*, Maurice Evans as the Emperor Antoninus in *Androcles and the Lion*, Sir Cedric Hardwicke as the Emperor Tiberius in *Salome*, George Relph as the Emperor Tiberius and Jack Hawkins as Consul Quintus Arrius in *Ben-Hur*, Sir Laurence Olivier as the dictator Crassus, Peter Ustinov as the *lanista* Batiatus and Charles Laughton as senator Gracchus in *Spartacus*, and Sir Alec Guinness as the Emperor Marcus Aurelius in *The Fall of the Roman Empire*. The same 'aural paradigm' for the same reason applied to Egyptian pharaohs, hence Michael Wilding as Akhnaton in *The Egyptian*, Jack Hawkins as Khufu in *The Land of the Pharaohs*, Sir Cedric Hardwicke as Sethi I in *The Ten Commandments* and David Farrar as Psussenes in *Solomon and Sheba*. In *The Robe*, the otherwise unknown New York actor Jay Robinson was cast as Caligula and made a big hit. As he revealed in his autobiography, he replaced at short notice the British actor John Buckmaster, who had originally been cast but had suffered a nervous breakdown. Robinson played the part with an impeccable British accent, which was one of his stage accomplishments.[8]

William Wyler's decision to strictly enforce the 'aural paradigm' on *Ben-Hur* necessitated the replacement after shooting had started of English actress Marie Ney, playing Ben-Hur's mother, by American actress Martha Scott.[9] On *Spartacus*, executive producer Kirk Douglas decided on a similar strict division between the Romans, to be played by British actors, and the slaves, to be played by Americans. So although the experienced Jean Simmons lobbied for the role of Varinia, Spartacus' wife, she was rejected on the grounds of her British accent in favour of an unknown German actress Sabine Bethmann, as Douglas wanted to stress the foreign origin of the slave wife. However, after only a couple of days shooting, Bethmann was deemed inadequate and Simmons was rushed into the role.[10] The casting of the beautiful but totally wooden American actor John Gavin as Julius Caesar, which also breaches the 'aural paradigm', was presumably a requirement of Universal for whom Gavin was a contract star being groomed for greatness – wisely he eventually abandoned acting to become US Ambassador to Mexico.

The success of faith-based historical dramas directly reflects the mindset of 1950s' America and explains the ideological thrust of many of these films and their success in the face of critical contempt. In 1949 the Protestant evangelist Billy Graham launched a religious revival in Los Angeles, declaring:

> Do you know that the Fifth Columnists, called Communists, are more rampant in Los Angeles than any other city in America? […] God is giving us a desperate choice, a choice of either revival or judgement. There is no alternative […] The world is divided into two camps. On one side we see Communism […] (which) has declared war against God, against Christ, against the Bible, and against all religion! […] Unless the Western world has an old-fashioned revival, we cannot last.[11]

His crusade vigorously promoted by the anti-Communist Hearst press, Billy Graham became a national celebrity. Stephen Whitfield has placed Graham in context:

> Graham's rise to prominence is unintelligible outside of the milieu of dread and anxiety in which he emerged. A preacher became more publicized than any American other than the president because of the message he delivered – mixing the fear of Armageddon with the assurance of redemption. The concerns he addressed, perhaps more than the solution that he provided, made Graham a phenomenon who seemed uncommonly attuned to the *Zeitgeist*.[12]

He had his own weekly television programme from 1952 and a syndicated news-paper column. The evils of atheistic Russia, whose creed he attributed directly to the influence of Satan, and Communist infiltration in the USA were a regular theme of his sermons. He backed Senator McCarthy's HUAC investigations.

It was not just Protestants who espoused anti-Communism, Catholics did too. In 1949 Pope Pius XII excommunicated Catholics who professed or promoted Communist ideas and Cardinal Spellman, the leading Catholic cleric in America and a fervent anti-Communist, denounced the menace of Communism both at home and abroad. He equated patriotism and anti-Communism and gave his enthusiastic backing to McCarthy.

Given the atheism associated with Communism, church membership became a way of affirming the American way of life in the 1950s and Christianity became equated with Americanism. In 1954 the phrase 'One nation under God' was by Act of Congress added to the pledge of allegiance to the USA recited daily by American schoolchildren. Church membership in the USA rose from 43 per cent of the population in 1921 to 49 per cent in 1940, to 55 per cent by 1950, to 69 per cent by 1960. Nine out of ten Americans believed in the divinity of Christ, according to a 1954 survey. Religious books, fictional and non fictional, featured in the top ten lists every year until 1959. (The distribution of faiths in 1957 was 66 per cent Protestants, 26 per cent Catholics and 3 per cent Jews.)[13]

The principal ideological purpose then of the 1950s' Roman Empire epics is an attack on the totalitarianism of Soviet Russia as an integral part of Cold War propaganda. So the continuing theme of the majority of the films is the conflict between tyranny and freedom. The Roman Empire is the ultimate totalitarian society, characterized by slavery, oppression, war, dictatorship and paganism. The Christians, Jews and slaves who oppose the Empire stand for democracy, brotherhood, peace and belief in the one God.

But, interestingly, the roots of the Roman Empire cycle lay in the desire during and immediately after the war to use Rome to denounce Nazism, appropriate enough in that Nazi buildings, ceremonial and even salute were modelled on those of Ancient Rome. First off the mark, in terms of cinematic release, was the old maestro Cecil B. De Mille who in 1944 reissued his 1932 Roman epic *The Sign of the Cross* with a newly filmed prologue, scripted by Dudley Nichols. The film detailed the persecution of the Christians by the Emperor Nero (Charles Laughton) and featured a romance between the proud pagan Roman aristocrat (Fredric March) and the chaste Christian maiden (Elissa Landi). It ends with her converting him to Christianity and both of them going joyfully to their death in the arena. The prologue has American bombers flying over Rome in 1944 and Catholic and Protestant chaplains aboard discussing Roman history and comparing the Allies' fight against Hitler to the Christians' resistance to Nero before the film flashes back to the 1932 film, suitably trimmed of its loucher elements (such as an attempted lesbian seduction) in order to conform to the stricter censorship regulations that had emerged since 1932.

The success of this reissue prompted Louis B. Mayer of MGM to order a production of *Quo Vadis*, based on the 1896 novel by Henryk Sienkiewicz, which had a virtually identical plot to *The Sign of the Cross* except that hero and heroine survive rather than dying in the arena. Arthur Hornblow Jr, a civilized and literate producer, was assigned, and scripting was begun. Classics scholar Hugh Gray, who was an MGM researcher, began the extensive research into the subject and the background which was the hallmark of Hollywood Roman epics. In 1949 John Huston was assigned as director. An experienced scriptwriter himself, he rejected the draft script he was presented with and suggested that he should write a new one with Gray, whom he described in his autobiography as 'an exceptionally cultivated man with a delightful personality'.[14] Huston made clear his intention in his autobiography:

> We wrote about half the script, and I thought it was quite good, but it wasn't what L.B. Mayer wanted. Mayer was after a De Mille-like religious epic. Gray and I were writing

a modern treatment about Nero and his fanatical determination to eliminate the Christians in much the same manner as his historic counterpart and fellow madman, Adolf Hitler, tried to destroy the Jews two thousand years later.[15]

Hornblow backed Huston when Mayer urged them to make a film which was a 'spiritual, uplifting experience, a C.B. De Mille picture' and they proceeded to pre-production, hopeful of bringing Mayer round to their way of thinking. Production was scheduled to begin in Rome in July 1949. Gregory Peck, Elizabeth Taylor and Peter Ustinov were cast in the leading roles of Marcus Vinicius, Lygia and Nero. But when Peck developed an eye infection and production was postponed, Hornblow and Huston withdrew from the production and moved on to make *The Asphalt Jungle*. In search of the kind of film he wanted, Mayer assigned a new team to *Quo Vadis*, director Mervyn LeRoy, producer Sam Zimbalist and screenwriters John Lee Mahin and S.N. Behrman. Hugh Gray's only contribution to the final script, credited to Mahin, Behrman and Sonya Levien, was the splendid lyrics he composed for Nero's songs. Huston concluded Mayer 'got the story he wanted all along. It was another dreadful spectacle, catering to the audience L.B. thought was there; L.B. was right; the audience was there.'[16] Huston is actually being grossly unfair to the film, which is a superb production and still contained a powerfully anti-fascist message in its imagery. Ironically Louis B. Mayer had been fired from MGM before the film was released.

LeRoy leaped at the chance to direct *Quo Vadis*, saying later: 'I had watched Cecil B. De Mille work [...] and I had always harboured a secret yen to make one of them myself.' During a brief acting career he had played one of the Israelites in the 1923 version of *The Ten Commandments*.[17]

The film was shot over a six-month period in 1950 at Cinecittà Studios in Rome, with a largely British cast. Italy was chosen partly for the authentic Mediterranean atmosphere, partly to utilize 'frozen funds' and partly because labour was cheap and the film required 30,000 extras. Much of 1951 was taken up with post-production at MGM Hollywood and MGM British. Press releases stressed the 'colossal' nature of the undertaking – the word 'colossal' became part of the advertising for the film – and quoted enormous figures for the costumes, props, numbers of extras, etc. Mayer stressed the film's topicality: 'never was the time more opportune to make such a film, when the world is once more confronted with the struggle of material and spiritual values'.[18]

The intelligent, literate and dramatically well-structured script evokes both the power of Rome and the nature of the challenge presented to it by Christianity. It is set out in the opening narration, spoken by Walter Pidgeon:

Imperial Rome is the centre of the empire and undisputed master of the world, but with this power inevitably comes corruption. No man is sure of his life. The individual is at the mercy of the state. Murder replaces justice. Rulers of conquered nations sur-render their helpless subjects to bondage. High and low alike become Roman slaves, Roman hostages. There is no escape from the whip and the sword. That any force on earth could shake the foundations of this pyramid of power and corruption, of human misery and slavery seems inconceivable. But thirty years before this day, a miracle occurred. On a Roman cross in Judaea, a man died to make men free, to spread the gospel of love and redemption. Soon that humble cross is destined to replace the proud eagles that now top the victorious Roman standards. This is the story of that immortal conflict.

Under the narration, we see images of Roman soldiers marching, slaves being whipped and herded and Christ in Jerusalem hauling his cross to his crucifixion.

The film, like the book and its stage adaptations, mingles the fictional love story of Marcus Vinicius, legate of the XIV Legion, and the Christian maiden Lygia and the parallel love story of his uncle, Gaius Petronius, *arbiter elegantiae* to Nero and his Spanish slave girl Eunice, with actual events of the reign of Nero (the Great Fire of Rome, the persecution of the Christians) and the exposition of Christ's teachings by Peter and Paul.

The main ideological thrust of the film is the contrast between Roman and Christian values. Roman values are embodied in the proud, ruthless soldier Marcus Vinicius. He fails to understand the Christian refusal to fight. He does not understand the freeing of his slaves by the Christian convert Plautius ('There always have to be slaves'). His personal philosophy is 'Conquest is the only method of uniting the world under one power.' He rejects Lygia's desire to learn and teach Christianity ('She wasn't born to think; she was born to feel') and compares taming a woman to taming a horse. He denounces Christianity as a religion of outcasts, slaves and aliens. Christian values are embodied in the gentle, loving Lygia, the foreign princess who is the ward of the old general Aulus Plautius and seeks to explain the new faith to Vinicius. The Christian message is spelled out by the apostle Peter in his address to a secret Christian gathering. He outlines the life of Christ, recites the Beatitudes and urges Christians to obey their existing rulers and the laws, to commit no acts of violence, to love their neighbours and to turn the other cheek.

During the course of the film Vinicius comes gradually to accept the truth of Christianity, humanized and softened by his love of Lygia, whom he marries. In his final exchange with his friend Fabius Nerva, after the death of Nero as they watch Galba's legions entering Rome to restore order, he concedes the vital importance of Christianity to society – a permanent society is not possible without a permanent faith.

The Nazi imagery is all there in the filming of the story. The sinister Praetorian Guard with their black robes and black plumes and their Nazi salute are evidently conceived as an analogue of the Gestapo. The sequence of Vinicius' triumph looks to be modelled directly on Leni Riefenstahl's *Triumph of the Will*. The various gods are invoked and receive ritual responses 'We worship you' with the crowd's arms raised. A woman in the crowd holds up her child to see the Emperor. Nero takes the salute from a balcony as the troops march past in perfect order and Vinicius from his chariot gives the Nazi salute. These are all vignettes present in *Triumph*.

The sequence of Nero with a huge model layout of his new Rome, Neropolis, duplicates exactly the sequence of photographs showing Hitler with models of the Nuremberg Rally Site, the rebuilt Munich and the planned new national capital, Germania. When Nero decides to make the Christians scapegoats for the Great Fire of Rome and declares: 'When I have finished with the Christians, history will not be sure they ever existed' and subsequently has Christians burned alive and thrown to the lions, the comparison with the Holocaust is inescapable. When Petronius says of the Christians' scapegoating 'People will believe any lie if it is fantastic enough' he is echoing Goebbels. The fact that director, producer and at least one scriptwriter were Jewish meant that the Holocaust parallel will not have been lost on them.

The detail is all of Nazi totalitarianism. This was evident to at least one critic, Jympson Harman of the *Evening News* (26 January 1952) who wrote: 'You think of Hitler when you see Nero, of the early Christians as the first underground Resistance Movement.' But without much stretch of the imagination, viewers could see the conflict between the dictatorial ruler of a pagan empire and the peace-loving democratic Christians as an analogy of the struggle between the godless, totalitarian Soviet Union and the democratic Christian west, with the NATO alliance represented by the casting of a British actress (Deborah Kerr) as heroine and an American actor (Robert Taylor) as hero, with Nero seen as a parody of Stalin.

A somewhat different resonance comes with Nero's dying line. Instead of the historically attested '*qualis artifex pereo*' (what an artist perishes with me), Ustinov's Nero expires with the words: 'Is this the end of Nero?' We can probably attribute this interpolation to Mervyn LeRoy, as it directly echoes the last words of dying Italian-American gang boss Caesar Enrico Bandello ('Is this the end of Rico?') in *Little Caesar*, the 1930 gangster classic which was Mervyn LeRoy's first big hit.

The role of Nero's artistic adviser Petronius takes on a contemporary ideological significance in the context of HUAC. For Petronius is an aesthete and novelist (author of the *Satyricon*) who in the atmosphere of oppression and terror goes along with mediocre art because it is produced by a powerful dictator. He finally commits suicide, urging the Emperor 'do not mutilate the arts', a martyr to freedom of speech and artistic expression. It may not be a coincidence that several of the victims of Hollywood blacklisting committed suicide. This parallel was spotted at the time. A review of the film in *Newsweek* (19 November 1951) equated Petronius with the journalist Walter Lipmann who had attacked McCarthyism.[19]

The ideology is expounded against a background of magnificently staged spectacle (triumphal processions, imperial banquet, a chariot chase with Vinicius and his pursuers lashing each other with whips as they draw level, the Great Fire of Rome and the execution of the Christians in the arena), which is a triumph of Technicolor photography, art direction and music. Much of the visual imagery recalls the Roman canvases of Alma-Tadema, continuing from the stage the inspiration of the painter's works.

Miklos Rosza's score made an important contribution, though as Derek Elley observes 'thanks to disgracefully bad dubbing, the many moods and finer details of the music are often rendered dramatically impotent'.[20] This is because the background music was banked down too much in certain scenes. Rosza, with the help of Hugh Gray, researched the authentic sound of ancient music. No Roman music had survived but he was able to utilize fragments of Greek melody and a collection of songs of Yemenite and Babylonian Jews as the basis of his score. He had soundless copies of ancient instruments made for use as props in the film and then utilized modern instruments approximating as closely as possible to the sounds that ancient instruments of that particular size and shape would have made: flutes, cors anglais, cornets and percussion, guitars and mandolins. He divided the music into three kinds whose interaction embodied the conflicts in the film. There was the music of the Romans (marches and fanfares chiefly); the dances and songs of the slaves (the wild, sensual Bacchanal; the fertility hymn; the Assyrian dance; Eunice's love song) and Christian hymns 'culled from early Jewish and Greek sources, the fountainhead of Ambrosian plain chant and Gregorian hymnody'.[21]

The acting is an equally important element of the film's success. Robert Taylor and Deborah Kerr are sound enough as the romantic leads, he tough and virile, she yearning and melting, though Taylor's American accent does jar from time to time with the British accents all around him. But the picture is stolen by the brilliant performances of Peter Ustinov and Leo Genn, both deservedly nominated for a best supporting actor Oscar, but thereby cancelling each other out. Ustinov is Nero to the life, petulant and posturing, by turns cowardly, cunning and vainglorious, singing his own composition while Rome burns, a prey to whims and arrogance. He makes the most of a series of memorable lines. He takes every comic opportunity offered but at the end even becomes a figure of pathos. Genn gives the performance of a lifetime, as the amused, cynical Petronius, an expert flatterer who beneath the courtier's veneer loves Rome and despises Nero. His manipulation of the Emperor is beautifully handled. But after the burning of Rome, he refuses to live on and has a superb death scene. After a last dinner with friends, he has his veins opened and as he dies composes a last letter to Nero, telling him he forgives him everything except for boring him to death with his dreadful songs. He frees his devoted slave Eunice and bequeaths her his property and is genuinely touched and astonished when she insists on dying with him.

There are notable performances too of integrity, faith and wisdom from Finlay Currie as Peter and Abraham Sofaer as Paul; of nobility and dignity from Felix Aylmer and Nora Swinburne, as Aulus Plautius and his wife Pomponia, Christian converts and later martyrs; with Patricia Laffan as an Empress Poppaea as predatory and feline as the leopards she leads round on golden chains and Rosalie Crutchley as a smoulderingly intense Acte, motivated by an unquestioning love for Nero.

As so often in this genre, critics and public were at odds. The critics excoriated the film. But having cost $7.5 million to make, it made more than $21 million worldwide. Following the London premiere of *Quo Vadis* at the Carlton Cinema on 25 January 1952, with usherettes dressed as Vestal Virgins, ushers in togas and a dozen legionary trumpeters to greet the arriving stars, controversy broke out. Christopher Mayhew MP (Labour, Woolwich) walked out, declaring the Colosseum scenes 'revolting' and the opinions of other public figures in the audience were canvassed. Lt Colonel Walter Bromley-Davenport MP (Conservative, Knutsford) said: 'I enjoyed myself immensely and there was nothing revolting about the film' and Constance, Lady Honywood said: 'The sacred scenes were sincerely done. It was an excellent film.'[22] The British Board of Film Censors, however, demanded big cuts if it was to receive an A certificate. MGM initially refused and the film was given an X certificate. However, after its West End run, MGM capitulated and cut 453 feet from the film for general release, gaining an A certificate thereby.

Peter Ustinov's experience of making *Quo Vadis* led him to 'the eventual conviction that no nation can make Roman pictures as well as the Americans'. This was because, although on the surface the films were critical of the Empire, Americans actually subconsciously identified with the Romans. Ustinov writes:

The Romans were pragmatic, a people of relaxed power with *nouveau-riche* lapses of taste. They too believed in the beneficence of atrium living, in pampering the body with steam and the laying on of heavy hands after the excesses of four-star cuisine. They too believed in dressing for comfort, and the intrigues in their senate matched anything in Washington while their total belief in Roman know-how led to a few ugly surprises, as did the total belief in American know-how in Vietnam. They too garnished their official walls with flags and eagles, and eventually the Roman way of life was all-important, being practised even when the later Emperors were of Iberian or Dalmatian origin; it mattered little, what mattered was a family feeling, a *modus vivendi* which was sometimes gracious, sometimes coarse, sometimes civilized and sometimes violent and cruel, and, yet, ever, unmistakably, Roman.[23]

MGM's follow-up to *Quo Vadis* was not, as producer Sam Zimbalist hoped, a remake of *Ben-Hur* but a film version of Shakespeare's *Julius Caesar*. It had its origins in the controversial and innovative Mercury Theatre Company stage production of 1937–8 in New York. Popularly known as 'the fascist *Julius Caesar*', it was the brainchild of theatrical *enfant terrible* Orson Welles and his production partner John Houseman. According to Houseman, Welles saw *Julius Caesar* as 'a political melodrama with clear contemporary parallels. All over the Western world sophisticated democratic structures were breaking down. First in Italy, then in Germany dictatorships had taken over; the issues of political violence and the moral duty of the individual in the face of tyranny had become urgent and inescapable'.[24] Welles himself said that the play was about the eternal dilemma of the liberal – Brutus in this case – who faced with the fact of dictatorship is driven to use the violence characteristic of dictatorship and is destroyed by it. Subtitled 'The Death of a Dictator', the play was ruthlessly cut to emphasize these themes. It came in at 109 minutes with no intermission, the battle scenes eliminated and the role of Antony reduced to give prominence to Brutus (played by Welles). It was performed in modern dress (fascist-style uniforms for the leading figures, street dress for the mob), deployed lighting and sound effects to intensify atmosphere and was performed with a cinematic fluidity and pace. It was a theatrical sensation and achieved a New York run of 157 performances, unequalled in the stage history of *Julius Caesar* in America.[25]

It was John Houseman, now a producer at MGM, who persuaded the new studio boss, Dore Schary, who had ousted Louis B. Mayer in 1951, to let him produce a film version of the play. Houseman decided against doing it in modern dress but still described it as 'a very sober and intimate political thriller'.[26] It remained relevant in the age of Soviet dictatorship. The civilized and literate Joseph L. Mankiewicz, already the winner of two directorial Oscars, was selected as director and he and Houseman set about shaping the play for the screen. They rejected the studio's suggestion that they shoot in colour. Houseman said: '*Caesar* is a tragedy of personal and political conflict; it calls for intensity and intimacy rather than grandeur; for direct, violent confrontations that do not benefit from a lush, polychrome background.'[27] Mankiewicz more succinctly said: 'I've never seen a good serious, dramatic movie in colour'.[28] Orson Welles, now living in Europe, got wind of the project. Always proprietorial about the play, which he had performed not only on stage but also on radio and on gramophone records, playing – characteristically – Brutus, Cassius and Antony in his time, tried to head off MGM, claiming that he was about to shoot a modern-dress version of *Julius Caesar* in Rome. But his intervention was ignored and his film version never appeared.

Mankiewicz and Houseman were able to persuade John Gielgud, who had played an acclaimed Cassius at Stratford in 1950, to repeat his characterization for the film. Mankiewicz suggested James Mason, who had played Brutus on stage much earlier in his career, for the role of Brutus. But they were unable to secure their first choice, Richard Burton, for Mark Antony. Houseman had a brainwave and contacted Marlon Brando to offer him the role. The film world was astonished, for Brando had only ever played modern-dress all-American roles and was characterized as a Method-acting naturalistic mumbler. But Houseman had seen him on the stage speaking perfect English and was confident he could play the role. Brando was to work hard at the part, studying recordings of Shakespeare performances by John Barrymore and Laurence Olivier, and receiving unofficial coaching from Gielgud. The resulting performance, delivered in clear and well-enunciated English, was to be a sensation. Houseman cast MGM regular Louis Calhern, whom he had directed on Broadway as King Lear, in the title role of Julius Caesar. MGM contract stars Greer Garson and Deborah Kerr took on the small roles of Calpurnia and Portia to add what was known as 'marquee value' – above-the-title star names – to the project. Houseman also brought in some Mercury veterans. Edmond O'Brien and Tom Powers, who had played Cassius and Brutus in a touring production of the Mercury's *Julius Caesar* were cast as Casca and Metellus Cimber. John Hoyt, who had played Decius Brutus in New York, recreated the role for the screen.

The film was budgeted at $2 million. But there still had to be economies. Villa interiors were recycled sets from *Quo Vadis*, crated up and shipped to California from Rome. A shortage of extras meant that the battle of Philippi was staged as a rather perfunctory western-style ambush, shot at Bronson Canyon, a familiar sight in cowboy films. MGM vetoed Houseman's desire to bring in Bernard Herrmann, the regular Mercury composer, to do the score and insisted on Miklos Rosza, who was already under contract. He provided a very effective score, having decided not to seek to recreate authentic Roman music, as he had for *Quo Vadis*, or Elizabethan music, as from the time of the play's composition, but to treat *Julius Caesar* as a film dealing with universal themes and provide 'interpretative, incidental music' in his own personal idiom. Similarly, Houseman hired as technical adviser not an archaeologist or ancient historian but P.M. Pasinetti, an associate professor of Italian at the University of California 'The idea was that the atmosphere of Rome in 44 BC was closer to that of an Italian city of any period than to anything else, and that a person with such memories could perhaps be less useless than a more conventional kind of expert'.[29]

The resulting film had all the sombre power, intelligence and pace of a first-rate political thriller. The theme is established from the opening titles in which a quotation from Plutarch explains that Caesar, having been granted dictatorial powers, became odious to moderate men. Then in the opening scene two tribunes speaking against Caesar to the crowd are arrested and hustled away by armed guards, creating the immediate feel of a police state. The drama of the conspiracy, assassination and flight and deaths of Brutus and Cassius then unfolds. When the film opened (its premiere was in Sydney, Australia on 11 May 1953), it received excellent reviews. *The Times* said: 'those who don't know the play will find it a tremendous experience; those who do, a remarkable one'.[30] Gielgud's Cassius, praised at the time, now seems stagey and mannered. It is easily outshone by Mason's Brutus. Mason was dissatisfied with his own performance and he is dismissed by Mankiewicz's biographer Kenneth Geist as 'colourless'.[31] In fact, his performance is superb, a piece of pure cinema acting, which allows the camera to see the intellectual processes at work mirrored in his face. As Kenneth Rothwell put it, Mason hits 'exactly the right note', a note of introspection and liberal angst.[32] The revelation of the film, however, was Brando who delivered a performance of such charisma and authority that he shifted the balance of the play. He is intended to be something of a political opportunist, and the sly smile he gives after the big funeral oration wins over the people; the scene in which he turns Caesar's bust sideways and occupies his chair hint at this. But looking like a Greek god and speaking English to the manner born, he has the audience rooting for him from the outset. Calhern makes a disappointing Caesar until you read that Houseman intended him to be 'an ageing, tired, nervous dictator rather than a triumphant one' and that is indeed how he comes across. But he does sound American and Mankiewicz was later to regret mixing British and American accents so freely in the film, evidence again of 'the aural paradigm'.[33] The film grossed $4 million worldwide and earned Oscar nominations for best film and best actor (Brando). In the event, it won one for best black and white art direction.

The Robe was based on a bestselling novel by Lloyd C. Douglas. Douglas (1877–1951) was a Congregationalist minister who turned to writing fiction after his novel *Magnificent Obsession* (1929) sold three million copies. By the mid-1930s he had become the most popular novelist in America with works which sought to promote spiritual values in contemporary society. His books *Green Light* (1935) and *White Banners* (1936) were, like *Magnificent Obsession,* snapped up by the Hollywood studios and turned into hit films. In 1942, however, he published *The Robe* which told a fictional story against the background of the rise of Christianity and its conflict with Imperial Rome. It sold three million copies and remained in the bestseller lists from 1942 to 1945. Independent producer Frank Ross, hearing of it from a literary agent, purchased the film rights for the book when it was only half written, for $100,000. RKO Radio Pictures undertook to produce it and in the context of the war it was yet another attempt, like *The Sign of the Cross* and *Quo Vadis,* to use the Ancient World to denounce modern Fascism. But RKO continually postponed production and eventually pulled out of the project. 20th Century-Fox stepped into the breach and agreed to produce it after the success of *Quo Vadis.* The intention was to shoot it in standard 35 mm format, with Tyrone Power in the lead and Mervyn LeRoy (fresh from directing *Quo Vadis*) as director, but by the time the script was ready both had moved on to other projects. Henry Koster, a refugee from Nazi Germany, known mainly for his comedies and musicals, was assigned as director, having impressed Zanuck with his handling of the romantic drama *My Cousin Rachel*.[34]

While the film was in pre-production, Fox had decided to deploy Cinemascope and Stereoscopic sound as its secret weapon to stem falling audiences, and *The Robe* was selected as the ideal story for the new format, which leant itself naturally to spectacle.[35]

Producer Frank Ross already had a script for *The Robe*. But Darryl F. Zanuck, the head of Fox Studios, insisted that Philip Dunne, who had scripted the top box-office hit of 1951, *David and Bathsheba*, should rewrite it. Dunne was not enthusiastic. As he recalled in his autobiography:

> *The Robe*, based on the somewhat simple-minded novel of that name, was an assignment I didn't want which resulted in a screen credit I neither wanted nor deserved.

Another reason he was reluctant to take on the project was literary snobbery:

> In their hearts, most screen writers value the approval of their colleagues above that of either the critics or the public. I might write enough to earn a screen credit or I might not; in either case I figured to lose, because to some of my sophisticated colleagues, a credit in such genres as biblicals and backstage musicals is less a credit than a debit.

But Zanuck twisted his arm, arguing that the whole future of the studio depended upon the success of this project and Dunne agreed:

> 'What do you want me to do with the damn thing?' I asked glumly. 'Put it in English' he replied. I knew what he meant. Dramatically the script was a vast improvement on the book, but a great many of the scenes were trite and De Millish. In other words, it was a typical biblical. There was no writer's name on the script. When I asked Frank Ross who had written it, he told me it was a medley of many scripts he had worked on over the years and I could assume that he himself was the author. I was able to contribute a good deal more than merely to 'put it in English'. I improved some of the characterizations, eliminated some of the religious hokum, interpolated some authentic Roman history, and sharpened the drama.[36]

When Dunne discovered he was to be given sole script credit, he objected. But Ross said he was the other principal writer and as producer did not want a writer credit. Dunne only discovered 20 years later that the script he had revised was largely the work of Albert Maltz, the blacklisted writer who was one of the 'Hollywood Ten' who had gone to prison for refusing to testify to HUAC. His co-writing credit was eventually restored to the DVD release of the film. But his involvement almost certainly explains a key sequence in the film.

The film was shot almost entirely on the Fox back lot in Hollywood, where Rome and Jerusalem were reconstructed. But Koster had to shoot every scene twice, once in Cinemascope and once in standard 35 mm format, because of fears that there would not be enough cinemas equipped to show the new process. A strong cast featured a large number of British actors in leading roles to conform to the 'aural paradigm' familiar from Ancient World epics (Richard Burton, Jean Simmons, Michael Rennie, Torin Thatcher, Ernest Thesiger, Dawn Addams).

Tribune Marcellus Gallio (Richard Burton), the archetypal proud pagan like Marcus Vinicius of *Quo Vadis* or Marcus Superbus of *The Sign of the Cross*, is posted to Judaea where he supervises the Crucifixion. He comes to believe he has been bewitched by Christ's robe and while searching for it to destroy it, he is converted to Christianity by St Peter (Michael Rennie). He returns secretly to Rome to organize the Christians. Arrested by the authorities, he declares that Christianity is not subversive and if the Romans were to embrace it the new religion would save the Empire. He is condemned to death by the Emperor Caligula (Jay Robinson) and goes joyously to his martyr's fate with Diana (Jean Simmons), the aristocrat who loves him and embraces his faith at the end.

The Christian message of love, peace and brotherhood runs through the film. The relationship between Marcellus and his Greek slave Demetrius (Victor Mature) changes from that of master and slave to friend and colleague, for Demetrius too converts to Christianity. The three leaders of the Christians in Rome are the Roman noble Gallio, the Greek slave Demetrius and the Jewish fisherman Peter. Demetrius denounces slavery ('To be a slave is to be a dog') and the humble origins of Christ and Peter (as carpenter and fisherman respectively) are stressed.

The totalitarianism is represented by the absolute power of the Emperors Tiberius and Caligula. Tiberius, fearing its effect on the Empire, rejects what Christianity stands for ('Man's desire to be free is the greatest madness of all'). But then a subversive message creeps in linking the dictatorship to McCarthyism, in a scene we can probably attribute to Albert Maltz (which is not in the book). Tiberius orders Marcellus to Jerusalem saying: 'I want names, the names of the disciples.' They are to be denounced and rounded up, like Communists in America. The detested process of naming names is a leitmotif in 1950s' films both by blacklistees and by liberals. The very next sequence in the film has an informer, another hated figure for the Left, a slimy Syrian merchant Abidor informing Marcellus where Christians are to be found.

When *The Robe* premiered in New York on 17 September 1953, the critics were enthusiastic about the new screen format ('breath-taking in comparison to normal screens' announced the *New York Herald Tribune*), the spectacle and the performances.[37] *Variety* declared it 'a big picture in every sense of the word. One magnificent scene after another, under the anamorphic Cinemascope technique, unveils the splendour that was Jerusalem and the time of Christ on Calvary [...] The performances are consistently good, Simmons, Burton and Mature are particularly effective, and Betta St John, Dean Jagger, Michael Rennie, Torin Thatcher and Ernest Thesiger likewise stand out in the other more prominent roles [...] the slave market, the freeing of the Greek slave from the torture rack, the Christians in the catacombs, the dusty plains of Galilee, the Roman court splendour and that finale "chase" (with four charging white steeds head-on into the camera creating a most effective 3-D illusion) are standouts.'[38]

The British critics were divided. Some welcomed both the new process and the film itself. The *Daily Mirror* (20 November 1953) called it 'a dignified, spectacular and very moving film' and praised the performances of Burton, Simmons and Mature. The *Daily Herald* (20 November 1953) thought that Cinemascope gave the audience 'a more complete illusion of something real happening before your eyes', praised Burton, Simmons and Robinson and concluded 'This film has a sincerity that makes you think about it long after you have seen it.' The *News Chronicle* (20 November 1953) thought it 'a triumph'.

Others expressed reservations about the process, in particular its unsuitability for conveying intimacy (thus the *Star*, 20 November, the *Sunday Chronicle*, 22 November, the *Financial Times*, 20 November). But perhaps the majority trotted out the usual criticisms of Ancient World epics. The comments included 'most of the film I found dull and the rest nauseating' (the *New Statesman*, 28 November 1953), 'fundamentally distasteful' (the *Daily Mail*, 20 November 1953), 'money down the drain' (the *Evening News*, 20 November 1953), 'boring, heavy-footed and ham-fisted' (the *Evening Standard*, 20 November 1953), 'tediously earnest and crushingly sentimental' (the *Sunday Express*, 22 November 1953) and 'a long, lachrymose high-class sleeping draught' (the *Financial Times*, 20 November 1953).

But as so often with Ancient World epics, the public had the last word. The film cost just over $4 million to produce, it took $17 million in domestic rentals and an estimated $36 million worldwide. It was the top box-office success of 1953.[39] This was helped by the fact that thousands of Catholic students were bussed to the film by their teachers, a process to be repeated in the reaction to Mel Gibson's *The Passion of the Christ* (2004).

Now that the ballyhoo surrounding the introduction of the new screen process has long subsided and the Ancient World epic has become a subject of serious academic consideration, it is possible to make a more balanced assessment of the film. It is not a great film in the way that *Spartacus* or *Quo Vadis* are great films. But it is a thoroughly professional one. It is sumptuously photographed in Technicolor by Leon Shamroy and superbly designed, deservedly winning Oscars for art direction and costume design. Interestingly, although the film itself, Richard Burton and Leon Shamroy were all nominated for Oscars but lost out, director Henry Koster did not receive a nomination. The new process of Cinemascope to a large extent dictated the style in which it was shot, full of panoramic long-shots and tableau groupings, minimizing the use of close-ups or fast intercutting, giving the film a stately pace and feel that was appropriate to its subject matter. It was pepped up by the action scenes (an exciting sword duel between Marcellus Gallio and centurion Paulus at Cana; the rescue of Demetrius from an imperial prison; and a carriage chase by Roman soldiers), but as the *Daily Telegraph* (18 September 1953) reported of the New York opening: 'Observers commented last night that some of the scenes were like Michelangelo paintings or highly coloured friezes come to life.'

The cast is uniformly excellent. Richard Burton successfully conveys the maturation of the tribune from tough pagan soldier to Christian warrior. Jean Simmons is beautiful and touching as the woman unwaveringly in love with Marcellus and eventually converted to his faith. Michael Rennie makes a powerful and dignified Peter, his stillness the measure of his quietly confident belief. Victor Mature, who got the best notices of his career, gives perhaps the best performance of his career as the Greek slave who is an early convert to Christianity. Torin Thatcher as Senator Gallio conveys the strength and stoicism of the old-style Roman, urging his son 'Be a Roman and a man of honour'. The hitherto unknown Jay Robinson, in his film debut, gives a scene-stealing performance as the evil Caligula, his malicious grin, wicked eyes, slouching walk and demented rages all perfect and providing a necessary counterpart to the goodness of the Christians.

An additional asset was Alfred Newman's score. Dismissed at the time by *The Times* as 'atrocious' (20 November 1953), it has since deservedly been re-evaluated. Christopher Palmer calls it 'a musical masterpiece'. Newman was experienced in providing music to accompany films with a spiritual theme, having scored *The Keys of the Kingdom*, *The Song of Bernadette* and *David and Bathsheba*. He adopted the customary Hollywood style of themes and motifs which recurred with variations to fit the mood of the scene. Among them are a brassy imperial march for Caligula, a wistful love theme for Diana, the Jewish rhythms of the Hymn for the Dead at Cana, an exhilarating escape theme for the prison break and for the exit of Marcellus and Diana the triumphant 'Hallelujah Chorus' Newman had composed for Quasimodo's rescue of Esmeralda in the 1939 *Hunchback of Notre Dame* and reused in *The Song of Bernadette* in 1944. But Christopher Palmer eloquently explained how the recurrent idea of the victory of faith over Roman might was achieved in the score:

Newman devised a harmonic sequence consisting of juxtaposed major and minor chords unrelated by key. This was a device patented by Debussy [...] and taken up by many later composers to suggest the remote, the mystical and the transcendental [...] Its roots lie in the medieval church modes of plainsong or Gregorian chant in which there seem to be no true closes. The effect is one of archetypal solidity and strength, a type of utterance to which Western man has been responding for centuries; and in that it represents the film's underlying concept. In essence it remains unchanged throughout, adapting itself to new situations through variations in orchestral colour and dynamic. We hear it on divided high strings with wordless voices in the background when Marcellus is finally convinced of the healing power of the Robe and is converted to Christianity by his slave Demetrius. Later, when Simon Peter brings Demetrius, on the point of death after being tortured by the Praetorian Guard, back to life, Peter emerges from the room where the slave has been lying and the 'chords' sound serenely in the brass, telling us more eloquently than words of the miracle which has been wrought. In the Procession to Calvary [...] the chords assume the character of a funeral dirge, punctuated by dragging drum-figurations and gong-strokes: against which high strings project a passionate, quasi-improvisatory melody of Hebraic cast. On Golgotha the wordless chorus takes up the melody imitationally [...] in a hypnotic manner suggestive of ritual keening. The orchestra gradually joins in to intensify the climax, and then the music fades into the natural sounds of a thunderstorm.[40]

Even while *The Robe* was in production, Fox took the decision to make a sequel, using the sets and costumes from *The Robe* and the surviving characters (Demetrius, Peter and Caligula) from the original. Producer Frank Ross, director Delmer Daves and screenwriter Philip Dunne devised a story and Dunne turned it into a script. 'It was a harebrained venture', he recalled, 'but somehow it worked [...] All in all, we came up with a good adventure yarn and, at least in my opinion, a far better pure movie than *The Robe*.' His script had 'an absolute minimum of religious hokum considering the nature of the story'. Since *The Robe* concerned a pagan converted to Christianity, he decided to make the new story concentrate on a Christian who loses his faith and to focus on the dilemma of a Christian, committed to non-violence, who is sent to fight in the arena. 'We also provided him with a Delilah-like temptress in the person of the notorious Messalina.'[41] The film was titled *Demetrius and the Gladiators*.

Dunne is correct in his assessment. In purely cinematic terms it does work better than *The Robe* and that is partly down to director Delmer Daves, who went on to craft a series of superior westerns (among them *Drumbeat*, *The Last Wagon*, *3.10 to Yuma* and *The Hanging Tree*), in which he demonstrated a flair for action, a good eye for visual composition and a sympathetic understanding of human frailty. All these qualities are on show in *Demetrius*.

Demetrius is condemned to the arena and, initially refusing to fight, loses his faith when Lucia, the girl he loves, apparently dies while on the verge of being violated by another gladiator. He goes berserk in the arena, killing half a dozen men, and wins immediate promotion to the Praetorian Guard as a tribune. He also embarks on a love affair with the promiscuous Messalina, wife of the Emperor's uncle Claudius. Meanwhile Caligula seeks the robe, which he believes has magical powers. When Demetrius discovers Lucia is not dead but in a trance, he prays to God to cure her and she revives. His faith is restored. Peter orders him to take the robe to Caligula in order to save Christian lives. When it fails to revive a dead slave, Caligula denounces the robe and is attacked by Demetrius. Demetrius is again condemned to the arena but there leads a Praetorian revolt against Caligula who is killed. Claudius is installed as Emperor. He declares that the Caesars have extinguished the virtues of the Republic and of true religious faith. He vows to restore them, promising an amnesty for Christians and justice for all. Messalina implausibly promises to abandon her immoral life and become a dutiful wife and empress.

The film has all the vigour of early De Mille, with its exciting gladiatorial contests, interspersed with fleshly pleasures, and there are distinct echoes of *The Sign of the Cross* in both content and characters. The film draws a contrast between sex (Messalina) and true love (Lucia) and between Christianity (democratic) and Imperial Rome (autocratic). Also, in a bold nod to civil rights at a time when the prominent black American Paul Robeson was being persecuted for his Communist beliefs, Dunne includes as a leading character the noble Nubian king Glycon (William Marshall). Having himself been sent to the arena, Glycon befriends Demetrius, converts to Christianity and is last seen as a leader on equal terms with the Greek Demetrius and the Jew Peter. Daves' pacy direction and Franz Waxman's robust score (incorporating several of Alfred Newman's themes from *The Robe*) keep things moving along nicely. Jay Robinson, Michael Rennie and Victor Mature successfully repeat their *Robe* characterizations of mad emperor, gentle and authoritative apostle and Christian convert turned action man. They are joined by Susan Hayward who is on fine form as the flame-haired nymphomaniac Messalina, swanning around in a succession of eye-catchingly vivid diaphanous gowns, and Barry Jones contributes a winning cameo of the elderly antiquarian Claudius, prudently concealing his intelligence beneath a mask of bumbledom until the time comes to assume the throne. The resulting film cost nearly $2 million to produce and netted a respectable though not outstanding $4.25 million in domestic rentals.[42] It was nevertheless the third most profitable Fox film of 1954.

In view of the success of *The Robe*, it must have seemed a good idea to Jack L. Warner to commission a film version of Thomas B. Costain's bestselling novel, which, like *The Robe*, centred on a Christian icon, in this case the cup used at the Last Supper, the Holy Grail. But the result, *The Silver Chalice* (1954), filmed in Cinemascope and Warnercolor and costing $4.5 million, was a resounding box-office flop.

The hero of *The Silver Chalice* is a young Greek sculptor, Basil, who is hired by Joseph of Arimathea to encase the simple cup in a silver chalice. The chalice is sought by Simon the Magician, who, using his magic tricks to perform 'miracles', seeks to create a rival religion to Christianity, backed by a sect of rebel Jewish zealots, the Sicarii. Simon plans to destroy the chalice as a sign of his victory over the Christians. But, intoxicated by his success in attracting disciples, Simon promises to fly from a great tower erected in the palace grounds of the Emperor Nero. He falls to his death. Basil is torn between the pagan temptress Helena, Simon's glamorous assistant, and Deborah, the devoutly Christian grand-daughter of Joseph. Eventually he settles for Deborah and Christianity, while Helena is thrown from the top of the tower on Nero's orders. The chalice disappears but St Peter predicts that it will return in the distant future when its inspiration will be needed.

Director Victor Saville attributed the film's failure to Jack Warner's injudicious cutting of the picture after its completion and to the miscasting of Paul Newman. It was Saville himself who had spotted Newman on the stage and hired him for his first screen role. Despite his classical profile, Newman was completely out of his depth as the young sculptor. When Newman himself saw the film, he declared himself 'horrified' and took out advertisements apologizing for his performance. He never acted in a historical costume picture again. The acting honours, such as they were, went to Jack Palance, intense and forceful as Simon the Magician. But there was more to it than that. It was Saville's decision to hire as production designer the Austrian Rolf Gerrard, who had designed opera productions for Sir Rudolf Bing at Covent Garden and at the Metropolitan Opera, New York. The highly stylized sets are hopelessly uncinematic and look indeed like a succession of modernistic stage sets. They give the whole production an air of arty-crafty artificiality. This is compounded by the tedium of an uninspired script and an uninvolved, largely American cast, with Jacques Aubuchon's Nero coming a long way behind Charles Laughton and Peter Ustinov, and the St Peter of Lorne Greene, the future star of *Bonanza*, failing to match Finlay Currie or Michael Rennie in the role. Only Franz Waxman's fine score attained the distinction Saville had hoped for in the production. He concluded sadly that the film did justice neither to Costain nor himself.[43]

Where Shaw's plays *Caesar and Cleopatra* and *Androcles and the Lion* had subverted and undermined the toga play genre in Edwardian England, the film versions of his plays failed to do the same for the toga film genre. Shaw had died in 1950 and Gabriel Pascal who had produced four screen adaptations of Shaw, embarked on his final screen adaptation, *Androcles and the Lion* in Hollywood in 1952 for RKO Radio Pictures. But the production was plagued by interference from the unpredictable and despotic studio boss Howard Hughes. Pascal was saddled with a director (Chester Erskine) he had not wanted. Unable to cast his first choice, Charlie Chaplin, as Androcles, he imaginatively substituted Harpo

Marx. But after several weeks of filming, Hughes shut down the production and insisted on replacing Marx with a young television comedian, Alan Young, who had impressed him. Finally, when the film was finished Hughes decided it needed pepping up and brought in Nicholas Ray to shoot 'a steamy Vestal Virgin bathing sequence' which outraged Pascal, provoked censorial intervention and ended up cut from release prints.[44]

In the event, Young was perfectly acceptable as the innocent, animal-loving Christian hero and Pascal surrounded him with a first-rate, largely English, cast. Jean Simmons, making her Hollywood debut, was spirited and meltingly lovely as Lavinia (she had had the non-speaking role of a harpist in *Caesar and Cleopatra*). The eminent Shakespearean stage actor and occasional film actor Maurice Evans played the Emperor. Other roles were filled by members of Hollywood's British colony (Robert Newton, Elsa Lanchester, Reginald Gardiner, Alan Mowbray). Victor Mature was borrowed from 20th Century-Fox to play the Roman Captain.

Shaw's 1912 play *Androcles and the Lion* was a precise parody of Wilson Barrett's play *The Sign of the Cross*, with the sympathies of the original reversed. Shaw's Romans are reasonable, pragmatic and regard sacrificing to the gods merely as a matter of good manners, and the Christians are fundamentalist fanatics, who march along singing 'Onward, Christian soldiers' and long for martyrdom. On to Aulus Gellius' fable (runaway slave encounters a lion, removes a thorn from his paw and when later captured and sent to the arena, encounters the same lion who spares his life) Shaw grafted his parody of Barrett highlighting hypocrisy and paradox. Spintho robs temples, confident that he will be forgiven when he eventually suffers Christian martyrdom. Ferrovius the blacksmith, the archetypal 'muscular Christian' abandons his pacifism in the arena and kills six gladiators. As a result, he joins the Praetorian Guard and returns to the worship of Mars. On the other hand, the Emperor, impressed by Ferrovius' fighting prowess, halts the persecution of the Christians and orders his gladiators to convert to Christianity.

Shaw's play constituted the core of the script, but it had only run for sixty minutes and for the film was expanded to ninety-eight minutes by Chester Erskine and Ken Englund. The arena scene in which Ferrovius kills six gladiators (only reported in the play) was included to provide a big action scene. Erskine fleshed out the arena scenes with footage from RKO's *Last Days of Pompeii*. The love story between the Christian maiden Lavinia and the pagan Roman Captain was given the full Hollywood treatment: dewy-eyed close-ups, emotional sincerity, surging background music. Most remarkable, however, and very daring, given Hughes' fierce anti-Communism and introduction of loyalty tests for employees, was the addition of a new subplot which is a disguised attack on McCarthyism. The film opens with a new character Cato (John Hoyt), commissioned to hunt down Christian subversives ('The enemy within is just as real as the enemy without'). He stalks through the film as a baleful presence, warning: 'Christianity is contagious. You never can tell when it will strike next.' He tells the Emperor that there are secret Christians even at his court. At the end he recommends throwing the Captain to the lions for associating with the Christian Lavinia. He slinks away when it is suggested he himself might be thrown to the lions. Substitute Communist for Christian and you have a contemporary message, evidently unnoticed by Hughes or anyone else.

Although Ferrovius' climactic unconversion and return to worship of Mars is cut, no doubt to spare the feelings of committed Christians in the audience, the mild satire on Christianity was evidently not to the taste of cinemagoers in the decade of devout epics. Significantly Simmons and Mature went on to star in a genuinely devout Christian epic, *The Robe*, that cleaned up at the box office, and the Ferrovius subplot turned up in *Demetrius and the Gladiators*, receiving serious treatment.

Columbia's contribution to the cycle was *Salome* (1953). It was conceived as a vehicle for Rita Hayworth, allowing her to add the Biblical temptress to her roster of soft-centred femmes fatales (Carmen, Gilda, Sadie Thompson). The screen story was provided by regular De Mille scriptwriter Jesse Lasky Jr, who had been asked by Columbia studio boss Harry Cohn to provide a vehicle for Hayworth ('something that has balls and is big'). It was turned into a script by Harry Kleiner.[45]

Rather than an adaptation of Wilde, like the silent film starring Nazimova, this *Salome* was an analogue of *The Robe* (Roman officer is converted from paganism by proto-Christ figure John the Baptist, defies Roman tyranny and converts the heroine). The basis of the story was the account in Matthew's Gospel, Chapter 14, which told how the seductress Salome danced for her stepfather, Herod Antipas, tetrarch of Galilee, on his birthday and he promised her anything she wanted in return for sex. She asked for the head of John the Baptist, on the instruction of her mother Herodias and duly received it.

During the later nineteenth century Salome had become a fin-de-siècle symbol of voluptuous and bejewelled female evil, depicted in Gustave Moreau's painting *Salome dancing before Herod*, in Oscar Wilde's play and Richard Strauss' opera, and a string of decadent and symbolist poems. In Columbia's version the story and character of Salome were turned upside down as Salome dances to save John the Baptist. It is her mother Herodias who successfully demands the head. The dance of the seven veils performed by Salome constitutes the film's climax, with a barbaric Orientalist dance, by turns seductively sinuous and passionately percussive, specially composed for the film by Daniele Amfitheatrof. The erotic dance is intercut with the lascivious reaction of Herod, previously manifesting sublime boredom at the procession of sword dancers, fire-eaters and acrobats paraded for his entertainment.

The film contrasts the preaching of John the Baptist and later Jesus – peace, justice and brotherhood – with the dynastic politics of the House of Herod and the ruthlessness of the hardbitten Roman military governor Pontius Pilate acting under the 'dictatorship' of the Emperor Tiberius.

Roman commander Claudius (Stewart Granger) falls in love with Salome as he escorts her from Rome back to Galilee. There her mother Herodias tries to use her to secure the death of John the Baptist who preaches constantly against her adulterous relationship with King Herod. Claudius, who believes in John's teaching, tries continuously to protect him but eventually after Salome dances for Herod, John is beheaded. Claudius and Salome leave the court and are last seen listening to the Sermon on the Mount being preached by Jesus, recognized by John the Baptist as the promised Messiah and earlier seen by Claudius curing a blind man and raising the dead Lazarus. The final title 'This was the Beginning' indicates the birth of Christianity.

The film conforms to a recurrent theme in the work of the director William Dieterle, an exploration of the anatomy of passion and the conflicts it induces. The passions here are on the one hand the worldly ones represented by Queen Herodias who has a passion for the throne which she is determined to secure for her daughter ('the throne is more than life to me'), by King Herod who desires to possess his stepdaughter ('I would give half my kingdom') and by Pontius Pilate who is preoccupied by the need to maintain order at all costs. On the other hand there are the holy passions embodied by John the Baptist, a wild-eyed, long-haired Old Testament prophet who has a passion for reform, denouncing immorality and violence and advocating peace and brotherhood. This new faith is also embraced by Claudius ('I've found a greater loyalty than Rome – humanity').

Salome, fetchingly played by Rita Hayworth in a succession of diaphanous gowns of old gold, royal blue, pure white, azure and apple green, is the pivotal figure converted from proud princess to humble Christian believer. Rita Hayworth is the only American among the stars who otherwise constitute a strong British contingent with Stewart Granger (borrowed from MGM) as Claudius, Alan Badel as John, Basil Sydney as Pontius Pilate, Charles Laughton as Herod, Sir Cedric Hardwicke as the Emperor Tiberius plus the Australian Dame Judith Anderson as Herodias. The strong cast, the massive and exotic palace sets and the glowing Technicolor photography which captures the vivid kaleidoscope of costumes in bright primary colours all contribute to the atmosphere. The critics were mainly unimpressed, the *New York Herald-Tribune* calling it 'the movie mixture presented many times before, a combination of musical comedy lavishness, dime novel melodrama and Biblical passion'.[46] The relatively modest returns on the four million dollar production led Columbia to abandon plans to film Frank Slaughter's novel *The Galileans* with Hayworth as Mary Magdalene.

In 1954 Hollywood's two principal interpreters of barbarism, Anthony Quinn and Jack Palance, simultaneously took on the role of the arch-barbarian, Attila the Hun, 'the scourge of god'. Quinn played the part in *Attila the Hun*, made in Italy by Lux, and Palance in *The Sign of the Pagan*, made in Hollywood by Universal-International. The Italian version was the more spectacular but the Hollywood version the more satisfying. Both centred on the threat to the Christian Roman Empire (the West) by a pagan barbarian horde from Eastern Europe (the Soviet Union) and the eventual defeat of the barbarians by the innate power of Christianity.

Douglas Sirk, Hollywood's master of melodrama and expert in 'women's pictures', was the somewhat unlikely director of *The Sign of the Pagan*. But it was a last-minute studio assignment when another director dropped out. Sirk tried to persuade Universal to let him make a film of Christopher Marlowe's *Tamburlaine*, but when this proposal was rejected he had Oscar Brodney's script rewritten by Barré Lyndon to give it classical gravity. Although it deployed Cinemascope and Technicolor, it was very economically filmed: the majority of the exteriors were shot in the studio, Universal's standing medieval castle saw service as the imperial palaces both of Rome and Constantinople and large-scale scenes of the Huns on the march were lifted from the 1951 film *The Golden Horde*.

What makes the film memorable is the striking performance by Jack Palance as Attila, ruthless, calculating and superstitious, but charismatic, dominating every scene in which he appears. Jeff Chandler makes a sturdy and convincing opponent as the Roman general Marcian. But as the beautiful princess Pulcheria, the ballerina Ludmilla Tcherina, is hopeless. Sirk recalled that the studio was seeking to promote her at the time: 'All she could do was dance [...] she had a good body, but she could do nothing with her face. Any emotion she may have had must have gone straight down to her feet.'[47] Her presence dictated the inclusion of an exotic and dramatically redundant dance, incongruously performed by the Princess before the assembled barbarian chiefs.

Although more concerned with court intrigue than military action, the film remains consistently watchable. The Cold War message is clear. The Christian Roman Empire is divided into two, with twin capitals at Rome and Constantinople. Its weakness and disunity are exploited by Attila, who unites the various barbarian tribes and plans to destroy Rome, become ruler of the whole world and return the world to its condition before the rise of the Roman Empire. The weak and selfish Eastern Emperor Theodosius plans to break away from Rome and to this end buys off the barbarian chiefs, agreeing to give them a free hand against Rome. The centurion Marcian, loyal to Rome and the West, organizes a coup which compels Theodosius to abdicate and installs his pro-Western sister Princess Pulcheria on the throne. He then leads the Eastern legions west to defend Rome. But it is Pope Leo, emerging from Rome, who persuades Attila, haunted by visions of the

Christian martyrs (who include his daughter Kubra, a convert to Christianity whom he has killed), to turn back from Rome. He is ambushed by Marcian as he retreats and killed by the captive Ildico, whom he has forcibly taken as wife. Pulcheria marries Marcian and elevates him to the throne.

The ideological conflict between the two sides is embodied in their recurrent symbols: the Christian cross which stands for peace, hope and faith and the sign of the pagan, a row of skulls on a tasselled banner which stands for bloodshed and slaughter. It is last seen burning after Attila dies in the shadow of the cross. The message is that the unity of the West, boosted by military preparedness and sustained by Christian faith, can defeat the barbarian hordes from the East. The meritocratic nature of western leadership is epitomized by Marcian, son of a humble sandalmaker, who rises from centurion to general and eventually emperor on the basis of his personal qualities.

Anthony Quinn's *Attila*, while telling a similar story, also looks back to Nazism as a version of totalitarianism. In this version the Huns have two different options, articulated by their joint rulers when a peace envoy, Aetius, arrives from Rome. Bleda advocates peace, agricultural settlement and alliance with Rome; his brother Attila calls for war, conquest and bloodshed. Attila has his brother assassinated and in a speech at his funeral pyre describes his objective – in words that deliberately echo Hitler – 'One race, one blood, one destiny. Today the Romans – tomorrow the world.' Rome is ruled by the neurotic and unstable Emperor Valentinian III. His ambitious sister Honoria (Sophia Loren) tries to get Aetius to overthrow him. When he refuses, she flees to Attila, hoping to use him to gain power. But Attila uses her and contemptuously casts her aside. Aetius leads the Roman army against Attila but is defeated and killed. As the Huns near Rome, Pope Leo emerges to confront Attila, already haunted by the deaths of his brother and his youngest son. The Pope prevails on him to turn back and as Attila retreats over the hill, the cross of peace appears in the sky. Despite the decadence of the imperial court, Rome has Christianity and that is the power by which the Huns are defeated.

The Roman Empire cycle essentially peaked at the end of the 1950s. By the mid-1950s MGM was in financial crisis, recording annual losses of $5 million. The studio decided to risk everything on a remake of *Ben-Hur*. Producer Sam Zimbalist, who had sought since 1952 to make the film as a follow-up to his successful production of *Quo Vadis*, was assigned to the production. A script was produced by the experienced screenwriter Karl Tunberg who had scripted the historical films *Beau Brummel* (1954) and *The Scarlet Coat* (1955) for MGM. The script was then worked on without credit by playwrights Maxwell Anderson and S.N. Behrman. Zimbalist recruited some of his collaborators from *Quo Vadis* to work on the film, notably the art director Edward Carfagno and the composer

Miklos Rosza. Several acting veterans of *Quo Vadis* (Finlay Currie, Marina Berti and Ralph Truman) were to reappear in small roles. As director, Zimbalist turned to William Wyler. Wyler was initially reluctant, not regarding the epic as his forte. But he changed his mind. His biographer Axel Madsen explains why:

> There was something in the clumsy, naive and nearly unreadable Victorian fiction that appealed to the Jewishness in him. As many men of his generation, he wore his Jewishness with nonchalance and distance. Somehow, it only came up in him when it was challenged. [...] Although he had never been there, he had applauded the creation of Israel and given generously to the cause. His empathy for Israel had just been aroused. In 1956, the Jewish state had started a pre-emptive war against Egypt [...] condemned by President Eisenhower and the United States and, therefore, stopped in its tracks. *Ben-Hur* told the same story – Jews fighting for their lives and their freedom. What had changed in two thousand years? Nothing. Instead of Romans, it was now Arabs; but the fight for a homeland hadn't changed.[48]

The film was shot at Cinecittà, like *Quo Vadis*, and took the best part of a year to make. It utilized 300 sets, 100,000 costumes and 10,000 extras. Wyler was, however, dissatisfied with the script and Gore Vidal was brought in to revise it and eventually it was being rewritten as the shooting proceeded. Vidal left after several months and the English poet and playwright Christopher Fry was engaged and remained with the production until the end, on set everyday for nine months to give the dialogue a more classical, and less twentieth-century colloquial, feel. Vidal famously suggested that Judah and Messala should have been lovers during their previous friendship and that Messala's subsequent hatred of Judah was partly inspired by Judah's rejection of that love. Vidal claims to have assured Wyler that this feeling would not be in the dialogue but in the attitude and reaction of Messala to Judah. Although Wyler and Heston both denied this story, if you examine the reunion scene carefully, Stephen Boyd is definitely looking at Judah with love in his eyes. Interestingly Christopher Fry quite independently told Heston: 'If I were writing an original screenplay instead of adapting a semi-classic novel [...] I wouldn't have the girl's role in the story at all. The significant emotional relationship is the love/hate between Messala and Ben-Hur. The audience knows this, and they're not interested in the Ben-Hur/Esther story'.[49]

The screenplay carefully streamlined the narrative of the original novel, eliminating for instance the romantic triangle of Judah, Messala and the Egyptian temptress Iras (which had figured in the silent version) and having Messala mortally injured in the chariot race rather than simply crippled and ruined as in the book. The focus was thus squarely on Judah's desire for vengeance on Messala, his search for his lost mother and sister and his encounters with Christ.

Wyler decided to enforce the 'aural paradigm' strictly and have the Romans played by British or British-sounding actors (Jack Hawkins, Andre Morell,

Terence Longdon, George Relph plus the Irishman Stephen Boyd and the Australian Frank Thring) and the Jews, apart from Israeli actress Haya Harareet as Esther, by Americans (Charlton Heston, Martha Scott, Sam Jaffe).

The film was shot in Panavision and Metrocolor, using the new 65 mm cameras which gave the images an unprecedented sharpness and clarity. The film was storyboarded first to ensure that Wyler got precisely the compositions he wanted. But perhaps the most memorable sequence in the whole film (and indeed one of the most notable in all cinema), the chariot race, was not filmed by Wyler. It was the work of the second unit. Veteran stunt director Yakima Canutt devised the action of the sequence with his son, Joe, doubling for Heston. The actual sequence was shot in five weeks by the experienced second-unit director Andrew Marton. The whole race was first shot complete using doubles for the stars and then Heston and Boyd came in to do close shots. Both had trained to drive a chariot for several weeks before shooting began. Marton admitted being influenced in part by his memories of the 1926 chariot race, and some of the camera set-ups are identical. The design of the spina in the centre of the circus with the bowed giants at each end is also very similar to that of 1926. The sequence remains literally breathtaking with its pounding pace, its panoramic long-shots, its exciting travelling shots, its close-ups of wheels, horses' heads and charioteers' faces intercut with vignettes of the action as chariots career round the circuits, interlocking, crashing, piling up and negotiating hair's-breadth escapes.[50] Marton also shot some of the exteriors in the sea battle, which is ironically less realistic than its 1926 counterpart, as the 1959 version made extensive use of model shots where in 1926 real galleys were used. The strain of overseeing such a massive production proved too much for Sam Zimbalist, who died of a heart attack aged only 57 on 4 November 1958, while the film was still being shot. Wyler took over as producer with experienced executive J.J. Cohn sent out from Hollywood to assist him.

Although *Ben-Hur* is subtitled 'A tale of the Christ', it is in fact the story of a Jewish prince, Judah Ben-Hur, and his conflict with Rome. However, the film opens with the Nativity and closes with the Crucifixion and at various key points the hero encounters Christ and is ultimately transformed by the contact. Central to the narrative is the emergence of Ben-Hur's Jewish identity, and this hinges on his relationship with Messala, who becomes the symbol of Roman totalitarianism. When Messala (Stephen Boyd), the boyhood friend of Judah Ben-Hur (Charlton Heston) and now a Roman tribune, arrives to take command of the Jerusalem garrison, he and Judah are joyfully reunited. But when Judah refuses to help Messala suppress Jewish rebels, they quarrel and part. When during the ceremonial arrival in Jerusalem of the new Roman governor Gratus, a tile is dislodged accidentally from the roof of the Ben-Hur palace and strikes the governor, Ben-Hur is arrested and sent to the galleys even though Messala knows he is innocent. Ben-Hur's mother and sister are imprisoned. Ben-Hur swears to exact vengeance on Messala. Passing through Nazareth on his way to the coast and parched with thirst like the other galley slaves, Ben-Hur is given water by a young carpenter. After three years in the galleys, Ben-Hur saves the life of the Roman consul Quintus Arrius (Jack Hawkins) during a pirate attack. He is adopted by Arrius as his son and becomes the champion charioteer of Rome. Although he adopts a Roman name (Young Arrius) and Roman dress, he eventually insists on returning to Judaea to search for his mother and sister. There he learns from Esther (Haya Harareet), the daughter of the family steward, with whom he fell in love some years earlier, that his mother and sister are dead. Hearing that Messala is now a champion charioteer, he signs on to drive the team of the Arab Sheikh Ilderim (Hugh Griffith). Mortally injured during the race, Messala tells Judah that his mother and sister are still alive but are lepers. Esther explains that they wanted him to be told that they were dead but Judah insists on being reunited with them. Meanwhile Esther, converted to Christianity by the Sermon on the Mount, seeks to bring mother and sister before Christ in hopes of a miracle. But Christ is arrested, tried and conveyed to Golgotha. He is crucified with Judah watching and at the moment of his death, mother and sister are cured and Ben-Hur, Esther and family reunited.

On one level, *Ben-Hur* tells the story of the conflict between totalitarianism and freedom that is common to so many of the Roman epics. When Messala arrives in Jerusalem, his weary and disillusioned predecessor Sextus (Andre Morell) tells him that the people of Judaea are drunk with religion, they refuse to pay their taxes, they destroy the statues of the Roman gods and they believe in the advent of a Messiah who will bring about an un-Roman paradise. 'How do you fight an idea?' he asks. 'With another idea' replies Messala. Messala has become imbued with the idea of the Romans as a master race. He has a mystical, quasi-Fascistic notion of Roman destiny: 'Fate chose us to civilize the world.' It was not just chance, he believes, that a village on the Tiber grew to be a world empire. It was meant to be. For him, the Emperor is God: 'He is real power, real power on earth.' He sees it as his duty to retain Judaea for the Emperor, even if it means exterminating the Jews to do it. He condemns his erstwhile friend to the galleys so that he will be feared by the people. None of this is in the book. The film contains impressive sequences demonstrating the power of Rome: Arrius' triumphal procession in Rome and the scene in which, impassively watching, he puts the galley slaves through their paces, constantly upping the rowing rate from normal speed to ramming speed.

Ranged against Rome are three forces, which become interlinked. There is Christianity, a religion of peace, love and universal brotherhood, preached by Jesus Christ. As in the 1926 version of *Ben-Hur* and also *The Robe*, Christ's face is not seen nor his voice heard. He is shot from the back or at a distance and his impact charted in the facial reactions of those watching him. There is Judaism.

From the outset Ben-Hur proclaims his Jewishness. When Messala asks his opinion on how to deal with the Jews, he replies: 'Withdraw your legions and give us our freedom.' Later he temporarily becomes a Roman. But when he returns to Judaea, he reverts to his original name, returns Arrius' signet ring and rejects the offer of Roman citizenship made by Pontius Pilate. (Neither of these scenes are in the book.) Having defeated Messala, he plans to raise a fighting legion to install Jesus as king of the Jews, until at the end he is converted to the Christian philosophy of non-violence. Finally, there are the pre-Muslim Arabs, despised like the Jews by the Romans and treated as second-class citizens. The Arabs are represented by the exuberant Welsh-accented Sheikh Ilderim, who allies himself with Judah and, in a significant scene, gives him a star of David to wear in the chariot race. So the Semitic peoples line up together against the Romans, a bold and symbolic move so soon after the reality of the Israel–Egypt conflict in the contemporary Middle East.

Just as the principal theme echoes that in previous epics, we also get the attack on McCarthyism, a sequence in which we can probably see the hand of Gore Vidal. For the sequence where Judah and Messala quarrel when Messala tries to persuade him to abandon his Judaism is not in the book. In the film, Messala asks for Judah's help in identifying the opponents of Roman rule. He wants him to name names. 'Would I retain your friendship if I was an informer? I would do anything for you except betray my own people', he says. Messala tells him 'You're either for me or against me.' Judah declares himself against, denouncing the Empire. 'Rome is an affront to God. It is strangling my people and my country, the whole earth. But not forever, and I tell you the day Rome falls there will be a shout of freedom such as the world has never heard before.'

The film premiered in America on 18 November 1959 and in Britain on 16 December 1959. Although a handful of self-confessed epic-haters both in Britain and America held out against it (William Whitebait, in the *New Statesman*, 26 December 1959; Dilys Powell in the *Sunday Times*, 20 December 1959; Dwight MacDonald in *Esquire*, March 1960, who called it 'bloody and bloody boring'), the majority of critics on both sides of the Atlantic bathed it in superlatives. In Britain it was proclaimed 'a masterpiece' by the *News of the World* (20 December 1959), 'magnificent [...] a screen landmark' by the *Daily Telegraph* (19 December 1959) and the *Daily Express* (15 December 1959) called it 'little short of a revolution in mass films'. The critics took up the same refrain in review after review, praising the unusually literate script, the astonishing spectacle – in particular of the chariot race – William Wyler's direction – tasteful, tactful, intimate – and the acting.

The public and the industry agreed with the critics. The film cost $15 million to make (the chariot race alone costing one million) and by the time of its first reissue in 1969 had netted $66 million. Nominated for 12 Oscars, it won 11: Best Picture, Best Director, Best Actor (Heston), Best Supporting Actor (Hugh Griffith),

Best Musical Score, Best Editing, Best Cinematography, Best Art Direction, Best Sound, Best Costume Design and Best Special Effects. It was a record not equalled until *Titanic* in 1997. It failed only to win Best Screenplay and that was because of the controversy surrounding the credit. Wyler requested the Writers' Guild of America to give Christopher Fry an equal writing credit with Karl Tunberg for *Ben-Hur*. They refused and Tunberg's name remained alone on the credits. But in his Oscar acceptance speech Heston conspicuously thanked Wyler, Zimbalist and Christopher Fry and there was a widespread feeling that Fry had been hard done by.[51] Rosza's Oscar-winning score, his third, was, he said, 'the one I cherish the most. The music of *Ben-Hur* is very close to my heart.'[52] Having vetoed Wyler's suggestion that he use the eighteenth-century 'Adeste Fideles' ('O, Come All Ye Faithful') over the Nativity scene, he proceeded to compose 110 minutes of music in the 'Roman' style he had perfected for *Quo Vadis*. It was one of his finest scores. Christopher Palmer calls the score Rosza's *magnum opus*.[53] As Derek Elley writes: 'there is scarcely a moment when its presence does not enhance the drama, commenting on the relationships, binding scenes into unified sequences and exposing characters' emotions in passages without dialogue'.[54] Interestingly the decision was taken to include no music in the chariot race, whose natural sound alone is used to enhance the excitement.

The film *Spartacus* (1960) opens with an establishing narration: 'In the last century before the birth of the new faith called Christianity, which was destined to overthrow the pagan tyranny of Rome and bring about a new society, the Roman Republic stood at the very centre of the civilised world [...] Yet even at the zenith of her pride and power, the Republic lay fatally stricken with a disease called human slavery. The age of the dictator was at hand, waiting in the shadows for the event to bring it forth.' It ends with Spartacus crucified and his wife Varinia, baby in arms, kneeling before his cross in the attitude of Madonna and child. But aside from these nods to Christianity, the rest of the film is resolutely secular, in marked contrast to its Ancient World predecessors.

Its origins lay not in a Victorian novel but in an unashamedly Marxist text. The Communist novelist Howard Fast was one of those sent to prison for contempt of Congress in 1950 when he refused to cooperate with the HUAC investigations. While in prison, he wrote a historical novel, *Spartacus*, setting out his intention in the preface:

> It is a story of brave men and women who lived long ago, and whose names have never been forgotten. The heroes of this story cherished freedom and human dignity, and lived nobly and well. I wrote it so that those who read it ... may take strength for our own troubled future and that they may struggle against oppression and wrong – so that the dream of Spartacus may come to be in our own time.[55]

The subject of the slave rebellion of 73–71 BC and its gladiator-leader Spartacus, who defeated a succession of Roman armies until finally defeated himself by Crassus, had acquired particular political resonance over the centuries. In the eighteenth and nineteenth centuries, Spartacus became a symbol and spokesman of the struggle for freedom from tyranny in France, Italy and America, and featured in plays and novels from those countries in this guise.[56]

In 1861, Karl Marx described Spartacus as 'the most excellent fellow in the whole history of antiquity, a great general [...] of noble character, a real representative of the proletariat of ancient times'.[57] The Communist movement, the *Spartakusbund*, which mounted an unsuccessful Communist coup in Berlin in 1919 took its name from the slave rebel. One of the principal cultural manifestations of Spartacus the Marxist rebel was Khachaturian's memorable ballet *Spartacus*, which premiered in 1956. The other notable manifestation was Howard Fast's novel. No publisher would touch it and so he published it himself in 1951 and it became a bestseller. It was also awarded the Stalin Peace Prize in 1954. It straightforwardly told the story of Spartacus as the struggle of a proletarian hero against Roman capitalism and imperialism. This was the work that Edward Lewis, a partner of Kirk Douglas in his production company, Bryna, brought to Douglas' attention in 1957. Douglas was immediately interested, but had resolved after *The Vikings* not to do another historical epic. But when MGM began casting *Ben-Hur*, Douglas felt that the title role would be perfect for him and lobbied William Wyler for the role. Wyler offered him Messala, having firmly decided on Charlton Heston for Ben-Hur. Douglas rejected the role but then turned his mind to a project that would equal *Ben-Hur*. He recalled in his autobiography: 'I was intrigued with the story of Spartacus the slave, dreaming of the death of slavery, driving into the armor of Rome the wedge that would eventually destroy her.'[58] Douglas optioned the book and set Howard Fast to prepare a script. He took the project to Arthur Krim at United Artists, for whom Douglas had produced *The Vikings*, confident of acceptance, only to discover that United Artists had their own Spartacus project underway, *The Gladiators*, based on Arthur Koestler's 1938 novel. It was being scripted by blacklisted leftist writer Abraham Polonsky and was scheduled to be directed by the liberal Martin Ritt and to star Yul Brynner and Anthony Quinn: there was a race on. Howard Fast's script turned out to be, in Douglas' words, 'a disaster, unusable' and so he and his producer Edward Lewis turned to another blacklisted screenwriter, Dalton Trumbo, one of the Hollywood Ten, who was not only talented (two of his pseudonymously written screenplays – *Roman Holiday* and *The Brave One* – had actually won Oscars in the early 1950s) but was also fast. Writing under the name of Sam Jackson, he began adapting the book. Although still without a director, after David Lean declined an approach, Douglas was able to get commitments from Laurence Olivier, Charles Laughton and Peter Ustinov to play the leading Roman parts. Universal-International Pictures took on the production and United Artists dropped out of the race to film the Spartacus story. With a 12 million dollar budget, 100 different sets, Technicolor and Super Technirama 70 and a cast of thousands, Universal insisted on the experienced Anthony Mann as director. Douglas resisted the choice, he felt: 'He was wrong for *Spartacus*. I like people who come up with ideas to make things better. Tony Mann had very little to say. He seemed scared of the scope of the picture. I fought with the studio to replace him [...] it ignored all my pleas.'[59] Shooting began on 27 January 1959 in Death Valley where the Libyan mine sequence was shot and which looks thoroughly assured and powerful. But by the time they began shooting the gladiatorial school scenes, Douglas says Mann had lost control of the production and Universal agreed to his removal and replacement by the young and comparatively untried Stanley Kubrick, who had directed Douglas the year before in the anti-war drama *Paths of Glory*. As if to prove Douglas wrong in his assessment of his directorial capacity, Mann went on to direct one of the greatest of historical epics – *El Cid* in 1961. Shooting of *Spartacus* went on for much of the rest of the year. The bulk of the film was shot on the Universal back lot, in the San Fernando Valley and the Californian hills, with William Randoph Hearst's San Simeon castle used as Crassus' villa and the battle scenes being shot in Spain in order to use 8,000 infantrymen from the Spanish army as extras. Vittorio Nino Novarese, professor of history, costume and drama at Rome's State School for Cinematographical Studies, was hired as historical and technical adviser to ensure authenticity – and spent 18 months researching the subject and period. It remained until the end a fraught production. Tony Curtis, who had asked to be included in the cast in order to get rid of a commitment to Universal for one more film on his contract, and for whom the role of Antoninus, not in the book, was created, recalled that most of the cast and crew thought Kubrick was a young upstart and he was particularly resented by cameraman Russell Metty: 'To Russ Metty, Kubrick was just a kid, barely shaving. "This guy is going to direct this movie? He's going to tell me where to put the camera? They've got to be kidding." That was his attitude.' But, says Curtis, Kubrick was 'a genius with the camera', used it creatively, took his time and got the shots he wanted by being obstreperous with the studio which was continually pressing him to speed up the shooting.[60] There was also permanent tension between Olivier and Laughton as rival grand British thespians. On top of all this, at various stages Curtis, Simmons and Douglas himself were off sick.[61]

Spartacus falls into two parts: the story of the slave revolt and the story of the emergence of dictatorship in Rome. This meant that the film could appeal equally to left and right. The film begins by establishing the evils of slavery. Spartacus, a Thracian slave working in the mines of Libya, is stretched on a rock to starve to death for helping another slave. Batiatus, the *lanista*, owner of a gladiatorial school at Capua, comes looking to buy gladiators, inspects their teeth as if they were horses and buys Spartacus. At the gladiatorial school, they are trained for the arena. Later, bored, decadent aristocratic Roman women, visiting the school, demand to see two pairs of gladiators fighting to the death semi-naked. When Draba the negro, having beaten Spartacus, refuses to kill him and aims his trident at the Romans, he is killed by Crassus, and later hung upside down like a piece of meat as a warning. The gladiators rebel and seize the school. Spartacus' rebel army is organized along democratic lines. It is a society without slaves. Each person is assigned to a job suited to his talents. He describes them as a brotherhood. Spartacus is given a domestic life which humanizes him. He falls tenderly and genuinely in love with the slave girl Varinia and she bears him a son. Their love scenes are characterized by tenderness and delicacy. He establishes a father–son relationship with the runaway slave Antoninus, killing him at the end to save him from crucifixion. They swear their love to each other as Antoninus dies. In the slave camp, long tracking shots pick out individuals, women, children, old persons, establishing it as a genuine community, and this sense of common brotherhood is affirmed triumphantly in the now famous scene when Crassus demands that the prisoners identify Spartacus and one after another they stand up, shouting: 'I am Spartacus', with a close-up of Spartacus' face with a tear trickling down his cheek. But, as Derek Elley has pointed out, Douglas has effectively transformed Spartacus from a Marxist rebel into a Zionist hero. For Spartacus stresses that he wishes not to attack Rome but to lead the escaped slaves out of Italy and back to their homes, for which purpose he does a deal with the Cilician pirates to use their ships – a deal thwarted when Crassus buys them off and forces the rebel army to turn back and attack Rome. Elley perceptively writes:

> What to Fast was a parable on equality became to Douglas one with specific Zionist leanings, with Spartacus as a Moses-Figure attempting to lead his brothers and sisters out of a repressive Italy (with Crassus as its Pharaoh) to an unspecified Promised Land.[62]

Proud of his Jewish background and heritage, Douglas made several films playing to this (notably *The Juggler* and *Cast a Giant Shadow*). The second part of the film, intercut with the first, charts the emergence of dictatorship in Rome. In Rome, the two sides of the political argument are embodied by the leader of the plebeians, Gracchus, and the pre-eminent patrician, Crassus. Gracchus is a hedonist, a cynic (he doesn't believe in the gods) and a pragmatist ('When a criminal has what you want, you do business with him') but he is also a democrat, committed to defending the rights of the Senate and determined at all costs to prevent Crassus becoming dictator. When he fails, he arranges for Batiatus to steal Varinia and her child from Crassus and convey them to safety, and then he commits suicide. Crassus is cold, ruthless and ambitious. He believes that Rome is 'an eternal thought in the mind of God'. He detests the mob and sees his mission as 'to cleanse this Rome which my fathers bequeathed me. I shall restore all the traditions that made her great.' He tells Antoninus 'There's only one way to deal with Rome [...] You must serve her. You must abase yourself before her. You must grovel at her feet. You must love her.' But by Rome, he also means himself. After several Roman armies have been defeated and the Senate turns to him to command their forces, he insists on his appointment as First Consul with dictatorial powers. Crassus announces that he will create 'a new Rome, a new Italy, a new Empire', based on the establishment of order. The kind of order he will impose is indicated by the intercutting of this speech with Spartacus' speech to his army: 'I know that we are brothers and I know that we are free', and then Crassus sending for Gracchus and telling him after the defeat of the rebels: 'As those slaves have died, so will your rabble, if they falter one instant in loyalty to the new order of affairs. The enemies of the state are known. Arrests are in progress. The prisons begin to fill. In every city and province, lists of the disloyal have been compiled. Tomorrow they will learn the costs of their terrible folly, their treason.' The young patrician Julius Caesar, who had been the protégé of Gracchus, has by the end of the film shifted his allegiance to Crassus and the audience will be aware that he too in time will assume dictatorial powers over Rome.

Crassus is obsessed with the destruction of Spartacus. 'It's not glory I'm after [...], it's Spartacus', he tells his officers. This involves his seeking the love of Spartacus' woman, Varinia, after he installs her as his prisoner in his villa. She escapes, as had Antoninus, the young Sicilian singer he had purchased as his body servant. In a delicately written scene, he had sought obliquely to seduce him sexually – prompting Antoninus' flight to the rebels.[63] Antoninus gives his love to Spartacus, once again snubbing Crassus. When they are captured, Crassus compels them to fight to the death. After Spartacus is crucified, Crassus orders his body burned and the ashes scattered, to destroy his legend. But as Spartacus tells him of Antoninus: 'He will come back and he will be millions.' As with previous epics, audiences could interpret this element of the film as an attack on either Fascist or Communist totalitarianism. But, unlike other epics, it could also appeal to Marxists and Zionists, in view of its origins in Howard Fast's novel and its development with Douglas' particular spin.

There is also the attack on McCarthyism that featured in other epics. When Crassus asks for the identification of Spartacus, his followers stand together to resist naming him. Even Batiatus, the cowardly *lanista*, refuses to become an informer. But Kirk Douglas took this defiance of McCarthyism one step further. When the news leaked out that Trumbo was scripting *Spartacus*, he prepared to give him the screenwriting credit in his own name for the first time since his blacklisting. Otto Preminger, for whom Trumbo was also scripting *Exodus*, getting wind of this, formally announced that he would break the blacklist by giving Trumbo a full credit. The release of these two films effectively broke the blacklist. The inclusion of the noble black gladiator Draba (Woody Strode) who dies rather than kill his beaten opponent also gave the film a timely civil rights dimension, like the inclusion of black warrior Glycon in *Demetrius and the Gladiators*.

Trumbo's intelligent, subtle and literate script was a distinct asset. So too was Kubrick's direction, graphic in its depiction of gladiatorial training, sweeping in the battle scenes, tender and lyrical in the love scenes (despite the obvious and rather stagey studio exteriors) and compelling in its political scenes. Douglas, in one of his finest screen performances, brought an intensity and power to his Spartacus which is mesmerizing. But he is matched scene for scene by Olivier's icily controlled, precisely enunciated aristocratic dictator whose mask only slips once when he finally confronts Spartacus and lets out a scream and slaps his face. Jean Simmons is sensitive and moving as Varinia, the slave girl, who humanizes Spartacus. Charles Laughton's sly, pleasure-loving, good-hearted democratic politician and Peter Ustinov's cowardly, roguish *lanista*, delivering with relish lines like 'The second best wine – no the best, but in small goblets', are a continual delight. Particularly enjoyable are their scenes together, rewritten by Ustinov with Laughton's approval. Only John Gavin's characterless Caesar and Tony Curtis' bland Antoninus fail to make an impression. As *Time* magazine (24 October 1960) put it Gavin is 'a rose-lipped, sloe-eyed young man who looks as though he never got to the first conjugation, let alone the Gallic Wars. And Antoninus, the Roman poet, is played by [...] Curtis with an accent which suggests that the ancient Tiber is a tributary of the Bronx river.' Alex North's music, despite sounding at times like the score for a Second World War movie, sought authenticity of sound by the use of ancient instruments, including the cithara, dulcimer, lute, bagpipes, Chinese oboe and mandolin.

Spartacus fared rather better with the critics than some of its predecessors. The three British actors got almost universally good reviews and there was praise too for Kubrick's direction. Paul Dehn, for example in the *Daily Herald* (5 December 1960) said that Kubrick deployed 'his cinematic genius (what close-ups, what camera movement, what cutting!) as majestically as Crassus deploys his legions for the huge battle in long shot which is the picture's climax' and he called the battle 'the best, the bloodiest and most technically clear of its antique sort since Olivier's Agincourt in *Henry V*'. But there was some concern expressed by older critics about the violence (the *Observer*, 11 December 1960, the *Daily Mail*, 9 December 1960). However these were minority opinions and for the most part there was enthusiasm for the film, the direction, the acting and the visual sweep (the *Sunday Express*, 17 December 1960, the *Guardian*, 10 December 1960, the *Evening News*, 8 December 1960).

Spartacus grossed more than $60 million worldwide. Interestingly, unlike *The Robe, Quo Vadis, The Ten Commandments* and *Ben-Hur*, it was not nominated for Best Picture in 1960, nor Best Director, Actor or Actress. This may well be as a result of the controversy attending its release. The American Legion called for a boycott of the film because of the credits given to known Communists Howard Fast and Dalton Trumbo. Right-wing groups picketed showings of the film, but newly elected President John F. Kennedy famously crossed the picket line to see the film in Washington, DC. The film did win the Best Supporting Actor award for Peter Ustinov and the Oscars for cinematography, art direction and costume design.

The Roman imperial cycle of epics came shuddering to a halt with the release of *The Fall of the Roman Empire* in 1964. It was the last historical epic to be produced by Samuel Bronston. The Russian-born American producer had set up his own studio in Madrid in 1959 and embarked on an ambitious programme of epic films, utilizing the varied landscapes of Spain as the settings, the Spanish army (which seems to have spent most of the 1950s and early 1960s on film locales in historical costume) as extras and a stable of blacklisted (and therefore cheap) Hollywood scriptwriters working under his head writer Philip Yordan. International stars and top directors were imported to work on *The King of Kings*, *El Cid* and *55 Days at Peking*.[64]

Bronston first conceived the idea of a film on the fall of the Roman Empire in 1960. Philip Yordan devised a storyline and Basilio Franchina and former blacklistee Ben Barzman developed it into a script. A top production team was assembled headed by director Anthony Mann, who had directed *El Cid*, and included 2nd unit maestro Yakima Canutt to oversee the action scenes, the design team of Veniero Colasanti and John Moore, Oscar-winning cinematographer Robert Krasker and Oscar-winning composer Dimitri Tiomkin, who had scored *55 Days at Peking*. Shooting in Ultra-Panavision and Technicolor began in the Sierra Guadarrama Mountains on 14 January 1963 and went on for 143 days with 69 days of simultaneous shooting on the action sequences by Yakima Canutt, with Andrew Marton (uncredited) taking on the sequence of the forest ambush of the Roman troops by the barbarians.[65] The film cost $16 million to produce.[66] In an article Anthony Mann explained what had drawn him to the subject:

> The reason for making *The Fall of the Roman Empire* is that it is as modern today as it was in the history that Gibbon wrote: if you read Gibbon, like reading Churchill, it is like seeing the future as well as the past. The future is the thing that interested me in the subject. The past is like a mirror; it reflects what actually happened, and in the reflection of the fall of Rome are the same elements in what is happening today, the very things that are making our empires fall.[67]

He did not, he said, want to make another *Quo Vadis* (revealing that he had shot the Great Fire of Rome sequence in that film) or any of the other films which pitted the Empire against Christianity, because the Empire was about so much more than just Christianity. 'Rome gave us greater law, greater understanding, greater concepts of peoples' and this was what he wanted to dramatize in the vision of Marcus Aurelius and the way in which it was systematically destroyed by his son Commodus.

The film contained many of the elements expected of the Roman epic: an exciting, wheel-grinding, tree-demolishing chariot race along cliff-edge roads with hero and villain whipping each other as well as the horses; full-scale pitched battles between Romans and barbarians and Romans and Persians; a lavish triumphal entry into Rome and an exciting final javelin duel between hero and villain. But it actually tried to do something different from the preceding epics by moving away from the Romans versus Christians conflict so characteristic of 1950s Roman epics. There is no mention at all of Christianity in the film apart from the single instance that, after his death, the Greek philosopher Timonides is found to be carrying the Christian chi-rho symbol.

Uniquely the film attempted to mount a debate on the nature of the Empire and on the reasons for its decline and fall. Historian Will Durant was employed as historical consultant and wrote the film's foreword: 'The fall of Rome like her rise was not due to one cause but to many. It was not an event but a process spread over three hundred years.' The film, however, dates the beginning of that process to the reign of Commodus (AD 180–92). The film took the inevitable liberties with history that all historical epics do: there is no evidence that Marcus Aurelius was poisoned; Commodus was not killed in single combat but strangled by a wrestler hired by his mistress Marcia while he lay drunk in his bedroom; his sister Lucilla did not marry the King of Armenia and did not survive him, being exiled and later murdered for plotting against Commodus; and the hero of the film, Gaius Metellus Livius, is completely fictional.

But the film does highlight several of the problems that historians have seen as contributing to the Empire's decline and fall: the manpower shortage, the uneconomic nature of slavery, the spinelessness of the sycophantic Senate, the extent of the frontiers and the continual barbarian pressure upon them, and the lack of a viable succession mechanism. Although Livius is fictional, the question of the adoption of the best man versus the succession of the eldest son, whether fit or not, had dogged the empire since the outset and contributed to its periodic instability.

The film opens in AD 180 on the northern frontier of the Empire. The Emperor Marcus Aurelius, depicted as an idealized statesman-ruler (his persecution of the Christians conveniently forgotten) seeks after 17 years of continual border war to transform the Empire from a state permanently at war to one that is permanently at peace. He calls all the kings and governors of the Empire to an assembly where he proposes to grant Roman citizenship to all, creating 'a family of equal nations', all dedicated to the preservation of the *Pax Romana*. It is in essence a blueprint for the United Nations. However, when it is learned that Marcus Aurelius plans to disinherit his degenerate and unstable son Commodus in favour of general Livius, who shares Marcus' ideals and also loves his daughter Lucilla, Commodus' cronies poison Marcus Aurelius before he can do so and Commodus duly succeeds to the throne. In a calculated reversal of his father's policy, he institutes a regime of oppressive taxation, brutal military repression and autocracy, having himself declared a god.

There is a distinct echo of the old Cold War ideology when in the Senate, the philosopher Timonides, the Greek ex-slave acting as Livius' spokesman, advocates a policy for the Empire which is based on freedom, equality, peace, common citizenship, the end of slavery and an open door for immigrants. In other words, he proposes to turn the Roman Empire into an idealized form of the United States. Commodus opposes the policy, preferring to turn the Empire into the Soviet Union, a cruel, militarist, totalitarian tyranny, his spokesman dismissing Timonides' vision as the creed of Greeks, slaves and Jews. However, the Senate votes for Timonides' vision and the captured Germanic barbarians are settled on Roman land and turn to a peaceful agricultural existence. Commodus punishes Livius by marrying Lucilla to King Sohamus of Armenia in an alliance of state and sending Livius back to the frontier. He is forced to recall him, however, when the East rebels against his oppression. Livius ends the rebellion but demands that Commodus institute Marcus Aurelius' vision for a New Rome. Commodus' answer is to destroy the barbarian settlements. The film ends with Livius killing Commodus in a duel. But when he is hailed by the legions as the new Emperor, he walks away with Lucilla, leaving rival claimants to bid for the throne and the support of the all-powerful legions.

Anthony Mann created on this narrative framework a succession of memorable visual sequences: the funeral of Marcus Aurelius, drums beating, torches flaring, snow falling; the spectacular battle of the four armies, the Northern and Eastern armies of Rome, the Persians and the Armenians, fought simultaneously on several levels; the delirious finale, with the now deranged Commodus emerging from inside a giant upright hand, as flagellant worshippers flog themselves, dissidents are burned at the stake as human sacrifices and the people are swept up in the collective madness of Saturnalia. The first part of the film evokes the dark north, with the predominant colours of brown, grey and white, a grim frontier fort of wood and stone, overcast skies, chill winds, gloomy forests stretching endlessly into the distance. This gives way in the second part firstly to Rome, all marble and gold, ornate palaces and temples, mosaics, statues and ceremonial, centred on Colasanti and Moore's magnificent recreation of the Roman Forum constructed on the plains of Las Matas, 16 miles from Madrid. Later, the action moves to the East with its permanently blue skies, vibrant colours and extraordinary Armenian fortress before returning to Rome for the finale. The stunning production designs and impressive direction are underpinned by Dimitri Tiomkin's full-blooded romantic score, one of his finest, with its fanfares, percussive battle music, lyrical love theme and sombre sonorous organ lament for the end of a civilization.

Although the romantic leads Livius and Lucilla (Stephen Boyd, in a role wisely rejected by Charlton Heston, and Sophia Loren) are bland and one-dimensional, there is compensation in the outstanding performances of Alec Guinness as the wise, witty and far-seeing Emperor Marcus Aurelius and James Mason as the articulate, peace-loving philosopher, who – in a memorable scene – survives torture at the hands of the barbarians but eventually sees reason overthrown by brute force. Christopher Plummer, in only his third film, enjoys himself hugely as the vicious and unbalanced Commodus, gradually growing madder and madder, until the inevitable end.

But, for all this, the film is fatally flawed. No hero worth his salt, having disposed of an evil tyrant and being offered the throne and the chance to implement Marcus Aurelius' vision and save the Empire, would simply walk away. Cinema audiences expect better of their heroes. But the scriptwriters faced the insuperable problem that there never was an Emperor Livius and the auction for the throne actually took place before the emergence of the Severan dynasty and the restoration of order and stability. Although the final, complete rejection of empire may have chimed with the views of the three scriptwriters, who were either liberal or leftist, Anthony Mann subsequently described the ending as 'defeatist' and at least one critic noted of Livius' abdication of responsibility that the film implied that 'this pusillanimous prig was indirectly responsible for the fall, and not Commodus'.[68]

The producers could hardly have asked for a better critical reception than they got from the British critics. 'The epic that has everything' declared the *Evening Standard* (19 March 1964), praising the 'magnificent sets, spectacular action, acting that proves … [that] only British actors should play Roman patricians – a story that grips without wrenching history in two, and even […] more than a modicum of visible and audible scholarship.' The *Evening News* (19 March 1964), heading its review 'At last! The epic grows up', said: 'It is all quite magnificently done […] a real breakthrough for an epic […] We get a taste of what it was really like to rule an Empire with 6,000 miles of frontier.' 'Visually this epic is really superb', trumpeted the *Sunday Express* (22 March 1964). The *News of the World* (22 March 1964) said: 'Here's every ingredient that ever went into any epic. But Mr Mann has blended them with a magic that makes them more than ever effective.' The *Observer* (22 March 1964) called it 'visually astonishing […] stunningly photographed' and declared the first half of the film 'a hundred times more dramatic than all the silly pomp of *Cleopatra*'. The *Daily Worker* (21 March 1964) declared it 'a very good epic: lively, colourful and exciting'. The *Financial*

Times (25 March 1963) found it 'literate', 'archaeologically careful', 'tastefully designed' and 'superbly photographed'. The *Sunday Telegraph* (22 March 1964) declared it 'a spectacular worth seeing' and praised Anthony Mann's 'superb use of weather and locations, which gives us an impression – solid and surely accurate – of the back-breaking job the legions must have had in patrolling their Empire'. Almost all the reviews praised the acting of Guinness, Mason and Plummer.

Despite these critical encomiums, the film was a total box-office failure. It bankrupted Samuel Bronston, who closed his Madrid studio and, despite his best efforts, never produced another film before his death in 1994. There was to be no new Roman imperial epic until 2000 when *Gladiator* triumphantly reinvented the genre.

What explains the fall of the Roman epic? To quote Will Durant, it was not so much an event as a process. The 1960s definitely saw a change in the tastes of cinema audiences. Between 1964 and 1970 the top successes at the US box office were *The Carpetbaggers*, *Mary Poppins*, *Thunderball*, *The Dirty Dozen*, *The Graduate*, *The Love Bug* and *Airport*. They were virtually all contemporary stories and, in the top 20 lists for these years, there are no historical epics. They are dominated by spy films, westerns, war films and the Disney family films.

Just as a set of political, social and cultural circumstances had given birth to the epic cycle, so changes in those circumstances underlay the demise of the cycle. The domestic atmosphere of fear and witch-hunting dissipated. The heyday of the HUAC hearings had been from 1947 to 1954. But in 1954 Senator McCarthy had overreached himself and was censured by the Senate after attacking the army and the President. McCarthy died in 1957, the HUAC hearings ended, but the blacklist continued until 1960. But also in 1960 a new young President, John F. Kennedy, was elected, the first Catholic to attain the office. His arrival presaged a spirit of optimism and youthfulness.

In a wider context, the first phase of the Cold War ended in 1965 and from then, until it revived in 1973, the United States embarked on a policy of détente. Culturally this was reflected in the fact that two of the most popular television series of the day, *The Man from UNCLE* and *Star Trek* both included sympathetic Russian characters as comrades of the American leads. The economies of both the superpowers were in trouble and it was in both their interests to de-escalate conflict. More significantly, America became embroiled in the Vietnam War and hoped to use the Soviet Union to put pressure on Ho Chi Minh, the Viet-Cong leader. So the propaganda imperatives of the Cold War weakened, and the need for Cold War warriors on film lessened.

During the 1960s too, wider social and cultural changes in the Western world affected Hollywood. The old Hollywood studios, already weakened by the 1949 court decision which forced them to divest themselves of their cinema chains and further undermined by the rise of television, began to break up and instead a wider range of independent producers emerged. At the same time the nature of the audience changed. Increasingly from the 1960s the core audience for films was perceived to be under 30. This had far-reaching ideological consequences. The old studio structure had by and large aimed at a cross-class, mixed-gender and all-age audience from six to 60 and had demonstrated in its films a commitment to the political, social and cultural status quo, dramatizing what it perceived to be widely held common values and seeking to avoid controversy. The new youthful cinema audience was assumed to be on the whole anti-Establishment and unsympathetic to the values and beliefs of the older generation. For many of the young, it was the USA, with its 'imperialistic' war in South Asia, which was now the 'evil empire' and not the Soviet Union. So the Roman Empire became ideologically irrelevant.

4

The 1950s and 1960s:

THE BIBLE

Despite the fact that most Hollywood movie moguls were Jewish, they were notoriously chary about sanctioning films on Jewish subjects, believing that pro-Semitic films would provoke an anti-Semitic reaction. Famously, in the film dealing with the Dreyfus affair, *The Life of Emile Zola*, no mention was made of the fact that Dreyfus was Jewish. Actors with obviously Jewish names regularly changed them to more acceptable Anglo-Saxon ones: thus Emmanuel Goldenberg became Edward G. Robinson, Julius Garfinckle became John Garfield, Issur Danielovich Demsky, Kirk Douglas and Bernie Schwartz, Tony Curtis. When the non-Jewish Darryl F. Zanuck of 20th Century-Fox decided to film *Gentleman's Agreement*, a novel about anti-Semitism in contemporary America, Jewish movie moguls tried to dissuade him. There were also attempts to dissuade the Jewish head of RKO, Dore Schary, not to film another attack on anti-Semitism, *Crossfire* (1947). Both Zanuck and Schary stood firm and the films were made, *Gentleman's Agreement* winning the best picture Oscar in 1948.[1] But America was not yet ready for films to tackle the holocaust and would not be so for another ten years, until *The Diary of Anne Frank* was made, again by 20th Century-Fox.

Israel represented another tricky problem for Hollywood. Hours before the British mandate in Palestine was due to expire on 14 May 1948, the state of Israel made a declaration of independence. The new state was immediately recognized by the United States and the Soviet Union and there was strong emotional support for the new state in the West, following the revelation of the events of the holocaust and because Israel immediately became the only western-style democracy in the Middle East. But Israel was immediately attacked by the combined forces of the Arab states of Egypt, Syria, Lebanon, Iraq and Jordan, an attack which was decisively defeated by the Israeli army by the end of 1948.

However, the creation of Israel became a subject too hot for Hollywood to handle, confirming the moguls' fears about pro-Jewish films. The first feature film to dramatize the creation of Israel was Universal-International's *Sword in the Desert*, which showed the Jews as heroic freedom-fighters, aided in their struggle by a lovable IRA bomber, and the British as stiff-upper-lip villains. When it was shown in London, there were riots in the cinema and the film was hastily withdrawn in the interests of public order. There would not be another film about the creation of Israel until Otto Preminger's *Exodus* in 1960.

However, in the absence of films about the present-day state of Israel and its struggle against powerful neighbours to maintain its independence, Hollywood was able to resort to a surrogate – the Bible. It is no coincidence that the 1950s and early 1960s was pre-eminently the decade of the Old Testament, seeing a succession of films about Jewish heroes (Samson, Moses, Joshua, David, Solomon) and heroines (Ruth, Esther). It is known that Adolph Zukor, the venerable president of Paramount Pictures, explicitly supported Cecil B. De Mille's desire to make *The Ten Commandments* because it was about a Jewish hero. Also, William Wyler took on *Ben-Hur* for a similar reason (see Chapter 3).

If support for Israel was the coded message of the 1950s' Old Testament epics, they had another upfront significance. The Bible was a potent weapon in the Cold War battle between an increasingly religious, not to say religiose, United States, officially from the 1950s one nation under God, and the godless totalitarian Soviet Union. But it was also the embodiment of a fundamental and basic belief system which entailed support for the family, marriage and sexual continence. The view of America as a country built on this belief system was rocked to its foundations by the publication in 1948 of Dr Alfred Kinsey's *Sexual Behavior in the Human Male* and five years later of *Sexual Behavior in the Human Female*. Both became instant bestsellers. They revealed the extraordinary range of sexual behaviour and of appetites, the virtual universality of masturbation in both sexes and the facts that 'a quarter of all white middle class women had committed adultery by the age of forty, and that nearly half had experienced intercourse before marriage'. The reports were widely denounced. *Life* magazine condemned the report as 'an assault on the family as a basic unit of society, a negation of moral law and a celebration of licentiousness'. Billy Graham said it was 'impossible to estimate the damage this book will do to the already deteriorating morals of America'. Several church sermons and newspaper editorials deliberately linked the book with Communism, saying it would 'pave the way for people to believe in Communism and act like Communists'.[2] Jonathan Gathorne-Hardy has attributed directly to Kinsey the development and eventual triumph of the idea that 'sexual activity was a good thing in itself and that no particular sexual activity was wrong'.[3] The Old Testament epics can be seen as a direct response to the concern provoked by Kinsey, for the principal films dramatize the conflict between sexuality and spirituality, coming down firmly on the side of obedience to the will and the commandments of God.

Once again, it was the old maestro Cecil B. De Mille who pioneered the revival of the biblical genre. He had long planned a film on the story of Samson and Delilah. He had famously said: 'I can make a picture out of any fifty pages of the Bible [...] except possibly the Book of Numbers.'⁴ But the story of Samson is actually based on four chapters, 13–16, of the Book of Judges, amounting to about three pages, and so De Mille fleshed it out by reference to the 1930 novel *Judge or Fool* by Zionist Vladimir Jabotinsky. He had been planning to film the story in 1935 with Henry Wilcoxon and Miriam Hopkins in the leading roles and he had a script prepared by Harold Lamb. But, after the failure of *The Crusades* to recoup its costs, Paramount was unenthusiastic, and De Mille was diverted to a series of films about American history.

De Mille judged the time was right for it in 1947 and he approached the executives at Paramount with the idea. They were still unenthusiastic, as he recalled in his autobiography:

> A new generation of executives had grown up since *The King of Kings*: and most of them greeted my suggestion of *Samson and Delilah* with the expected executive misgivings. A Biblical story, for the post World War II generation? Put millions of dollars into a Sunday school tale? Anticipating this familiar chorus, before the meeting held in my office to decide on my next production, I asked Dan Groesbeck to draw a simple sketch of two people – a big, brawny athlete and, looking at him with an at once seductive and coolly measuring eye, a slim and ravishingly attractive young girl. When the executives trooped in, ready to save me and Paramount from the ruinous folly they were sure I had in mind, I greeted them, saw them to their seats and brought out the Groesbeck sketch [...] They were enthusiastic. That was movies. That was boy-meets-girl – and what a boy, and girl!⁵

The dual level of appeal that De Mille saw in all his Biblical and religious films was summed up succinctly when he told his staff: 'We'll sell it as a story of faith, a story of the power of prayer. That's for the censors and the women's organizations. For the public it's the hottest love story of all time.'⁶

As always with De Mille, the script had to be completely written and thoroughly researched before he started shooting. Jesse Lasky Jr and Fredric M. Frank completed the script, based on Harold Lamb's treatment and Jabotinsky's novel, and Henry Noerdlinger undertook the research, which De Mille was keen to stress took two years and involved consulting 2,000 volumes.⁷ De Mille cited Gustave Doré, Rubens, Michelangelo and Solomon as his sources of visual inspiration. The influence of Doré's picture of Samson slaying the Philistines with the jawbone of an ass and him bringing down the temple can certainly be seen in the equivalent scenes in the film.

When it came to casting Samson and Delilah, De Mille recorded: 'I selected two players quite deliberately because they embody in a large part of the public mind the essence of maleness and attractive femininity, Victor Mature and Hedy Lamarr.'⁸ He was to have cause privately to regret both choices as Henry Wilcoxon recalled. Wilcoxon, who was now playing Ahtur, the Philistine commander and

Samson's rival for the hand of Semadar, and was shortly to become De Mille's associate producer, recorded that Mature was strongly averse to strenuous action scenes. He was called upon to wrestle an elderly lion in the lion hunt sequence of the film. He steadfastly refused and so he had to be doubled in long shot by a wrestler named Kay Bell who tackled the live lion, with intercut close-ups of Mature struggling with a very obviously stuffed lion. De Mille was so concerned about the critical reaction to this sequence that, after the film's initial release on 21 December 1949, he shot five more days of new material in January 1950 and had them inserted in a recut lion sequence.[9] But De Mille also had concerns about Lamarr who, he complained, was radiantly beautiful but had only one facial expression. By dint of constant coaching he extracted from her what Wilcoxon considered her best ever screen performance.[10] Despite this, the acting honours went to George Sanders as the suavely sardonic Saran of Gaza, the king of the Philistines. De Mille, as always, filled his supporting cast with silent-screen veterans, among them William Farnum, who had starred in the original stage version of *Ben-Hur*, Victor Varconi (Pontius Pilate in *The King of Kings*) and Julia Faye (Pharaoh's Wife in the silent *Ten Commandments*). The film was shot between 4 October and 22 December 1948 at a cost of just over $3 million.

The film's opening narration, delivered by De Mille himself, sets the story in the Cold War context of the struggle for freedom from tyranny. Over the revolving globe, shrouded in mist, De Mille intones his historical analysis, equating tyranny with idolatry:

> Before the dawn of history, ever since the first man discovered his soul, Man has struggled against the forces that sought to enslave him. He saw the awful power of Nature arrayed against him [...] enslaving his mind with shackles of fear. Fear bred superstition, blinding his reason. He was ridden by a host of devil gods and human dignity perished on the altar of idolatry. And tyranny rose, grinding the human spirit beneath the conqueror's heel. But deep in Man's heart still burned the unquenchable will for freedom. When the divine spirit flames in the soul of some mortal [...] his deeds have changed the course of human events and his name survives the ages.

Thereafter the story unfolds with the characteristic De Mille mixture of sex, action and piety, all superbly photographed in Technicolor (George Barnes) amid memorable sets and costumes (both deservedly awarded Oscars in 1950). There are four big action highlights: the lion hunt, Samson slaughtering the Philistine wedding-feast guests, Samson killing the Philistine soldiers with the jawbone of an ass and the final destruction of the temple of Dagon by the blinded Samson – a special effects' tour de force created by Gordon Jennings. In between Samson, judge of the Danites, experiences his struggle against sensuality. Having courted the Philistine maiden Semadar (Angela Lansbury) and won her hand in marriage, he sets a riddle for the guests. She teases the answer out of him and gives it to her unsuccessful suitor Ahtur. This provokes a riot, in which Samson kills the guests and Semadar is killed. Seeking vengeance for her dead family and her own rejection by Samson, Delilah (Semadar's sister) offers to discover the secret of his strength in return for a fortune in silver, which the Saran promises her. After she successfully seduces him, learning that his secret lies in his uncut hair, she has his hair shorn and he is seized and blinded by the Philistines. Repenting of her part in his humiliation, she tries to persuade Samson to escape with her. But he seeks to expiate his sin by death and by destroying the temple of the heathen idol Dagon. She assists him and together they and the Philistines are all killed by the crashing masonry as he dislodges the two columns sustaining the building. But Samson has made a prophecy about the future, indicating that the sturdy boy Saul (Russ Tamblyn), who has manifested courage and commitment to his homeland, will in time become king of an independent Israel.

In general terms, the story highlights the fight for freedom against tyranny, the victory of religious faith over sexual sin: propaganda for the American way of life in the Cold War. But the fact that it is Israel that is being oppressed by the Philistines (the film opens with Philistine soldiers beating up an old storyteller relating the tale of Moses the liberator to a group of children) and that the leading Philistines are played by British actors (George Sanders, Henry Wilcoxon, Angela Lansbury) suggests that we might also see this as an analogue of the British occupation of Palestine and the Jewish struggle to create an independent state.

One or two critics welcomed the film. The *Daily Express* (22 December 1950) called it 'vulgar, fascinating and enjoyable' and the *Daily Mirror* (22 December 1950) called it 'majestic' and predicted 'a box office block buster'. There was frequent praise for the temple collapse sequence and the acting of George Sanders. But for the most part the critics reached for the familiar adjectives: 'tawdry [...] bore' (*Evening Standard*, 22 December); 'bad taste' (the *Daily Telegraph*, 22 December); 'dialogue beneath contempt' (the *News of the World*, 24 December); 'stupendously null, colossally void' (the *Daily Mail*, 22 December); 'childish stuff, meant for illiterates' (*Public Opinion*, 29 December 1950); 'a tastelessness, supine and void, ravages the eye, ear and mind for 127 minutes' (the *News Chronicle*, 22 December). A couple of critics, pointing out that it was the pantomime season, compared the film to a pantomime (*Sunday Graphic*; *Sunday Chronicle*, both 24 December). Virginia Graham in *The Spectator* (29 December 1950) displayed a nice sense of critical schizophrenia: 'It would be easy to mock this film, to debunk its pseudo-biblical script, its extravagances and vulgarity, but the fact remains that it is not only gigantic, stupendous, colossal and dazzling, but also highly enjoyable. It is everything I dislike most and I loved it.' Despite the critics, the film netted $11 million and became the top box-office success of 1950.

Impressed by the success of *Samson and Delilah*, Darryl F. Zanuck commissioned Philip Dunne to write a script based on the life of King David. Dunne was chary of the assignment and told Zanuck 'not to expect a De Millish script: no miracles, no chorus of heavenly voices, no actors – as Victor Mature once put it – 'making with the holy look', no sadism; and as for sex, a mature love story and nothing more'. Zanuck agreed, saying 'Okay, as long as you give me some of those De Millish grosses at the box office.'

Dunne settled on the story of David and Bathsheba, as told in the Second Book of Samuel, believing it to be a contemporary account of the reign, 'a forthright and sometimes brutally frank account of David's triumphs and defeats, his generosities and sins: a portrait of a complex, attractive and intensely human individual'. Dunne concluded that it was 'one of my better efforts [...] if only because it isn't a biblical epic at all, but a modern-minded play which explores the corruptions of absolute power and its effect on the character of one of the most colourful and attractive monarchs in all history'.

Dunne proposed Laurence Olivier and Vivien Leigh for the leads but Zanuck preferred to use the Fox contract stars Gregory Peck ('Peck' he said 'has a biblical face') and Susan Hayward, who both turned in effective and convincing performances.[11] The director assigned was Henry King who had achieved successes with religious drama (*The Song of Bernadette*), paeans to American democracy (*Wilson*) and slices of pastoral Americana (*Tol'able David*, *State Fair*, *Jesse James*). There were elements in the script which drew on all these generic traditions. A key role is played by the Ark of the Covenant which is brought in procession to Jerusalem and established in a tabernacle outside the gates. David is portrayed as a democratic monarch. He stresses the fact that, although chosen by God to be 'shepherd of his people', he was elected by the elders of all the tribes. He tells his son Absalom: 'I am bound by the law. With our people the law is everything.' He tells Bathsheba that, although he is the king, he has never taken anything or anyone by force; only by consent. The film also sets up a contrast familiar in American cinema between the innocence and wholesomeness of the countryside and the corruption of the city. David admits to Bathsheba that he has become detached from his pastoral roots. He recalls his days as a shepherd boy when he found God in nature and lived a simple family life, gradually losing touch with that life and its values when he moved to the city, became involved in court intrigue and took on the burdens of kingship. Symbolic of this loss is the scene in which he tries to demonstrate to Bathsheba his former prowess with a sling shot but fails to hit a tree, something effortlessly accomplished by a shepherd boy they encounter in the fields.

The film hints at the embattled situation of the contemporary state of Israel in the opening sequence. Israel, only recently united by David, is at war with its traditional enemy, the Amorites, and is besieging their stronghold of Rabbah. King David goes out on a scouting raid with his troops, demonstrating his commitment to the military struggle to defend Israel's independence. The war remains in the background for much of the film until Rabbah is taken. During the course of the film he conducts negotiations with the Egyptians but is suspicious of their motives, suspicion confirmed when they refuse to aid Israel during the famine.

But after the opening, there are no more action scenes and the film concentrates on the love story of David and Bathsheba. David, while walking on his terrace, sees Bathsheba bathing and falls in love with her. They embark on an affair but when she becomes pregnant, he is driven to dispose of her husband, Uriah the Hittite, by ordering him set in the forefront of the battle and then abandoned to be killed. Thereafter they marry but God curses the land with drought, famine and dust storms and causes their first-born son to die. Nathan the prophet demands that Bathsheba be stoned as an adulteress, but David submits himself to the will of God, entering the tabernacle of the Ark and asking God to take his life but to spare Bathsheba. God pardons him and sends the rain.

Dunne puts a thoroughly modern interpretation on the affair of David and Bathsheba. He shows both of them trapped in loveless marriages. David is married to Michal, daughter of King Saul. It had been a marriage of state to secure the allegiance of the Northern tribes; she is depicted as bitter, shrewish and snobbish, dismissing David as merely a 'shepherd's son'. Bathsheba was married to Uriah by her father and first saw him on her wedding day. They have only been together for six days during their seven-month marriage – he has been serving with the army meanwhile – and she admits that there is no love in the marriage. David and Bathsheba are drawn together by genuine love. She insists she wants to be his wife and not his mistress and he gives a very twentieth-century definition of his needs: 'I am only a man, Bathsheba. I need someone to understand that. I need the kind of understanding that only one human being can give to another. I need someone to share my heart.'

It is made clear that Uriah has no understanding of his wife's needs when David sounds him out about his attitude to his wife. Uriah declares 'My wife is nothing beside my duty.' He is unconcerned about her point of view and he would certainly consent to her stoning if she were to be found guilty of adultery. David delivers an eloquent plea for consideration to be given to the wife's feelings:

> Is it possible that you believe that she does not think or feel? A woman is flesh and blood, Uriah, like us. Perhaps even more so, because we give her so little to think of but matters of the flesh. In all our history only a handful of women have been permitted to write their names beside the men: Miriam, Deborah, Jael, perhaps one or two more. A woman's occupation is her husband and her life is her love, but if her husband rejects her love, she puts another before him.

But Uriah is unmoved by this declaration of a woman's rights. Both David and Bathsheba are haunted by guilt after Uriah's death. When they see an adulteress being stoned and begging for pity, their own predicament is underlined; as when their son dies. But David will not give up Bathsheba to the law, even when she is denounced for adultery by Michal and Absalom. David offers to give up the throne and flee to Egypt with Bathsheba but she will not allow him to abandon the position for which he has been chosen. He turns in the end to God for judgement.

Dunne's David is a very modern man: self-questioning, sceptical and pragmatic. Dunne, who himself was a non-believer and did not accept the existence of miracles, has David say at the siege of Rabbah: 'There are no Joshuas among us to cause the walls to fall down.' When the soldier Uzza touches the Ark and is struck dead and Nathan proclaims it the will of God, David suggests he died of natural causes brought on by a combination of the heat of the sun and the fact that he had been drinking wine. When Nathan blames David's sin for the drought, David says: 'There have been droughts before.' However, in the film's climax, David goes to the tabernacle and prays. He asks God to remember his innocent boyhood (there are flashbacks to his anointing by Samuel and his slaying of Goliath), repents of his crimes ('In all things have I failed thee'), and asks God to free his people from the misery put upon them for his sins. Finally, he asks God to take his life and puts his hands on the Ark as had Uzza earlier. There is a flash of lightning and the rain starts to fall. Outside the people sing the 23rd Psalm, composed by David and recited by him earlier ('The Lord is my Shepherd'). Dunne's explanation of this was 'I left it to the audience to decide whether the blessed rain came as a result of divine intervention or simply of a low-pressure system moving in from the Mediterranean.'[12] But it looks distinctly like a miracle in the film.

Several critics recognized it as a conscious and, they believed, laudable attempt to escape from the De Mille biblical epic formula (the *News Chronicle*, 31 October 1951; the *Manchester Guardian*, 3 November 1951). But most of them seemed to miss the old formula and remained unmoved and unimpressed: 'dull as ditchwater' (*Empire News*, 4 November 1951); 'dull' (*Sunday Graphic*, 4 November 1951); 'ponderous' (the *News of the World*, 4 November 1951); 'long drawn out and tedious' (the *People*, 4 November 1951); 'soporific' (the *News Chronicle*, 31 October 1951); 'somniferous' (the *Daily Telegraph*, 2 November 1951).

Some recognized the modern spin put on the story. The *Daily Mail* (2 November 1951) noted disapprovingly that the story had been adapted to 'the pattern of modern American adultery at country club level [...] only the clothes and camels are there to remind us that this is Jerusalem, Israel and not Jerusalem, Connecticut'. The *Daily Express* (2 November 1951), alluding perhaps to his previous role in the wartime drama *12 O'Clock High*, thought Peck played David 'like a bomber pilot torn between the safety of his crew and the WAC he has left behind'.

From others there were howls of outrage. The *Daily Graphic* (2 November 1951) said the whole thing was 'as outrageous a piece of monstrous misrepresentation and howling hypocrisy' as had ever been put on the screen. The *Evening News* (1 December 1951) said 'Hollywood's phoney Code of film morality has never been so completely exposed as by the whitewashing of the "hero" in *David and Bathsheba* [...] Far from protecting young people from seeing an immoral story on the screen this Code-satisfying film becomes pernicious glorification of the intrigues and meanness of David and Bathsheba. All under the guise of a Great Love. Basic facts are reversed to condone the evil of the guilty lovers and both are presented as heroic characters helplessly in the grip of a perfectly understandable passion. The British censor should have given the picture one of his "X" certificates to prevent young people from having their moral values debased.'

In fact the Hollywood censors, the Breen Office, had been worried about the script. Dunne recalled: 'When the boys from the Breen Office said: "Adultery? Murder? The man gets away with both?" I merely smiled and pointed to my authority: the Old Testament itself.' The 'divine' origin of the story, plus approval from a panel of rabbis, apparently quelled the doubts of the Breen Office, if not of the *London Evening News*.[13]

The public seem to have been less concerned. Produced at a cost of $2 million, it achieved the required 'De Millish' returns. It grossed $7 million in domestic rentals alone and became the top American box-office success of 1951.[14] It received Oscar nominations for Dunne's script, Alfred Newman's surging and melodic score with its distinct echoes of Richard Strauss' *Salome* (another biblical tale of illicit love), photography, sets and costumes – though in the event it won none.

MGM's contribution to the sex and spirituality cycle was *The Prodigal* (1955), directed by the efficient journeyman Richard Thorpe in Cinemascope and Technicolor. Based on the parable told by Christ in St Luke's Gospel 15:11–32, the film expanded the story (younger son takes his portion, goes to the city, wastes it in riotous living and returns to a forgiving father who kills the fatted calf to welcome him) into a full-blown Ancient World epic. Set in Joppa and Damascus in 70 BC, *The Prodigal* is constructed on the contrast between the simple, monotheistic spirituality of Judaism and the orgiastic paganism of the god Baal and the goddess Astarte, whose fertility cults embrace human sacrifice and temple prostitution. Linked to the contrast of faiths is a contrast of political and social philosophies, with Judaism standing for freedom and paganism for slavery. Micah, the younger son of Jewish farmer Eli, becomes besotted with Samarra, high priestess of Astarte, takes his portion of the family wealth and goes to Damascus to court her. She refuses to marry him because of her vocation ('I belong to all men') and she recounts the list of the rulers with whom she has had sex (though when she includes the Caliph of Baghdad she is several centuries too early). Eventually Micah loses everything because of his obsession with her and is sold into slavery. She offers him his freedom if he will publicly renounce his God. He refuses and instead leads a slave revolt which results in the deaths of both the tyrannical high priest of Baal and of Samarra, who hurls herself into the sacrificial fire as the temple is stormed by the rebels. Sadder and wiser, Micah returns home to his family.

The unfortunate Edmund Purdom, who had just starred in one big budget Ancient World flop, *The Egyptian*, found himself playing a similar role in the same earnest manner in *The Prodigal*. Lana Turner is completely out of her depth as Samarra. With her blonde hair, 1950s make-up and spangled dresses, she gives the impression of someone auditioning for a role in the latest Broadway musical. A reliable supporting cast (Francis L. Sullivan as a genial moneylender, Louis Calhern as the tyrannical High Priest and Joseph Wiseman as a good-natured rascal) do their best but no one can rise above the derivative script, uninterested direction and one-dimensional characterization. Produced at a cost of $5 million, the film failed at the box office.

Far more successful was Cecil B. De Mille's *The Ten Commandments* (1956), the remarkable culmination of a remarkable career. In his autobiography, De Mille recorded that the stimulus to make it came from the many letters he received after the Second World War urging him to remake his silent epic *The Ten Commandments*:

> The world needs a reminder, they said, of the law of God; and it was evident in at least some of the letters that the world's awful experience of totalitarianism, fascist and communist, had made many thoughtful people realize anew that the law of God is the essential bedrock of human freedom.[15]

Rather than have a modern story with a flashback to the story of the Exodus as in 1923, De Mille decided to concentrate the whole film on the story of Moses. He had a definite political agenda:

> The Bible story was timeless. It was also timely. It is a story of slavery and liberation, two words that the world's experience since 1923 had saturated with more vivid meaning, with more real fear and more anxious hope. When Moses stood before Pharaoh, voicing the divine demand, 'Let my people go!', the same two forces faced that confront one another today in a world divided between tyranny and freedom. When Moses led his people to Mount Sinai, they learned, as the world today must learn, that true freedom is freedom under God.[16]

De Mille expanded on this in an address he gave at a luncheon at the Plaza Hotel, New York, just prior to the film's opening:

The Ten Commandments given on Mount Sinai are not laws. *They are The Law.* They are the expression of the mind of God for His creatures. They are the charter and guide of human liberty, for there can be no liberty without the law. The motion picture, *The Ten Commandments*, is the most modern picture I have ever made, because the struggle between the forces represented by Moses and those represented by Pharaoh is still being waged today. Are men free souls under God or are they the property of the state? Are men to be ruled by the law or by the whims of an individual? The answers to these questions were given some three thousand years ago on Mount Sinai.

Despite the importance of the message, he also added what was in effect a summary of his approach to the Bible as source material:

The story is human, the greatest human story I have ever directed. The purpose of the theatre is to entertain, not to preach. If you were to strip the drama of all its spiritual elements, it would still remain the second greatest story ever told. When you dip beneath the Elizabethan English of the Bible, the men and women in it are men and women of flesh and blood. They love and hate; they mourn over the death of a child; arrogant ruthless men try to over-ride their fellows; the women of the Bible are women of virtue and women of vice, women of treachery and women of faith – just the same in the Bible as men and women are today. Moses is Everyman [...] the life of Moses was a life of struggle and defiance, of daring and sorrow, a life of love and battle, of sacrifice and murder, a life of achievement and disaster, humiliation and glory.

But he insisted on its ultimate authenticity:

We did not invent what you see on the screen. We translated it from the written word into visual form. [[...] We tried not to make it 'a movie', but a living experience, as real humanly and spiritually as it is authentic historically.[17]

But before he even started shooting he had to get the approval of Paramount Studios. He appeared before the board in 1952 to explain that he had five projects currently in development, four of them were epics (*Helen of Troy, Alexander the Great, The Story of Esther* and *The Ten Commandments*); the other was a biopic of Lord Baden-Powell, the founder of the Boy Scouts. The project he currently most favoured was *The Ten Commandments*. The majority of the Board were hostile to the idea. The studio president, Barney Balaban, was particularly scornful, dismissing the idea as old-fashioned and wanting him to come up with something modern like his recent circus film hit, *The Greatest Show on Earth*. Production chief Y. Frank Freeman intervened to point out that De Mille always knew 'which way the wind was blowing with the moviegoing public'. But it was the venerable studio founder and board chairman, the 80-year-old Adolph Zukor, who made the decisive intervention. He pointed out that more than once Paramount had been saved from receivership by the revenues of a De Mille picture and that De Mille was the most consistently bankable director working in Hollywood. But he added:

> After we have just lived through a horrible war where our people were systematically executed, we have a man who makes a film praising the Jewish people, that tells one of the great legends of our Scripture – and he isn't even a Jew. We should get down on our knees and say 'Thank you!' And now he wants to make the life of Moses? I've had to sit here all morning and listen to nothing but screaming and yelling about how *awful* that would be! You should be ashamed of yourselves [...] What kind of Jews are you? I, for one, think it's a good idea, not a stupid idea.[18]

Permission was given and De Mille initiated the research. He always laid the greatest stress on research and authenticity. The research for *The Ten Commandments* was coordinated by Swiss-born Henry Noerdlinger. He had joined De Mille to research *Unconquered* in 1945, stayed on for *Samson and Delilah* (1949) and began work on *The Ten Commandments* in 1952. Noerdlinger's input was crucial. He attended all the daily script conferences and was permanently on hand to ensure that the historical background remained accurate. The publicity for the film stressed that 30 libraries and museums had been contacted, 1,644 publications consulted and 30,000 photographs studied. The results of the research were to be published under the title *Moses and Egypt* by the University of California Press. It has been called 'an outstanding example of pseudo-history' which made no attempt to evaluate and compare the sources and reconcile any contradictions.[19] Sometimes Noerdlinger was required to produce historical justification for something De Mille wanted, as when he was tasked with producing evidence that Delilah would have worn a bra. He was able to come up with a photograph 'showing a Minoan woman whose dress had a bra-like sweep to the upper portion'. It was enough for De Mille.[20]

De Mille worked closely with his writers, laying out plot and motivation, ruling on mood and pace. Phil Koury, his executive assistant for seven years, recalled:

> Melodrama burned brightly in DeMille's mind. If he warred, rather than worked with his writers it was because he wanted them to feel the scenes as deeply as he did. He constantly hammered at the emotional meaning. Once he cried: 'There's terrific power in this scene. You can get the audience so worked up they can't bear it. What I want here is something that would make Shakespeare say, "Why didn't I think of that"!'[21]

He made a distinction between 'narrative' and 'dramatic situation'. He believed in the motivating force of conflict, 'the only thing that will keep an audience awake' (the dramatic situation), and broke down the story into its action highlights (the narrative), which were placed regularly throughout the script. He delighted in devising his own bits of dialogue which he inserted in the script and fiercely protected.[22]

Lest there be any doubt about the fact that the film was the gospel according to De Mille, he would himself be present throughout the film. The trailer was constructed around De Mille in his office explaining with extracts the nature and purpose of the film. The film itself opens with a shot of drawn red curtains, echoing footsteps are heard and De Mille emerges from behind the curtain to address the audience directly, insisting on the film's historical accuracy and explaining that the film is about the birth of freedom, the decision whether men shall be free souls ruled by God's law or by the whims of a dictator, 'a struggle still being waged in the world today'. Thereafter the film is narrated by De Mille with a narrative steeped in biblical cadences and delivered with patriarchal gravity.

The evidence for De Mille's evangelical mission further lies in the fact that he offered a print of the film to every prison in the United States and free distribution of the film in the USSR as long as it remained uncensored – an offer never likely to have been taken up. He also sent copies of *Moses and Egypt* to every library in the United States.[23]

Many writers found themselves unable to stay the course with De Mille. He was fond of quoting Dion Boucicault's maxim: 'Plays are not written. They are re-written', and his scripts went through draft after draft until he was satisfied. For, as Jesse Lasky Jr, regular De Mille scriptwriter, testified, the final script had to be a total blueprint for the epic, fully annotated with source references and detailing props, costumes and camera set-ups. *The Ten Commandments* script ran to 308 pages.[24]

For *The Ten Commandments* there were four scriptwriters. Jesse Lasky Jr and Fredric M. Frank had worked for De Mille before. Lasky had co-written *Union Pacific, Northwest Mounted Police, Reap the Wild Wind, Unconquered* and *Samson and Delilah*. He knew the routine with De Mille. Frank had co-written *Unconquered* and *Samson and Delilah*. They were joined on *The Ten Commandments* by Aeneas MacKenzie and Jack Gariss. Lasky characterized his fellow-writers in his autobiography. Frank, a former New York advertising account executive, was 'a devout Republican, a compact logician, a mule-stubborn scriptwriter as hard-headed as the boss. His conservatism was deep-rooted and practical'. Aeneas MacKenzie was a 'peppery Scotsman who had drifted to Hollywood after World War One, attached himself to the young film industry and never gone home again. Aeneas was a fine film dramatist and a walking encyclopedia of obscure information [...] When he joined us he was ageing and nearly blind, but he had never forgotten anything he had ever seen, heard or read – not a bad trait for a screenwriter.' His screen credits included *Juarez* (1939), *The Private Lives of Elizabeth and Essex* (1939), *Buffalo Bill* (1944), *The Spanish Main* (1945), *Captain Horatio Hornblower R.N.* (1951) and *Against All Flags* (1952). *The Ten Commandments* would be his last. Jack Gariss 'had recently emerged from William De Mille's Film Department at the University of Southern California. He was huge and bearded, and both looked and was a tower of erudition, exuding infinite tranquillity and mysticism.' It would be his only screen credit. Lasky concluded that 'no previous De Mille writing team had ever been better equipped to survey the forest of research for *The Ten Commandments*'.[25] They were required to steep themselves not only in the Bible, the Qur'an, the Talmud and the Midrash but also the works of Eusebius of Caesarea, Philo and Flavius Josephus. Whatever De Mille said about absolute accuracy, the writers were confronted with the fact that there was a gap of 30 years in the life of Moses. This gap was filled by reference to the romantic novel *Prince of Egypt* by Dorothy Clarke Wilson (1949), whose conjectural life of Moses as an Egyptian prince and the favoured heir of Sethi I, could, argued Noerdlinger, be supported by the known facts. They also drew on ideas from Revd J.H. Ingraham's *Pillar of Fire* (1892) and Revd A.E. Southon's *On Eagle's Wings* (1937). The script was three years in the writing and that work proceeded with the inevitable rows and reconciliations between De Mille and his writers. De Mille acknowledged this, praising his two new recruits as 'both of them men of strong and independent mind, able to hold their own in the long, hard process of forging a story with a finished screenplay. In our story conferences, producer and writers may alternate in the role of hammer and anvil. If sparks fly sometimes, it is good when they glow with the intelligence and wit of writers like the four who worked with me on this film.'[26] Meanwhile, Edith Head and her staff were designing the costumes, John P. Fulton was preparing to execute the special effects (The Angel of Death Visiting Egypt, The Pillar of Fire, The Parting of the Red Sea, The Earthquake) and LeRoy Prinz, the choreographer, was studying Egyptian wall-paintings in order to choreograph the dances. De Mille had the whole thing visualized before he began, having 1,200 storyboards prepared by artists which would then be effected by his cameramen on location or on the sets at Paramount. Hal Pereira and Walter Tyler, the art directors, based their set designs on Henry Noerdlinger's research and on Paul Iribe's designs for the 1923 film, which De Mille admired still.

The casting was crucial and here De Mille was prepared to take risks. Charlton Heston, a comparative newcomer, had starred in De Mille's *The Greatest Show on Earth* but he had only made his Hollywood debut in 1950 and thereafter had been seen mainly in modern-dress roles or westerns. But De Mille was convinced of his ability to play the part by his resemblance to Michelangelo's statue of Moses and by viewing his performance as Mark Antony in a low-budget 16mm film of *Julius Caesar* in which he had appeared in 1949. He found the perfect Rameses II in Yul Brynner, then appearing on the New York stage in the role which made him a star: the King of Siam in *The King and I*. He surrounded them with a raft of stars, among them Sir Cedric Hardwicke as the Pharaoh Sethi I. Hardwicke would recall in his autobiography: 'I enjoyed working with De Mille, who of all the directors I have known was the only one who really knew what he wanted – he and Olivier.'[27] Edward G. Robinson was under consideration for the role of Dathan, the Jew who collaborates with the Egyptians and later leads the Jews into worship of the Golden Calf. Robinson, labelled a 'premature anti-fascist' and someone who had links with left-wing organizations, had in the witch-hunting atmosphere of the early 1950s been 'gray-listed', which led to his being confined to B pictures. Robinson recalled of De Mille:

> No more conservative or patriarchal figure existed in Hollywood, no one more opposed to communism or any permutation or combination thereof. And no fairer one, no man with a greater sense of decency and justice […] somebody suggested I would be ideal (for the part of Dathan) but under the circumstances I was, of course, unacceptable. Mr De Mille wanted to know why, coldly reviewed the matter, felt I had been done an injustice, and told his people to offer me the part. Cecil B. De Mille returned me to films. Cecil B. De Mille restored my self-respect.[28]

It may be too cynical to suggest that casting a known leftist as the 'enemy within' the Jewish people might be seen to be making a point about contemporary subversion in the United States. Other leading roles were filled by Anne Baxter, Martha Scott, Nina Foch, Vincent Price, Judith Anderson, Debra Paget, John Derek, Yvonne de Carlo, Henry Wilcoxon and John Carradine. Apart from the stars, De Mille maintained a stock company of supporting players, many of whom had been with him since silent days and for whom he regularly found parts in his sound epics. Among them was Julia Faye, an everpresent in his casts, who had played Pharaoh's Wife in the 1923 *Ten Commandments* and now played Elisheba. One of the most moving moments in the whole film comes when the now frail and elderly H.B. Warner, who had played Christ in the silent *King of Kings*, is carried on as the dying Amminadab to participate in the Exodus.

Only three of the stars, Heston, Wilcoxon (who was also associate producer) and Brynner (very briefly) accompanied the production team to Egypt where the exterior locations were shot, and where the City of Per-Rameses was constructed at Beni-Youssef, and the Egyptian Army Cavalry Corps doubled as Pharaoh's army. De Mille and company were there from 14 October to 13 December 1954. The company were welcomed by the Prime Minister, Colonel Gamal Abdel Nasser, who told De Mille that his film *The Crusades* was much admired in Arab countries for its fair-minded portrayal of Sultan Saladin.[29] 20,000 extras were utilized in the recreation of the Exodus and two second-unit teams under Henry Wilcoxon and Arthur Rosson supplemented the work of the main unit under De Mille. During the course of shooting, De Mille suffered a heart attack but recovered sufficiently to complete the demanding schedule. The rest of the film was shot on the Paramount back lot between 28 March and 13 August 1955. It was then edited by his 75-year-old regular editor Anne Bauchens.

Along with historical authenticity, De Mille believed in telling a story visually, and for inspiration he turned regularly to Victorian paintings. His associate producer Henry Wilcoxon recalled:

> I suppose, more than anything, Mr De Mille was seeking to recapture the Victorian passion plays of his youth with *The Ten Commandments*. Everything has a style and pageantry faithful not only to ancient Egypt, but to the Victorian painters of the late nineteenth century as well. Biblical paintings and biblical illustrations in books and magazines of that day were immensely popular. Painters travelled to the Holy Land for background for their work and came home with furniture, rugs, clothing, and artifacts that they used with models in their studios. One of De Mille's favourite Old Testament theme paintings was Sir Lawrence Alma-Tadema's *Finding of Moses*. Compare the colour and light in that painting to our film. Alma-Tadema really did his homework and so did De Mille. We discovered when we travelled to Egypt that Alma-Tadema's eye matched the camera's.[30]

The fact is that Alma-Tadema did not visit Egypt before doing his Egyptian paintings, though he did research the trappings of the pictures. It is nevertheless true that De Mille matches Alma-Tadema's colours and patterns in his Technicolor photography. One can see the Victorian inspiration in scene after scene. Poynter's great *Israel in Egypt* canvas lies behind the scenes of the Jews in captivity hauling the great monuments, and the Exodus sequence. The finding of Moses is based on the paintings by Edwin Long and Frederick Goodall. Alma-Tadema's *Finding of Moses* actually inspires the visit of Nefretiri to the brickfields. The scene of Nefretiri and Sethi playing a board game is modelled on Alma-Tadema's *Egyptian Game* and his *Death of Pharaoh's First Born* influences the similar scene in the film. Moses on a rock above the Red Sea summoning the parting of the waves is a realization of Christoph Eckersberg's *The Crossing of the Red Sea* (1813). Frederick Bridgman's *Pharaoh's Army engulfed by the Red Sea* (1900) is similarly realized in that sequence. Doré's Bible illustrations inspired the sequence of Moses with the Ten Commandments and the effects created by John Martin's apocalyptic painting of The Golden Calf and The Parting of the Red Sea can be seen also in De Mille's staging of those events. It is also worthy of note that many of the sequences from the Exodus onwards are copied directly in terms of camera angle and staging from the identical scenes in the 1923 version.

The film opens with Pharaoh Rameses I (Ian Keith), learning of a prophecy that Egypt's Hebrew slaves will be freed by a newly born Deliverer. He orders all new-born Hebrew male children slaughtered. But Jochabel (Martha Scott) floats her newly born son in a basket on the Nile. He is rescued and adopted by Pharaoh's widowed and childless daughter, Bithiah (Nina Foch). Thirty years later Moses (Charlton Heston) is an Egyptian warrior hero and, as Pharaoh's nephew, the rival to Pharaoh's son Rameses (Yul Brynner) for the hand of Princess Nefretiri

(Anne Baxter) and the succession to the throne of Sethi I (Cedric Hardwicke). Sethi, who favours Moses for the succession, commissions Moses to complete the building of his treasure city, and Rameses to find the fabled Deliverer who is still spoken of by the Hebrew slaves. Moses completes the building of the city, treating the Hebrew slaves with compassion. But he kills Baka the master builder (Vincent Price), when Baka tries to flog the slave Joshua (John Derek) after making off with Joshua's sweetheart Lilia (Debra Paget). Hebrew collaborator Dathan (Edward G. Robinson) informs Rameses that Moses is of Hebrew origin and is the promised Deliverer. Rameses delivers him in chains to Sethi, who broken-heartedly exiles him for life. Crossing the desert, Moses is taken in by the family of desert sheikh Jethro and marries his daughter Sephora (Yvonne de Carlo). Speaking from the middle of a burning bush, God commands him to return to Egypt and free the slaves. Moses and his Hebrew brother Aaron (John Carradine) make successive appearances before Rameses, now Pharaoh and married to Nefretiri, to urge him to 'let my people go'. A succession of plagues fails to move him until the Egyptian firstborn are all killed. The Hebrews are freed and depart Egypt joyously. But Nefretiri persuades Rameses to bring them back. He pursues them with his host. Moses parts the Red Sea, allowing the Hebrews to cross, before the waters close over the pursuing Egyptians. Moses leads the Hebrews to Mount Sinai and he then goes up into the mountain to receive the Ten Commandments. Below, Dathan persuades the Hebrews to set up and worship a Golden Calf. Moses returns to find an orgy underway and, declaring 'Those who will not live by the law shall perish by the law', hurls the Ten Commandments at the Calf, causing an earthquake which swallows up the evildoers. For forty years the Hebrews wander in the wilderness until they are permitted to reach the Promised Land. But Moses may not enter, he hands over the leadership to Joshua, bidding him 'go, proclaim liberty throughout all the lands' and goes up into Mount Nebo to die.

The film opened in New York on 8 November 1956 and in London on 28 November 1957. The review in *Time* magazine (12 November 1956) typified the critical reaction of the big city critics, when it called *The Ten Commandments* 'the biggest, the most expensive and in some respects, perhaps the most vulgar movie ever made'. The film was compared to a chorus girl, 'pretty well put together, but much too big and much too flashy'.

The trade press was more enthusiastic but even *Variety* (10 October 1956) thought 'De Mille remains conventional with the motion picture as an art form. The eyes of the onlooker are filled with spectacle. Emotional tug is sometimes lacking. *Commandments* is too long [...] Scenes of the greatness that was Egypt, and Hebrews by the thousands under the whip of the task-masters are striking. But bigness wearies. There's simply too much.'

Although the film was praised by the *Daily Mirror* and the *Daily Telegraph* (both 28 November 1957), the British critics were mainly disparaging. The *New Statesman* (7 December 1957) and the *Daily Express* (28 November 1957) dismissed it as a 'bore'. The *Daily Mail* (28 November 1957) said the film left you 'more exhausted than uplifted'. It was 'far too long' and lacking in 'the poetic magic to convey the full spiritual inspiration of the spectacle'. *The Times* (28 November 1957) called it 'a brightly coloured postcard magnified into a mural'. The *Star* (28 November 1957) called it 'the best made bad film I have ever seen but it is corn in Egypt. Golden Corn but corn.'

So often had De Mille been accused of producing corn, that he had an answer ready:

> Be proud of corn [...] corn is soul, corn is that which makes you cry and laugh. Corn is all humanity. Yes, my pictures have corn and I am proud of it.[31]

The critical reaction demonstrated the truth of the lament of one Paramount insider: 'Nobody likes De Mille's film except the public.' It received seven Oscar nominations but won only one Oscar for special effects. By 1960, 80 million people had seen *The Ten Commandments*.[32] Costing $13,272, 381, it had by 1979 made $90,066,230.[33]

Granted the occasional jarring element (Jethro's daughters, played as sex-starved 1950s American teenagers, are particularly tiresome), *The Ten Commandments* remains, whatever the critics at the time said, a stupendous achievement. The building of Sethi's treasure city with hordes of slaves hauling statues and a massive obelisk being set upright remains a truly magnificent sequence. So is the Exodus with the Jews pouring out in their hundreds, men, women, children and animals, between the rows of sphinxes. For this, De Mille used three cameras, one at ground level, one in medium shot and one in long shot, so that the resulting footage could be mixed to give a three-dimensional impression of the event. The Egyptian footage was then supplemented by character vignettes shot in Hollywood to show the reactions of individuals to the granting of freedom. This was always an important aspect of De Mille's approach and gave a dimension of humanity to the epic events. It was achieved by a technique learned from D.W. Griffith, as Henry Wilcoxon explained:

> It was on the set of *Intolerance* that De Mille observed Griffith's method of costuming his assistant directors and assigning them perhaps 250 or 300 extras to 'oversee'. Each extra knew his assistant director, each assistant director was charged with the duty of seeing to it that his 'extras' behaved like 'actors'. With perhaps as many as twenty A.D.s working in a crowd, everyone stayed on his toes, everyone acted and reacted as one [...] During our Exodus, we had twenty-two Egyptian A.D.s from Misr Studios in Cairo who spoke several languages and kept in contact with De Mille and one another by hidden walkie-talkies. That is the reason neither Griffith's nor De Mille's crowd scenes ever look like an unruly

mob. *Everyone* is acting. Everyone has a job and is doing it. It's easy to stand there and pick out individuals and follow their 'little story' along the way.[34]

It is possible to see *The Ten Commandments* as the triumphant cinematic culmination of the Victorian stage tradition of Ancient World melodramas. The visuals are throughout compelling, their Victorian painterly inspiration always obvious, underlined by De Mille's use of panoramic long-shots and tableau groupings for his characters. There is apocalyptic splendour from the very opening scene in which a great stone statue is hauled along by thousands of slaves against a blood-red sky, a visual encapsulation of the reality of Hebrew bondage. This same feeling permeates the sequence of the Passover and the visitation of the Angel of Death; in the crossing of the Red Sea, with Moses standing on a rock, black thunder clouds swirling round him, as he orders the waters to part, the Hebrews crossing and the Egyptian army engulfed; in the granting of the Ten Commandments and the destruction of the Golden Calf by the avenging patriarch. But there are moving intimate moments too stressing the humanity of the protagonists (Sethi's death, Jochabel's acknowledgement that Moses is her son, Moses' declaration of love for his adoptive mother Bithiah, the death of Pharaoh's first-born son).

Victorian too in inspiration is the extravagantly ornate dialogue, which would not have been out of place in a nineteenth-century melodrama. Choice examples abound: Moses telling Nefretiri 'Your fragrance is like the wine of Babylon', Nefretiri declaring: 'Moses, Moses, you stubborn, splendid, adorable fool', Rameses (to Nefretiri): 'You sharp-clawed, treacherous little peacock [...] You will be mine, mine, like my dog or my horse or my falcon. Only I will love you more and trust you less.' They are lines to relish and to cherish.

The impression created by the combination of visuals and dialogue is superbly complemented by the musical score. Victor Young, who had scored every De Mille film since *Northwest Mounted Police* (1940), was too ill to undertake *The Ten Commandments*. So De Mille called on a young new film composer Elmer Bernstein. It was Paramount music director Roy Fjastad who suggested Bernstein to provide the music needed for a Bedouin dance during the Hollywood filming. De Mille liked it well enough to offer him the whole film to score. But Bernstein had to play each theme of his score through to De Mille on the piano before it could be orchestrated. The result was a notable epic score with a luscious love theme, stirring epic theme, joyous Exodus music and inspiring music for the crossing of the Red Sea with its characteristic Jewish rhythms. Bernstein employed the shofar (ram's horn), theremin, cymbals and sistrum to get the ancient texture of Egyptian and Hebrew music right.[35]

The actors make a major contribution to the success of the film. Heston and Brynner are perfectly cast as the protagonists in the principal conflict of the film. Heston imbues with power and strength both his proud Egyptian warrior prince and his blazing Old Testament patriarch. He is matched scene for scene by Brynner as the virile, arrogant and ruthless Rameses, swaggering and flashing-eyed. They are splendidly supported by Sir Cedric Hardwicke as the wise and good-natured Pharaoh Sethi, John Derek as a swashbuckling Joshua, Yvonne de Carlo as the patient and loving Sephora, Vincent Price as the suave, sneering master-builder and Edward G. Robinson, playing the collaborator Dathan as a sardonic, scented Jewish gangster. Anne Baxter hams up the role of Nefretiri deliciously, eye-rolling, lip-smacking and barnstorming as she vamps Moses enthusiastically, and ruthlessly murders the slave Memnet who threatens to expose his Hebrew origins. It is one of cinema's over-the-top performances but one entirely in the spirit of full-blooded Victorian melodrama and thus totally in keeping with the project.

By the time the next drama of the conflict between spirituality and sexuality reached the screen, Israel had been involved in another war. In 1956, following the nationalization of the Suez Canal by Egypt's President Nasser, Britain, France and Israel attacked Egypt. The attack was called off after the United States refused to support it. But the invasion was followed by armed clashes along the Israel/Jordan border with King Hussein personally commanding the Jordanian troops.

This situation was directly reflected in the film *Solomon and Sheba* (1959), along with the characteristic 1950s' message about the threat to religious faith from unbridled sexuality. Like previous Ancient World epics, *Solomon and Sheba* was filmed in Spain, shot in Technicolor and Technirama 70 and employed 5,000 soldiers from the Spanish Army to fight the ancient battles. It cost $5.6 million to make.

But the production was blighted by tragedy. Three-quarters of the way through the filming, Tyrone Power, who was playing Solomon, collapsed and died of a heart attack on 15 November 1958 aged only 45. The decision was taken to reshoot Power's scenes with another actor and Yul Brynner took over the role. But this changed the nature of the character. The director, King Vidor, felt that Brynner resisted the interpretation of the character Power had given, a poet rather than a soldier and a man troubled by his desires. Brynner wished to dominate every scene he was in and his performance, while convincingly authoritative, lacked the depth and complexity that Power would have given it. Nevertheless the film made $5.5 million at the American box office and $10 million in Europe, putting it comfortably into profit.

It was the last film from director King Vidor, who had over the course of his long career moved from making small-scale films characterized by documentary realism and naturalistic acting (*The Crowd, Our Daily Bread*) in the 1920s and early 1930s to large-scale, full-blown grandiose epics, almost operatic in their extravagance (*Duel in the Sun*, *War and Peace*) in the late 1940s and the 1950s. *Solomon and Sheba* was the culmination of his 'operatic' phase, containing as it did a pagan orgy (admittedly rather tame), the destruction of the temple at Jerusalem and several pitched battles, culminating in the spectacular destruction of the Egyptian army.

The politics of the contemporary Middle East lie behind the script, as the opening titles make clear: 'This is the border between Israel and Egypt. As it is today, so it was a thousand years before the birth of Jesus of Nazareth.' The film begins with a border skirmish between the Egyptians and the Israelites, the Israelites being led by the two sons of King David, Adonijah and Solomon, characterized respectively as warrior and poet. News arrives that King David is dying. Adonijah proclaims himself King while Solomon races back to be with his father. David, who has so recently united the 12 tribes in a single state ('Israel has hardly begun' he says), now seeks to preserve the unity and integrity of the new kingdom. He is clear about the method. 'Defend but never attack' he advises and declares that God has told him 'Only in peace can Israel prosper and be made great.' It is an echo of the American rebuke for the allies' attack on Egypt. To the fury of Adonijah, David declares Solomon his heir and he is anointed as King, with the consent of the tribes. In order to keep the peace, he appoints Adonijah commander of the army and sets out to build a temple for God.

Meanwhile, the Pharaoh of Egypt plots the destruction of the young state of Israel, organizing a simultaneous attack by Moab, Chaldea and Egypt from the north, the south and the east, exactly like the 1948 war. The Queen of Sheba, however, offers to seduce Solomon and destroy him. For she sees her absolute rule threatened by the democratic and egalitarian doctrine espoused by Solomon and Israel. Her chancellor Baltor tells her: 'Nothing is more dangerous than a man with an idea – the one god who teaches that all men are equal and none are slaves'.

Much of the film is taken up with the Queen of Sheba using her wiles to enslave the devout Solomon. He does his best to resist but eventually succumbs and both permits and attends the orgiastic pagan festival of the god Ragon, where they make love. But God destroys the pagan idol with thunder and lightning; and then the newly built temple, as a sign of his displeasure. Killed in the temple is Abishag, the adopted daughter of David, who had pleaded with Solomon to remember his duty to his people. Now she had prayed to God to take her life and spare Solomon and he had.

Solomon is rejected by the people for his blasphemy. Adonijah uses the opportunity to defect to Egypt and lead the Egyptian army in an attack on Israel. Solomon is advised by God to have his army burnish their shields, so that they blind the advancing Egyptian host, which plunges to its destruction in a ravine. Solomon subsequently kills Adonijah in a sword duel. Solomon is restored to the throne and wants Sheba to share it. But she had vowed to God that if he preserved

Solomon's life and gave him victory, she would return to Sheba and introduce monotheism. Sadly but obediently she leaves. So the film ends with democratic Israel triumphing over absolutist Egypt, monotheism over paganism and duty over the desires of the flesh.

The film boasted handsome sets (Richard Day), superb colour photography (Freddie Young), and an excellent and largely British supporting cast, headed by George Sanders as Adonijah and Finlay Currie as David. Reassuringly, even God when he speaks does so with a British accent. Gina Lollobrigida, however, makes an indelibly Italian Queen of Sheba.

The theme of sex versus duty continued to be expounded but with diminishing box office returns until the early 1960s after which it was submerged by the arrival of the new morality of the 'Swinging Sixties': chic, cynical, consumerist and individualist, with little time for the ethic of restraint, self-sacrifice and self-denial.

By the time of *Solomon and Sheba*'s release, the British critics had perfected their attitude of amused contempt towards the genre. So the *Daily Herald* (30 October 1959) declared: 'As a spectacle, it is splendid. As a piece of biblical history, it is a gigantic joke. And [...] it offers some of the most lunatic dialogue it has ever been my privilege to hear.' The *Financial Times* (2 November 1959) said: 'In the special style of Hollywood spectacles, this one turns the grandeur of the old Bible stories into a mixture of epic set-pieces [...] and bathetic domesticity.' The *News of the World* (1 November 1959) said: 'BARNUM AND BAILEY in all their glory never dreamed up a circus show of such monstrous immensity as the much-vaunted *Solomon and Sheba*.' *Time and Tide* (7 November 1959) said: 'Probably the best thing to do with *Solomon and Sheba* is to take a large pinch of salt, keep as far away as possible from the house-speakers which emit the voice of God at intervals, and sit back and relish its absurdities.' The *Guardian* (31 October 1959) declared: 'This *Solomon and Sheba* is always tasteless and sometimes funny. It is vast, loud, awful and likely to achieve its relentless purpose of enormous popular success.' The *People* (1 November 1959) reported: 'King Vidor's *Solomon And Sheba* is stupendous but dull. Fabulous sets dazzle the eye; but the film fizzles out in long stretches of tedium.' The *Sunday Express* (1 November 1959), pronouncing it 'a stinking awful film', added: 'Compared with the Bible story this is hokum, and while some people feel tolerantly that the cinema has now established a licence to rewrite the Bible to make it bigger, brasher and sexier entertainment, I don't agree [...] the script [...] is so banal that never for a moment is one's wonder tempered by anything but an embarrassed incredulity. The actors [...] are so dazed and adrift that not a single scene has even a tinkle of truth.' Leonard Mosley devoted almost the whole of his review in the *Daily Express* (31 October 1959) to lamenting the inadequacy of the orgy.

Veteran director Raoul Walsh produced, directed and co-wrote (with Jewish journalist Michael Elkins, later the long-serving BBC correspondent in Jerusalem), *Esther and the King* (1960) which celebrated one of the rare Jewish heroines of the Old Testament. It was filmed in Italy at the Titanus Appia Studio in Rome, produced by the Italian company Galatea but released in the United States by 20th Century-Fox, who provided two of its contract stars, Richard Egan and Joan Collins, to play the title roles. Apart from them and the Irish actor Denis O'Dea, who gave the best performance in the film as the noble and dignified Mordecai, the rest of the cast were Italian, many of them regulars in the Italian 'sword and sandal' epics of the 1960s. With its one-dimensional characters, risible dialogue and narrative that was a mélange of heavy religiosity (appeals to Jehovah, speeches about religious freedom), gaudy pomp (gyrating dancing girls, feasting courtiers, parading soldiers) and labyrinthine political conspiracies with nobles seeking to unseat the King, it was virtually indistinguishable from the host of historical epics coming out of Italy in the late 1950s and the 1960s. Walsh was renowned as an action director but the film boasted very little action and for much of its length was sluggish and slow-moving.

The story of Esther was recast in such a way as to emphasize twentieth-century parallels. In the absence of King Ahasuerus on campaign, the Jewish community in Persia is oppressed by Prime Minister Haman and General Klidrates. Their villages are destroyed and their people scattered in what Jewish leader Mordecai anachronistically describes as 'a holocaust'. When the King returns, divorcing his wife, Queen Vashti, for adultery, Mordecai ensures that Ahasuerus marries Esther, Mordecai's niece. Under her influence, the King institutes an enlightened regime of fair taxes, freedom of speech, religious toleration and no punishment without trial. But Haman fakes documents (the ancient equivalent of the Protocols of the Elders of Zion) to prove that the Jews have been having treasonable dealings with the Greeks. The King renounces his wife and leaves for Persepolis. Haman and Klidrates plan to assassinate the King and eliminate the Jews. But the King survives the assassination attempt, the Jews barricade themselves in their temple and Ahasuerus returns in the nick of time with his troops to save them and to hang Haman. He is reunited with Esther.

Joan Collins recalled the film in her autobiography: 'It was not a good film. It was full of pseudo-biblical, banal, Hollywood dialogue, and, with the exception of Richard Egan, Denis O'Dea and myself, an all-Italian cast who spoke their dialogue in Italian to which we replied in English […] It really was crap.'[36] Raoul Walsh omits any discussion of the film in his autobiography.

Henry Koster's *The Story of Ruth* (1960), produced by 20th Century-Fox in Cinemascope and De Luxe Colour, is a slow, lumbering and laborious slice of Sunday school soap-opera with a sermonizing script, mechanical direction and earnestly conscientious performances by a cast of young hopefuls (Elana Eden as Ruth, Tom Tryon as Mahlon and Stuart Whitman as Boaz). It was Israeli actress Elana Eden's first film – she had been discovered playing Anne Frank on the stage in Tel-Aviv.

Ruth is a Moabite priestess who comes to question the cruelty of the worship of the god Chemosh, which involves the sacrifice of children. She is converted to Judaism by the Jewish goldsmith Mahlon, who is condemned to the quarries for his pains. She arranges his escape but he is mortally wounded and dies soon after they are married. Ruth flees with her mother-in-law Naomi to Bethlehem where she suffers from anti-Moabite prejudice, being put on trial for paganism but acquitted when her accusers turn out to be false witnesses. She also survives the marital designs of a wealthy kinsman before settling down with Boaz, the man she has come to love.

Liberal scriptwriter Norman Corwin uses his script to call for racial tolerance. Ruth is converted from paganism to Judaism, survives the initial racial hostility against her and has an interracial marriage with Boaz, a passing holy man predicting that their line will produce King David and in due course the Messiah. There are also the familiar Cold War themes of anti-totalitarianism, with Moab characterized by idol worship, human sacrifice and slavery and Judah by monotheism, freedom and democracy, and anti-McCarthyism, with the hounding of Ruth by informers. These messages were not lost on the *Daily Telegraph* (16 July 1960), where the film critic said that the High Priest looked 'like Mr Kruschev, behaving in an unpleasant totalitarian fashion' by sending Mahlon to the quarries, the Moabite equivalent of the salt mines, and the trial of Ruth smacked of 'a McCarthy-like investigation'.

Viveca Lindfors as a waspish, chiffon-clad Moabite priestess and Thayer David as the sneering, shaven-headed High Priest of Chemosh are clearly dying for some villainy to get their teeth into, but the script does not oblige them. An escape from the quarries, a harvest festival dance and a glimpse of child sacrifice are the only spots of excitement in what is otherwise a deadeningly reverential and seemingly interminable 132 minutes. The exquisite, evocative Franz Waxman score deserved a better setting. The film cost $3 million to make and recouped nearly that amount in domestic rentals; the overseas returns being all profit.

Time magazine (4 July 1960) said *The Story of Ruth* was 'that rare film, a Bible story done with taste and without lions [...] the picture is commendably unepic [...] *The Story of Ruth* is simpler than life, but it is also a warm and moving film, several cuts above the religious films that cinema viewers have been accustomed to.' This set the tone for the British reviews. The critics divided over whether they appreciated the film's 'unepic' nature or not. The film's intelligence and restraint were praised by some: the *Guardian* (16 July), *Time and Tide* (23 July), the *Daily Worker* (16 July), and the *Sunday Times* (17 July). Others found it 'a tedious confection'

The perennial ingredients for the Ancient World epic were:

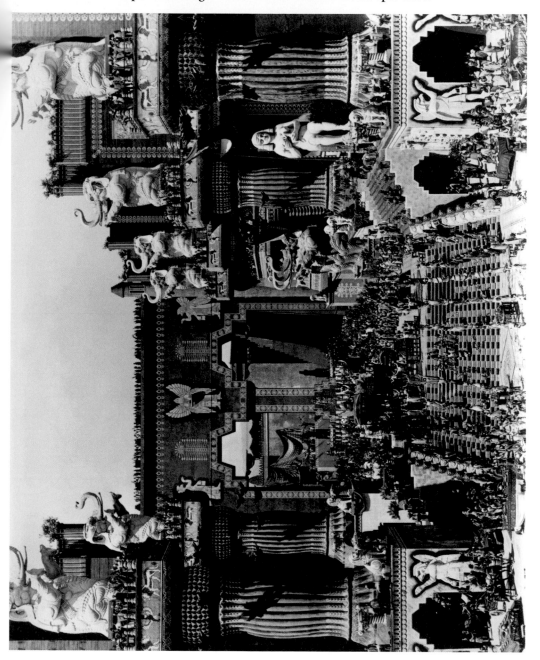

1. Spectacle (*Intolerance*)

2. Action (the 1926 *Ben-Hur*)

The Roman Empire was a recurrent metaphor for society.
Under an evil emperor, it was a textbook totalitarian society.

Under a good emperor, it was the blueprint for the United Nations.

Old Testament epics detailed the creation of the state of Israel.

Above: 7. Charlton Heston as Moses in *The Ten Commandments*

Opposite page (top): 5. Charles Laughton as Nero in *The Sign of the Cross*

Opposite page (bottom): 6. Alec Guinness as Marcus Aurelius in *The Fall of the Roman Empire*

8. Jeffrey Hunter as Jesus in *The King of Kings*

Ancient world cinema returned regularly to the key myths.

9. The Trojan War in *Helen of Troy*

10. The slave revolt in *Spartacus*

(the *Daily Telegraph*), 'totally devoid of the least speck of life or imagination' (*The Times*, 14 July), 'long, boring, and without imagination' (the *Financial Times*, 18 July), 'sad, trivial, artificial' (the *Sunday Express*, 17 July). Veteran actress Peggy Wood, playing Naomi, received most of the acting plaudits.

Following his production of *Barabbas* (1961), Italian producer Dino de Laurentiis conceived the grandiose idea of filming the whole of the book of Genesis, with a prestige roster of directors taking on individual episodes: Robert Bresson, the Creation and the story of Adam and Eve, Orson Welles, Abraham and Isaac, Luchino Visconti, Joseph and his Brethren, Federico Fellini, the Flood. There were equally grand casting suggestions (Rudolf Nureyev, Maria Callas, Olivier, Gielgud and Richardson), none of which actually materialized. De Laurentiis envisaged John Huston as the overseer of the whole project. But when Huston was contacted, he told De Laurentiis that to film all of Genesis was too large an undertaking, and he outlined his conception of a film of the first 22 chapters of Genesis: 'the picture should describe man's emergence from the mists of mythology and legend into the first light of history. To me that meant starting with the Creation and going as far as Abraham, the first figure in the Bible of whose existence we have historical proof'.[37] De Laurentiis was convinced, and gave Huston the job of directing the whole film. Christopher Fry provided the script which duly articulated this vision of Genesis. But it was very much Huston's project. He not only directed it, he narrated it, he provided the voice of God and when his first-choice actors for the role of Noah (Charlie Chaplin and Alec Guinness) proved unavailable, he successfully took on the part himself. Huston's conception was highly artistic and he employed the services of a group of eminent practitioners to assist in its realization; the painter Corrado Gagli to design the Tree of the Knowledge of Good and Evil and the impressive ziggurat-style Tower of Babel; the artist Mirko to design Sodom; the sculptor Giacomo Manzù to fashion the figure of Adam as created by God from the dust; and the Japanese composer Toshiro Mayuzumi to provide the striking, innovative score.

Inevitably the result was episodic and lacking in dramatic coherence, something emphasized by the adoption of different styles for each of the episodes; a *National Geographic* magazine version of the Creation; a coy 1950s' naturist film version of the Garden of Eden with a blond, blue-eyed Adam and Eve; charming folksy comedy for the story of Noah and his ark; and straightforward naturalistic story-telling for Abraham. This final and longest episode, the story of Abraham, largely concerned with his attempts to beget a son and heir, is, despite a powerful performance by George C. Scott as the patriarch, ultimately tedious. It is, however, briefly enlivened by the story of Lot in Sodom, with the city surrealistically conceived as an oppressive shadowy labyrinth, home to half-glimpsed depravities and with leering, painted orgiasts emerging from the shadows with the intention of debauching the Angels of God. Despite the disparate styles, the message was clear. Those who disobey or defy God (Adam and Eve, Cain, Nimrod) cause havoc and disaster; those who obey him unquestioningly (Noah, Abraham) receive blessings and rewards.[38]

The film was released with the title *The Bible ... In the Beginning* (1966), cost $18 million to make and took $15 million at the American box office after mixed reviews, with *Variety* praising its 'consummate skill, taste and reverence' and other papers dismissing it as a glorified Sunday school picture book.[39]

The British critics, most of whom enjoyed the Noah episode, were in the main dismissive of the film as a whole. The *Daily Express* (7 October 1966) thought that, despite the talent and effort lavished on the film, 'The Good Book became the Dreary Film.' The *Spectator* (14 October 1966) called it 'a long and ponderous, slow-moving and unmoving movie'. The *Observer* (9 October 1966) characterized it as 'obscurantism without mystery and slow without pomp' and said 'most of the acting seems half-asleep'. The *Sunday Telegraph* (9 October 1966) found it to be 'Gloomy as an old-fashioned Sunday school [...] In the whole three hours of this long, slow-moving pageant, there is not one loving, yes-saying moment.' De Laurentiis made no more Biblical films after this and, despite its title, *The Bible ... In the Beginning* marked the end of the Old Testament cycle.

One of the most misconceived of Ancient World epics was *Sodom and Gomorrah* (1962) (US title: *The Last Days of Sodom and Gomorrah*). The film was initiated by producer Goffredo Lombardo of Titanus Film, who joined forces with Joseph E. Levine, who had made a fortune promoting the Italian muscle-man epic *Hercules Unchained* in America. They hired the top American director Robert Aldrich to direct it and it was filmed partly in Rome at Cinecittà Studios and partly on location in Morocco.

No one involved in the film was subsequently to have a good word to say for it. Robert Aldrich described it as 'a terrible film', one of his discontents being that his four-hour film was eventually cut to 153 minutes for release.[40] During the course of it he fell out with the producer, and production costs escalated from $2 million to $5 million. Sergio Leone, who had just begun his career as a director with *The Colossus of Rhodes*, agreed to head the second unit because of his admiration for Aldrich's work. He worked on the film for eight weeks, shooting the spectacular battles between the Hebrews and the Helamites. But then he and Aldrich quarrelled and he left the production. Aldrich imported an American director, Oscar Rudolph, who shot some inserts for the battle scenes and received the second-unit director credit on the American print.[41] Miklos Rosza, commissioned to do the score, wrote in his autobiography: 'the film was like a parody of the genre, a wretched script, bad acting, some passable battle scenes, some interesting photography; but I was stuck with it, and with close to two hours of music. However, the producer was a friend, the studio was paying me well and I hoped I might be able to help a bit.'[42] In fact he produced a fine score, drawing on the themes and rhythms of the music of the Babylonian and Yemeni Jews he had researched for his previous Biblical epics. It complemented the various moods of the film perfectly.

Aldrich, dissatisfied with the script, sent for Hugo Butler, the Communist former blacklistee with whom he had worked before, to rewrite it. Butler did so and it is almost certainly to him that we can attribute the anti-capitalist message of the script. But his widow Jean Rouverol recalled that he was 'unsatisfied with the result and also at how Bob planned to shoot it'.[43] Production designer Ken Adam, who worked on the film for a year and a half, recalled 'We had one disaster after another' including the fact that Rosanna Podesta, playing one of Lot's daughters, developed a heart problem and had to leave the Moroccan location and shoot her scenes in Italy, where a section of Sodom had to be reconstructed.[44]

Finally, the actors hated it. Stanley Baker recalled 'It was one of the most agonising experiences of my life. That location! We were in a terrible place called Ourzazate in Morocco. I tell you, when you weren't being chased by scorpions and horned vipers, you were being eaten up by flies and roasted by the sun.' Stewart Granger, who injured his back during the filming, would greet visitors to the set with the words 'Welcome to Hell.'[45]

The subject was fraught with pitfalls. One inevitable problem was going to be the straitjacket of censorship. Given that Sodom and Gomorrah were a byword for unspeakable sins, how were the film-makers going to depict them and avoid the wrath of the censors? Robert Aldrich subsequently railed against the censors for their interference but admitted that all he could manage were 'oblique [...] tasteful references to denote immoral behaviour'.[46] The most he could muster was the opening scene, a long dolly-shot across a sea of sprawled bodies in the aftermath of an orgy, and very discreet hints at lesbianism (Queen Bera and her handmaidens) and incest (the Queen and her brother Astaroth). With the exception of a scene in which Astaroth offers Lot's daughter Shuah to his captain who says: 'I have served your person and your desires these many years and I deserve more respect from you than this', implying a previous sexual relationship, there is no sign of the sin to which Sodom gave its name.[47] Early in the film, the Helamite leader warns the Prince's messenger 'Be careful of Sodomite patrols' which provokes interesting speculation that remains unfulfilled. The fact that Queen Bera of Sodom is in fact King Bera in the Bible may also be a clue of some kind to fathomless perversion – or perhaps not. The philosophy of the Sodomites is articulated by the Queen's slave Ildith: 'Where I come from nothing is evil, every-thing that gives pleasure is good.' But Queen Bera seems to take most pleasure in watching prisoners being tortured to death and burned alive – apparently a censorially more acceptable activity than unbridled sexual perversity.

In the absence of sexual sin, the film concentrates on the more respectably Marxist subject of the capitalist exploitation of a captive people. The Sodomites' wealth and power lies in their trading of salt, which is mined by an army of slaves. The film therefore sets up a contrast between the simple God-fearing Hebrews, who live a pure nomadic and pastoral life, and the citizens of Sodom, characterized by cruelty, wealth, slavery and sexual licence. Their attitude to slavery is what divides them, Lot telling Ildith: 'For one human being to own another is wrong – evil.' Queen Bera establishes the Hebrews in the valley outside Sodom as a buffer against the hostile desert tribe, the Helamites, agreeing to their request that they may give sanctuary to runaway slaves. Initially they keep clear of Sodom, but when they defeat the Helamites in battle, partly by destroying the dam they have built to irrigate their land, their settlement and crops are destroyed. However, they accidentally discover a rich vein of salt and believing this to be God's will, Lot leads the Hebrews into Sodom to become peaceful and honest merchants. However, they are corrupted by life in Sodom. Symbolically they take on the exotic fashions and hair styles of the Sodomites which they had previously condemned. When his son-in-law Ishmael plans a break-out of the slaves, Lot refuses to help, describing them as 'the property' of their hosts. Ishmael goes ahead anyway but the fleeing slaves are denied sanctuary by the Hebrews, rounded up and eventually executed. When Lot learns that both his daughters have been debauched by the Queen's brother Prince Astaroth, he kills Astaroth in a fight, sword against shepherd's crook, and is imprisoned by the Queen. He now sees the error of his ways and is released by divine agency and ordered to lead his people out of Sodom and not to look back. They leave and Sodom is destroyed but Lot's wife, Ildith, the former slave of the Queen, does look back and is turned into a pillar of salt. The Hebrews are resuming their old, simple, decent, uncorrupt and non-capitalist life. So in this version, the conflict of sexuality and spirituality is yoked to a conflict between on the one hand pastoralism and capitalism and on the other slavery and anti-slavery.[48]

There are capable performances from Stewart Granger as the Hebrew leader Lot, Anouk Aimée as the shrewd and scheming Queen Bera and Stanley Baker as her treacherous brother Prince Astaroth. Many of the critics had fun with the absence of depravity from the film. The *Evening Standard* (29 November 1962) commented: 'it is disconcerting to find that people who were reputedly so corrupt should have had such a dreary time in Sodom' and the *Monthly Film Bulletin* (29 December 1962) said: 'The depravity of the Sodomites is depicted in remarkably mild, not to say prudish terms […] Only Anouk Aimée's Queen Bera seems aware – judging by the knowing looks she gives her handmaiden from time to time – that the Sodomites have some kind of reputation to keep up, even if only off screen.' There were the customary critical dismissals: 'a sumptuous farrago which has a bare minimum of connection with either scriptures or legend' (the

Sunday Telegraph, 2 December 1962); '2½ hours of almost unrelievedly sub-standard Biblical tedium' (the *Daily Herald*, 1 December 1962). But there was a perhaps surprising level of praise from other critics: 'a thundering good picture, packed with spectacle' (the *News of the World*, 2 December 1962); 'rattling good entertainment' (the *Daily Express*, 28 November 1962); 'colourful and exciting' (*Evening News*, 29 November 1962). The *Daily Mail* (28 November 1962) praised 'the visual splendour' achieved by Aldrich. Several picked up on the anti-capitalist message (*Scene*, 29 November 1962; the *Daily Telegraph*, 1 December 1962). There was also praise from many for the battle scenes, the destruction of the twin cities and the acting of Granger and Baker. But box-office returns were modest in Britain and America and certainly not enough to repay the original investment, not just of money, but of time and effort.

If the 1950s was the decade of the Old Testament, the 1960s was that of the New Testament. Samuel Bronston's independent production operation in Spain, having begun with a misfire, the tedious and overlong but patriotically flag-waving naval epic of the American War of Independence, *John Paul Jones*, in 1959, hit its stride with the much more satisfying *King of Kings* (1961). It was the first full-length life of Christ since De Mille's silent film of the same title, although Christ had been glimpsed, usually from the back or in the distance in *Quo Vadis?*, *The Robe*, *Ben-Hur* and *Salome*.

Bronston hired Nicholas Ray to direct *King of Kings* and it was Ray who suggested Philip Yordan, who had written Ray's *Johnny Guitar*, as scriptwriter and Franz Planer, who had photographed his 1954 television film *High Green Wall*, as cinematographer. (Planer had to be replaced halfway through the film by Milton Krasner when he went down with heatstroke.) It was also Ray who suggested Jeffrey Hunter for the role of Jesus. Hunter had played Frank James in Ray's *The True Story of Jesse James* (1957). Ray said of that performance: 'I noticed then a quality of genuine gentleness in his conduct with people, and I remembered *that* when we first began discussing the role of Jesus. In Jeffrey there was an honest warmth which came across on the screen. I thought he was superb as Christ. And above all he had remarkable eyes. You notice them from the first, as indeed you must have done with Christ. That is the feature that I tried to emphasise.'[49] Close-ups of his eyes figure at key points in the film. The distinguished theatre art director Georges Wakhevitch designed sets and costumes, though there was an immediate setback when before filming began the huge Jerusalem temple set was blown down in a storm and had to be completely rebuilt, taking three months to complete. Bronston said the film was meant to be 'non-denominational' and to have 'universal appeal' and he appointed Catholic, Protestant and Jewish advisers and secured the Pope's blessing on the production. (*Weekend*, 12 November 1961, the *Daily Herald*, 20 June 1961).

The Cold War still lurked in the background as the prologue printed in the film's souvenir programme revealed:

As it is today, so it was in the turbulent times before Christ, that the menace of pagan tyranny shadowed the hearts of men who would be free. In their quest for truth, their unquenchable thirst for knowledge and faith, they brought down the wrath and might of Roman blasphemy. Amid this barbaric world seethed conflicts of human drama, of violent passions, which tore asunder the high places and trembled the foundations of false idolatry. Into this troubled world came Jesus of Nazareth, who feared none, nor even death, to bring forth enlightenment and triumph, and He was crowned King of Kings.

It is probably the most political and action-packed life of Christ to have been filmed. The direct allusions to the present and the recent past were deliberate. Ray said: 'I was constantly trying to make things real and relatable to the present day.' So the central theme of the film is the oppression of the Jews.[50]

Uniquely, the film opened in 63 BC, with the Roman general Pompey taking Jerusalem and violating the temple in search of treasure. In a striking image, he rides his horse up the steps of the temple and through the silent ranks of white-robed priests. When a line of priests try to deny him entry to the Holy of Holies, he has them cut down by his spearmen. This massacre of the priests and the profanation of their temple, like the later slaughter of the zealots in the courtyard of the fortress Antonia by the steadily and inexorably advancing Roman war machine, evoke memories of the Nazis.

Orson Welles' subsequent narration over further scenes of burning and slaughter sets the political and social context for the film:

Thus for more than fifty years after Pompey's invasion, the history of Judaea could be read by the light of burning towns. If gold was not the harvest, there was a richness of people to be gathered; the battalions of Caesar Augustus brought in the crop. Like sheep from their own green fields, the Jews went to the slaughter; they went from the stone quarries to build Rome's triumphal arches.

The Romans also play a second role as analogues of the British occupiers of Palestine. But the British Romans have two different faces. Pontius Pilate is a ruthless, ambitious military governor, played with aristocratic hauteur and a British accent by Hurd Hatfield, best known for playing the title role in *The Picture of Dorian Gray*. Unhistorically, his wife Claudia (Viveca Lindfors) is made into the daughter of the Emperor Tiberius, resulting in Pilate having imperial ambitions. But there is a 'good' Roman, the centurion of the Crucifixion, who is given a continuing back story in the film. Centurion Lucius, movingly played by the Australian actor Ron Randell in a career-best performance, is first encountered expressing reluctance to undertake the Massacre of the Innocents ordered by Herod the Great, later turns a blind eye to Jesus' survival from the massacre, allows Jesus to see John the Baptist in prison, attends the Sermon on the Mount, speaks on Jesus' behalf at his trial, respects his zealot enemy Barabbas and finally recognizes Jesus as the son of God at the Crucifixion.

The 10,000 zealot rebels are the Ancient equivalent of the Irgun and Stern gangs of Jewish terrorists who fought against the British in Palestine. They first appear in a vigorously staged action scene ambushing Pontius Pilate's column as he arrives in Judaea. The film also references the current plight of the state of Israel, threatened by its Arab neighbours. Again unhistorically, the film makes Herod the Great, appointed King of Judaea by the Romans, and his son and successor Herod Antipas, Bedouin Arabs and they grievously oppress the Jews. Herod the Great crucifies hundreds of Jewish rebels and a scene of Jewish bodies being shovelled into a pit onto heaps of corpses inevitably summons up images of the Nazi death camps. Later it is Antipas who, succumbing to his lust for Salome, orders the execution of John the Baptist.

The film is constructed around the question of how the Jews are to deal with their oppression and equal screen time is given to Jesus and Barabbas, described by the narrator as respectively 'the Messiah of Peace' and the 'Messiah of War'. The narrative interweaves the familiar episodes from Jesus' life (the miracles, the preaching, the recruitment of the disciples) and the military activities of the zealots, led by Barabbas (Harry Guardino) against the Romans. Barabbas recognizes that they both seek freedom for the Jews but by different methods. The link between them is Judas Iscariot (Rip Torn) who having been the right-hand man of Barabbas becomes a follower of Jesus and betrays him to the authorities, not for money, but to force his hand so that he will use his wonder-working powers to defeat the Romans by a miracle, achieving freedom by peaceful means. When Jesus does not do this but dies on the cross, Judas hangs himself.

The key point of contrast between the two philosophies lies in the prominence accorded to the Sermon on the Mount, the principal statement of Christ's teachings, a sequence which involved eighty-one camera set-ups and twenty-one days' shooting, and the attempt by the zealots to seize the fortress Antonia which is crushed by the Romans. The way of Jesus is love, peace and brotherhood; the way of Barabbas war, violence and resistance. But Barabbas is nevertheless seen by the film as a Zionist hero, dedicated and sincere in his beliefs, even if ultimately mistaken in his methods by comparison with Christ. The Jews are acquitted of responsibility for Jesus' death, which is squarely laid at Pilate's door, with Pilate showing no remorse – the famous hand-washing scene is omitted.

The finished film, shot in Super Technirama 70 and Technicolor, is full of striking images: Pompey's invasion of the temple; the bold overhead shot of the death of Herod; Salome's dance before Antipas; the Sermon on the Mount; the ambushes and battles; the agonizing procession to Calvary with the cross catching regularly on the stepped and cobbled street; the raising of the cross with the camera behind the head of Christ to give his point of view of the event.[51] Ray himself said that he had not, like previous directors, sought inspiration in religious paintings:

> The compositions had to come from the situation, time, the truth of the scene as I saw it, or else I would have not been making a film, I would just have been recreating a series of tableaux, familiar tableaux ranging throughout possibly twelve centuries in style and, more importantly, I would have violated the concept of the film as taking place for the first and only time, that it was of *that* moment, not of a Renaissance moment, not of a Flemish moment, not of a Byzantine moment.[52]

But what happened after the completion of the film understandably distressed him. Samuel Bronston, in need of money to make his next film, *El Cid*, sold a share of *King of Kings*, together with distribution rights to MGM, and MGM decided that the film was too long and cut 45 minutes, removing the entire role played by Richard Johnson, a cosmopolitan Jew called David who returns from Rome to Jerusalem and engages in debate with Pilate about monotheism. The role of Claudia, who is gradually converted to Christianity along with Lucius, was also heavily cut back. Ray thought the editing 'atrocious'.[53] Miklos Rosza, who was brought in to score the film, was faced with two dilemmas. One was that he found the edited-down version incomprehensible: 'What were we to do with this nonsensical biblical goulash? How were all these isolated episodes, some of them as poorly acted as they were directed, going to be shaped into a coherent whole?'[54] The second problem was to write new music for scenes he had so recently scored in *Ben-Hur* – the Nativity, the Way of the Cross, Golgotha, the Resurrection.

The first problem was solved by knitting the film together with a linking narration, composed by Ray Bradbury and reverently delivered by Orson Welles. The second was resolved by focusing on the central character of Christ, who had only been glimpsed in *Ben-Hur*. Rosza composed a lyrical and moving score, making full use of inspiring choruses. The central theme of 'Christ the Redeemer' recurred throughout the film, usually accompanied by female chorus. There were leitmotifs for John the Baptist, the Virgin Mary and Satan, a single lullaby for the Nativity, strong rhythmic marches for the Romans, festive Hebrew music for the Palm Sunday entry into Jerusalem and an exotic barbaric dance for Salome.[55]

When the film was released in Britain, one or two critics were able to appreciate its visual qualities and the artistry of Nicholas Ray. The *Daily Herald* (14 November 1961) thought it did '*not* travesty the book of the film' and was 'not unworthy of its great subject. The result deserves our gratitude and our patronage.' The *Daily Telegraph* (14 November 1961) praised the 'commendable simplicity' of the storytelling and the 'visual splendours' of Ray's direction. The

Sunday Telegraph (19 November 1961) thought the *mise-en-scène* 'magnificent' (the battles 'superlatively well-ordered', the Sermon on the Mount 'marvellously staged') and the 'appeal to the senses is prodigious', but added: 'the appeal to the imagination is restricted [...] the appeal to the spirit is faint to the point of nullity'.

The rest of the critics reached for the vitriol. The *Spectator* (24 November 1961) called it 'negative, limp, spiritually empty' and *Time and Tide* (23 November 1961) called it 'a resounding flop' with 'no single moment of real power from beginning to end'. The *Daily Express* (14 November 1961) called it 'a sorry and sometimes unseemly travesty [...] appallingly spoken and acted' and pronounced the hope that it would be 'a flop of flops'. The *Evening Standard* (14 November 1961) also called it 'an abysmal travesty of the Christian story', describing it as 'the most theologically dubious, religiously vapid, historically unlikely view of the Redeemer I have ever encountered'. The *Guardian* (18 November 1961) thought 'it intended to give no offence to Jew or to Christian of whatever denomination and succeeded [...] in giving offence to everyone because of its lavish tastelessness'. The *Observer* (19 November 1961) thought 'there is not an element in it that is not crude, square or irreligious'. The *Daily Worker* (14 November 1961) thought it 'painstaking, impersonal and dull'. Such plaudits for the acting as there were went to Ron Randell and Hurd Hatfield, but there was almost universal dissatisfaction with Jeffrey Hunter: 'a marvel of miscasting' (the *Spectator*), and 'an affront even to non-Christians' (the *Observer*) were typical of the comments. Many critics complained about the slaughter and bloodshed which attended the Barabbas subplot.

When the film came out, cynics mocked it under the title 'I was a teenage Jesus'. But the film's programme had insisted on the youth of the protagonists: Jesus died at 33, the disciples were all young men, Mary was 14 at the time of the nativity and Salome 15. In fact, Jeffrey Hunter is the perfect blue-eyed Pre-Raphaelite Christ, summoning up images of Millais and Holman Hunt. But by the 1960s that image was passé and the excellence of Hunter's performance was overlooked. There were fine performances too from Frank Thring as a sneering, sleazy, ringleted Herod Antipas, Hurd Hatfield as the icily aloof Pilate, Siobhan McKenna as a radiant Irish-accented Mary and Ron Randell as centurion Lucius. Costing $8 million to produce, it garnered $7.5 million in US domestic rentals and putatively as much again in overseas rentals. It is a film which improves on each viewing and, despite its production difficulties, remains an original and powerful telling of the Jesus narrative.

Bronston's great European rival in the production of epics was the Italian film producer Dino De Laurentiis. His answer to *King of Kings* was *Barabbas* (1961) which conjectured the otherwise unknown future life of the criminal released by

Pontius Pilate instead of Christ at the demand of the Jewish crowd. It was based on the novel, published in 1951, by the Nobel Prize-winning Swedish novelist Pär Lagerkvist which had been described by one critic as 'an intellectual poem'. De Laurentiis had long wished to adapt it for the screen. He said:

> I saw in *Barabbas* the opportunity to make a film entirely different from any other with its source in the Bible. I was fascinated by the problem of transforming this admittedly difficult work into a motion picture without losing any of the literary value and profound religious spirit. Then there was the essential modernity of this creature of Lagerkvist's imagination who epitomised, it seemed to me, the doubts and torments of modern man, with his spiritual conflicts, and his struggle with the problem of the supernatural.

He therefore sought as screenwriter someone who was a poet and a Christian, but also well-versed in creating cinematographic narrative. He found him in Christopher Fry, who had achieved a notable success with *Ben-Hur*. As director, he chose Richard Fleischer, who had demonstrated his mastery of the epic form in *The Vikings* (1958). Fleischer was intrigued by the story: 'I felt that *Barabbas* offered an opportunity to make a rare kind of film best described in such contradictory terms as "an intimate spectacle". Against the vividly coloured background of Roman pomp and the awesome pageant of the Crucifixion, we were undertaking a dramatic analysis of one of the most enigmatically complex characters in literature.'

'Authenticity was a prerequisite' says the film's souvenir programme and records that the film took five years from conception to completion, with sets, costumes and artefacts painstakingly researched and recreated. Shooting began on 15 February 1961 in order to capture an actual total eclipse needed for the Crucifixion scene. The scenes in the sulphur mines were shot on Mount Etna and the surviving Roman amphitheatre at Verona was used for the gladiatorial scenes. Designer Mario Chiari recreated Rome and Jerusalem in three-dimensional solidity on the studio back lot. The film was shot in Technicolor and Technirama at a cost of $10 million.[56]

Visually the film is constructed on a consistent polarity of darkness and light. The theme is the search of Barabbas for enlightenment as to why he was spared and Christ died in his place, but that life is marked by repeated retreats from the light into darkness. He is first seen in the darkness of an underground prison cell, from which he emerges, dazzled by the light, to see Christ condemned, scourged and forced to drag his cross to Calvary. After celebrating his release in a tavern, he becomes convinced he has been struck blind – but it is the effect of the total eclipse which accompanies the Crucifixion. Reverting to his previous career as a bandit, Barabbas is arrested and condemned to toil in the Sicilian sulphur mines, living in permanent semi-darkness for years, until an earthquake destroys the mine and releases him and fellow slave, the Christian Sahak (Vittorio Gassman). Taken to Rome, Barabbas and Sahak are trained as gladiators. The brightly lit arena with its spectacle and violence is contrasted with the dark, narrow corridors backstage. When Sahak refuses to kill because of his Christian beliefs, he is condemned to death. Barabbas denies he is a Christian and later kills in the arena the psychotic gladiator Torvald (Jack Palance) who executed Sahak. Taking Sahak's body to the catacombs, Barabbas becomes lost there in the darkness, emerging to find Rome on fire. Believing that this is God's will, he sets fire to a storehouse and is arrested by the troops who are rounding up all the Christians. In prison, he learns from Peter (Harry Andrews) that the fire was not God's will and asked why he had been chosen to live, Peter answers 'Because being furthest from Him, you were the nearest.' Crucified with the others, Barabbas gives himself up to Christ and the promise that he will dwell in the light eternally.

Anthony Quinn, in the title role, doing his familiar uncouth peasant act, remains an entirely unsympathetic character, shambling and inarticulate. Christopher Fry was aware of the difficulties entailed in adapting Lagerkvist's novel. He said:

> Was it possible to translate the bare brooding atmosphere of the novel into film terms? Was it possible to make a visually arresting version without destroying the strength of the novel? The problem [...] was how to make Barabbas talk. In the novel he is a taciturn man; his character is built up by descriptions of his emotions and thoughts; there is very little dialogue. But clearly an actor can't go through a film without speaking [...] so, a way had to be found to make the inarticulate articulate.

Sadly it did not work. The hellish scenes in the sulphur mines and the exciting scenes of gladiatorial training and combat are visually arresting. But the film as a whole fails to move. Christianity emerges as a joyless masochistic faith that invites non-stop suffering – flogging, crucifixion, stoning and spearing. It never becomes clear why Barabbas should opt for it at all, whatever the gnomic utterances of St Peter. Perhaps not surprisingly the film was a box-office failure.

The majority of the critics greeted the film with revulsion. The *Observer* (10 June 1962) complained 'the acting is leaden and the scenes of violence had no more moral force than a car smash; in the context they leave one simply with a sense of desolation and nausea'. The *Guardian* (9 June 1962) thought the film set two records, 'one for tastelessness; the other for goriness'. The *Evening News* (9 June 1962) lamented that the film contained 'the bloodiest games ever staged in the Christian era'. *Time and Tide* (14 June 1962) thought the film 'unsophisticated, crude and hence merely revolting'. The *Daily Mail* (9 June 1962) called it 'a mammoth Grand Guignol of terror, torture, death and destruction'. *The Times* (5 June 1962) called it 'a riot of large-screen delight in the cruel, the brutal, the inhuman'. The *Spectator* (15 June 1962) complained: 'all that is surprising, apart from the script by Christopher Fry, is the extent of its nastiness, the hypocritical glee, with which, in the name of spiritual values and the God of love, it invites us to gloat over pain'.

Originally released at 144 minutes, it was cut by 20 minutes for general release, losing the scene which the *Sunday Telegraph* (10 June 1962) called 'a remarkable and memorable five minutes as Lazarus (Michael Gwynn) [...] tells Barabbas what it is like to be dead. This [...] is Mr Fry's best scene.' Although missing from the video release, it has been restored in the DVD release.

At the same time as Samuel Bronston was producing his life of Christ in Spain, another life of Christ was being planned in Hollywood. While he was making *The Diary of Anne Frank* in 1958, George Stevens was commissioned by 20th Century-Fox to film Fulton Oursler's 1949 book, *The Greatest Story Ever Told*, on a budget of $6.5 million, with the film to be delivered by 1960. Stevens had been filming the American advance into Germany in 1945 when he arrived at Dachau two days after its liberation. It had a lasting effect on him and inspired him with the idea of making a film with a message of love and universal brotherhood, 'the ultimate movie on Jesus'. It eventually took him six years to make and was a labour of love that ended in box-office disaster. The script was prepared by Ivan Moffat, James Lee Barrett and Stevens himself, with dialogue being polished by the poet Carl Sandburg. In 1961 Fox, totally preoccupied with *Cleopatra*, pulled out of the deal. But United Artists agreed to distribute it and put up some of the costs, with George Stevens Productions raising the rest of the finance. Filming eventually began on 28 October 1962 and lasted until 1 August 1963. The filming was slow and laborious as Stevens sought perfection in every sequence. It fell so far behind schedule that two other directors had to be drafted in to direct without credit scenes in the film: Jean Negulesco did Jewish street scenes and David Lean the Herod scenes, with a favourite actor Claude Rains playing Herod at his request. Charlton Heston directed the scene of his own arrest as John the Baptist.[57] It took 17 months to edit and the film was finally released in 1965 in Cinerama. It ran for 225 minutes on its roadshow release. But for its British release and big-city showings in America, Stevens reduced it to 193 minutes and for its general release he cut it further to 141 minutes.

Stevens had made two controversial innovations. Having scouted locations in Israel, he did not find them grand enough and so filmed in Utah and Arizona. The result was pictorially impressive, with magnificent dawns and sunsets, and awe-inspiring mountainscapes, but you constantly expected to see tribes of Indians appearing pursued by the US cavalry. In a bid to bring in the audience, Stevens peopled his cast with cameos by a host of Hollywood stars, leading many critics to ignore the message and play 'spot the star'. However, the heavy cutting led to some big names being reduced to bit players with just one line or sometimes no lines at all: Richard Conte as Barabbas, Angela Lansbury as Claudia, Carroll Baker as Veronica and Shelley Winters as the Woman with No Name among them. John Wayne as the centurion at the Crucifixion was much mocked for his delivery with evident embarrassment of his one line: 'Truly this man was the Son of God.'

The film emerged as long, slow, obviously sincere, always beautiful to look at, but lacking the dynamism and vigour of *King of Kings*. Only occasionally was the audience swept up into the events emotionally by the staging and performing of the various episodes of Christ's life, notably the Massacre of the Innocents, the raising of Lazarus and the Crucifixion. Max von Sydow could not have been more different as Jesus from Jeffrey Hunter, more Byzantine icon than Pre-Raphaelite matinée idol. He spent the film intoning the best-known sayings of Christ from the Gospels. Charlton Heston scored as a blood and thunder John the Baptist, vigorously dunking the soldiers sent to arrest him in the river while shouting 'Repent'. Claude Rains was briefly impressive as the aged, fearful and ruthless Herod the Great. But most of the stars had little to do but lend their familiar features and voices to small roles. No explanation is given for Judas' betrayal. But the Jews are acquitted of guilt in the death of the Christ as events are manipulated by a Satan figure, The Dark Hermit, played as a quirky Pinteresque tramp by Donald Pleasance. The casting of a black man, Sidney Poitier, as Simon of Cyrene, who helps carry the cross, gave a timely Civil Rights dimension to the story. Alfred Newman composed what many have seen as one of his finest scores, but it was seriously compromised when Stevens insisted on replacing his 'Hallelujah Chorus' with Handel's from *The Messiah* and his 'Via Dolorosa' music with Verdi's *Requiem*. As the film was steadily reduced in length, so the music had to be truncated. Newman declared sadly: 'It's my name but it isn't my score. I'd be happy if my name were removed from the credits.'[58]

It received mixed reviews in America. The *New York Daily News* called it 'a magnificent film [...] handled with reverence, artistic appreciation and admirable restraint'. But the *New York Herald Tribune* said: 'it does not succeed ultimately in elevating its theme visually or intellectually beyond the dime-store-picture-Sunday-school-holy-primer level to which its predecessors have accustomed us.' *Newsweek* called it 'a farrago of solecisms' and the *New Yorker* called it 'a disaster'.[59]

The British critics turned on it virtually to a man. The *Spectator* (16 April 1965) called it 'a disaster – slow, ponderous, dead and even insultingly boring'. The *Sunday Telegraph* (11 April 1961) said it was 'a thousand leagues from being the greatest picture ever made' and thought it told the story of Christ 'stagily, statically, and without a glimmer of imagination'. The *Financial Times* (9 April 1965) thought 'its reverence and pictorial care [...] sap it of any vitality'. *The Times* (8 April 1965) dismissed it as 'deadly slow, heavy and dull, mixing styles uncomfortably as it suggests one famous biblical painting after another and fatally omitting to develop any style of its own'. The *Daily Telegraph* (9 April 1965) dubbed it 'The Passion Without Passion'. The *Guardian* (9 April 1965) pronounced it 'admirably restrained, supremely reverent, and in very good taste. It is, however, dead' and declared Pasolini's *The Gospel According to St Matthew* 'immeasurably superior'. The *Daily Mail* (8 April 1965) sighed that it was too often 'the longest […] story ever told'. The *Evening News* (8 April 1965) thought it 'desperately lacks subtlety, mystery, appeal to the imagination'. The *Sunday Express* (11 April 1965) called it 'one of the most monumental failures the epic cinema has ever known'.

It had cost $20 million to produce and made only $6.9 million at the box office.[60] Stevens' biographer Marilyn Ann Moss concluded sadly but accurately: 'The times were not receptive to a film as long, as laboured, and as reverent as Stevens' story of Jesus.'[61] The ethos of the 1960s was at odds with Stevens and sealed the fate not only of the film but of the cinematic genre. The Biblical epic ground to a halt at more or less the same time as the Roman epic, extinction similarly dictated by the box office.

5

The 1950s and 1960s:

GREECE AND EGYPT

Hollywood showed little interest in Ancient Greece and Ancient Egypt. This in part reflected audience reaction, as the Roman and Biblical epics drew the crowds whereas Greek and Egyptian ones did not. That in its turn reinforces the interpretation that one of the appeals of Ancient World epics was religious as the Roman epics generally dealt with the Christian, and the Biblical epics with the Jewish, struggles against tyranny. The Greek and Egyptian epics dealt exclusively with pagans. The main exception to this was the success of *The Ten Commandments*, and that was specifically Bible-based.

Although Greece was celebrated as the birthplace of democracy and Western civilization, Hollywood was interested primarily in empires and not in small, often warring city-states. It is no coincidence then that the principal ventures by Hollywood into Ancient Greece in the 1950s were to tackle Alexander the Great and the Macedonian Empire, and the Trojan War, which since the days of Homer had the vital epic characteristics of war, romance, spectacle and the fall of kingdoms. Even these two stories ran up against another taboo for 1950s Hollywood – the cultural centrality to Greek life of sexual relationships between older men and youths, 'the unspeakable vice of the Greeks' as it was called by the Victorians.

Alexander appeared on stage before he reached the screen, as Terence Rattigan made him the subject of his play, *Adventure Story*. It opens with Alexander dying and wondering where it all went wrong. Rattigan interpreted the story as one of a man who gained the whole world and in so doing lost his soul. Rattigan's ear for dialogue was attuned to that of the twentieth-century English middle class and one critic thought his Alexander was 'in speech and thought [...] like a daring fighter pilot of World War Two'. Lavishly staged with sets by George Wakhevitch and music by Benjamin Frankel, it opened at the St James's Theatre on 17 March 1949 with Paul Scofield as Alexander and Gwen Ffrangcon-Davies as the Persian Queen Mother. The critics mainly saw it as a 'gallant failure' and it closed after 108 performances, never to be revived except as a BBC television production in 1959 starring Sean Connery. Rattigan summarized the reviews as saying that the play 'lacked the language of the poet and the perception of the philosopher'. The censorship of the time also dictated the elimination of Alexander's homosexuality and the consequent concentration on his relationship with a mother substitute, Queen Sisygambis.[1]

The combination of the poetic language, psychological insight and philosophical sophistication lacking in Rattigan's interpretation, together with the sympathetic and convincing integration of homosexuality into his personality, were all to be found subsequently in Mary Renault's trilogy of novels about Alexander and her non-fictional *The Nature of Alexander* (1975): the best evocation of Alexander to date.

The film *Alexander the Great* (1955), produced, directed and written by Robert Rossen and featuring a largely British and British-dubbed Spanish supporting cast, was filmed in Cinemascope and Technicolor in Spain over an eight-month period. It was budgeted at $2 million, but exceeded it. It was planned as a three-hour epic with an intermission, but the distributor (United Artists) took fright at the length and forced Rossen to cut it to 141 minutes, which he claimed later had eliminated some of the complexity of the story. Rossen explained his attraction to and interpretation of Alexander in an interview.

> A man born before his time, a catalytic agent, he emerged from an era of warring nationalisms to try for the first time in history to get the peoples of Asia and Europe to live together. But he became a destructive force and in the process of destroying other people while attempting to unify them, he destroyed himself.[2]

While virtually all his previous work as writer and director had been set in modern America, the story of Alexander conformed to a theme that preoccupied Rossen in his own work: the process by which an idealist is corrupted by power, a theme notably explored in his Oscar-winning political drama *All the King's Men* (1949). It is a theme which Alan Casty suggests proceeded directly from his own political journey. A Communist Party member from 1937, he had been progressively disillusioned with the party post-war and disengaged from it in the period 1945–7.[3] However, the film has another contemporary resonance. It opens with Alexander as a troubled adolescent with a dysfunctional family – an estranged mother and hostile father competing for his affections. He becomes a rebel with (rather than without) a cause, reflecting the preoccupation of 1950s' cinema and of American society in general with teenage rebellion and juvenile delinquency.

The film falls into two halves. The first half, with the young Alexander devoted to his possessive mother Olympias, charts the wary relationship between him and his father, King Philip of Macedon, as the latter conquers and unites Greece. Although Alexander saves Philip's life at the battle of Chaeronea and Philip makes him regent of Macedon, they are estranged when Philip divorces Olympias to marry the youthful Eurydice. Olympias stirs up Pausanias, who hero-worships

Alexander, to murder Philip. Alexander kills Pausanias and is hailed King by the army.

The second half of the film details Alexander's ten years of Asiatic campaigning – most of which is described in a single voice-over – and the process by which he becomes more and more autocratic, proclaiming himself a god and brooking no opposition to his insistence on marching to the end of the world. However, after he drunkenly kills one of his oldest companions, Cleitus, he turns back to Babylon and begins to fulfil his dream of uniting Europeans and Asiatics, an objective urged on him in the dying words of Darius, the defeated Great King of Persia. But, after a mass-marriage ceremony, uniting Macedonians and Persians, he dies, bequeathing his empire to 'the strongest'.

The film is superbly photographed on grand Spanish locations and boasts a literate and well-informed script. But the film has its weaknesses. The battle scenes are for the most part perfunctory, apart from Gaugamela, where the staging of the action demonstrates Alexander's bold tactics. Alexander's love life is given short shrift, for the very pertinent reason that Alexander was an inconvenient hero for 1950s' America. The conqueror of half the world preferred sex with men rather than with women. Although he did his dynastic duty by impregnating two princesses, one Persian (Stateira) and one Bactrian (Roxane), his most substantial and fulfilling relationships were with men: his boyhood companion Hephaestion, whose death literally deranged him, and his 'Persian boy', the eunuch Bagoas. Hephaestion, a long way down the cast list, barely appears and Bagoas is not seen at all. Rossen amalgamates Stateira and Roxane, making the latter Darius' daughter instead of the former. The brief love interest is confined to Barsine, whom Alexander takes as his mistress after her husband, the renegade Athenian general Memnon, is killed.

A further weakness lies in Richard Burton's performance as Alexander. Thirty years old and sporting a blond wig, Burton is too old for the 18-year-old Alexander at the start, though right for the 33-year-old world-conqueror at the end. But, alternately brooding and ranting, he gives no hint of the legendary personal charm that caused his troops to love him devotedly and follow him unquestioningly. Without this, the performance seems one-dimensional.

Danielle Darrieux and Fredric March are effective in the first half, she as the beautiful, imperious, scheming Olympias and he as the rough-hewn barbarian Philip, though his American accent sometimes jars in the context of the British cast around him. Almost no one else in the large cast gets a chance to shine, with the exception of Harry Andrews as King Darius and Peter Cushing as the Athenian Memnon, both of whom succeed in imbuing their roles with dignity and authority.

Mario Nascimbene's score is a distinct asset. Deciding to confine his music to only those instruments available to the Macedonians, he dispensed with strings and provided a score with drums, horns and trumpets for the action scenes and woodwind for the gentler passages. The richly percussive brass and timpani passages, echoing the crash and thunder of battle, evoked the primitive excitement of ancient conflict and contrasted effectively with the woodwind and haunting Oriental melodies, inspired by ancient Jewish synagogue music, which accompanied the brief Alexander–Barsine love scenes and the flight and death of Darius.

The British critics were mainly unimpressed: 'a crashing flop and a colossal bore' (the *Daily Express*, 24 March 1956), 'mostly gore and bore' (the *Daily Herald*, 23 March 1956), 'an endurance test' (the *Sunday Express*, 25 March 1956), 'monotonous' (the *Daily Mail*, 23 March 1956, the *Daily Telegraph*, 24 March 1956), 'dull' (*The Times*, 21 March 1956). One or two critics differed, with the *Spectator* (30 March 1956) pronouncing it 'immensely exciting [...] an achievement of outstanding intelligence and power' and the *News of the World* (25 March 1956) praising its 'scenes of majesty and magnificence'.

There was the same reaction to Burton's Alexander. The *News of the World* declared: 'I have never seen acting of finer quality' and the *Sunday Dispatch* (25 March 1956) thought Burton 'a manly and finely spoken Alexander'. But the main consensus was that his Alexander was 'dull' (the *Daily Express*, the *Daily Herald*, and the *Financial Times*, 26 March 1956). The *News Chronicle* (23 March 1956) headed its review 'Alexander the Mediocre'. It failed at the box office.

Helen of Troy (1955) was one of two epics produced by Warner Brothers in Italy to utilize 'frozen funds' – film rentals which by law could not be removed from the country. (The other was *Land of the Pharaohs*.) It was shot at Cinecittà in Cinemascope and Warnercolor and it boasted impressive sets for Troy, inspired by the Minoan remains in Crete, and a surgingly romantic score by Max Steiner. But these assets failed to redeem what is a turgid retelling of key episodes from Homer's *Iliad*: Helen, Queen of Sparta, eloping with Prince Paris of Troy; the Greeks invading to reclaim her; Hector killed by Achilles and Achilles killed by Paris; Troy taken by the Greeks, concealed in a gigantic wooden horse; Paris killed and Helen returned to Sparta.

It is fatally handicapped by its pallid and unexciting leads, Italian actress Rosanna Podesta as Helen and Lithuanian-born French actor Jacques Sernas as Paris, both of them dubbed with impeccable but passionless English accents. They are supported by a distinguished British cast (among them Sir Cedric Hardwicke as Priam, Nora Swinburne as Hecuba, Stanley Baker as Achilles, Harry Andrews as Hector and Torin Thatcher as Ulysses), most of whom can do little with the stilted script.

The epic genre was not the forte of director Robert Wise and, having devoted a year to *Helen of Troy*, he never tackled it again. Veteran director Raoul Walsh had to be flown into Rome to take charge of the action sequences and provided some spirited battle scenes. But the film lost $4 million.

There is a fundamental, insuperable problem with the story of Troy for modern audiences. The modern sensibility does not respond as readily as the ancients to the concepts of divine vengeance, malign fate and tragic grandeur, all integral to the Homeric original. Also, modern audiences require a happy ending and in *Helen of Troy* the 'bad guys' win. The Trojans are honourable, noble and peace-loving; the Greeks treacherous, greedy and cynical. They plot an attack on Troy, describing it as 'a war of defensive aggression'; they violate an agreed truce and they stab Paris in the back. Their leaders are on the whole deeply unpleasant: Achilles is sulky, Agamemnon thuggish, Menelaus greedy, Ulysses crafty. The Achilles–Patroclus relationship is carefully de-sexualized. It all makes for an unsatisfactory outcome.

The year before *Helen of Troy*, the other great Homeric epic the *Odyssey* had been filmed as *Ulysses*. Unlike *Helen*, however, it was not the work of a Hollywood company but an Italian one (Lux), though it received distribution in both the USA (Paramount) and the UK (Archway). It boasted two Hollywood stars (Kirk Douglas as Ulysses and Anthony Quinn as Antinous) with a largely Italian supporting cast. The narrative had Ulysses, cursed by Cassandra for desecrating the temple of Neptune, condemned to wander round the Mediterranean for years, encountering the Cyclops Polyphemus, the enchantress Circe and the sirens, before returning to Ithaca to rout the suitors harassing his wife Penelope. The film is a ponderous bore with pedestrian direction and a stilted script, about which there is nothing to add to the verdict of the *Monthly Film Bulletin*:

> The army of scriptwriters (there were seven, four Italian, two American and one English) have succeeded in cunningly telescoping a number of unrelated episodes from the *Odyssey* into the main ones of the Cyclops, Circe, the Sirens and Nausicaa. In devising an idiom for the dialogue of the English version, however, they have settled for a pedantic, lifeless standard-English, which lands the performers with long, dreary speeches. These speeches are not brightened by the full, inexpressive faces and (dubbed) voices of the leading characters. Tried performers though they are, the principals – Kirk Douglas, Silvana Mangano, Anthony Quinn and Franco Interlenghi – seem to have been deliberately presented as the traditional wooden-heroes of spectacle films; for the film is consciously presented as a spectacle. Unfortunately its spectacular elements are markedly inadequate. The use of models, trick photography and sectional sets (e.g. the *head* of the giant horse, the *legs* of the Cyclops, the limited area of the deck of Ulysses' ship) is much more obvious than the spectacular effect it achieves. Either as the *Odyssey* without Homer or a spectacle without anything spectacular, Ulysses is a long, dull let-down. If there is any consolation, it is in the excellent photography and colour (Hollywood veteran Harold Rossen) and the sudden unexpected vigour of Ulysses' rout of the suitors.[4]

Perhaps the best of Hollywood's Greek epics remains the largely forgotten *The 300 Spartans* (1961). It centred on the battle of Thermopylae in 480 BC when the Spartan King Leonidas and his personal bodyguard held the vital mountain pass against the invading army of the Persian King Xerxes until they were wiped out to the last man. But their example inspired the Greeks to unite and Thermopylae was followed by the victory of the Athenian fleet over the Persians at Salamis, preserving freedom in Greece.

Intelligently scripted by George St George and magisterially directed by Rudolph Maté (with Richard Talmadge heading the second unit), *The 300 Spartans* is one of the finest recreations of an ancient battle put on film. Impressive panoramic long-shots make it possible to follow with absolute clarity the progress of the battle, as successive waves of Persians, cavalry, charioteers and infantry hurl themselves against the Spartan lines until the surviving Spartans, outnumbered and surrounded, are finished off by the archers. The film also benefits from the genuine Greek locations and the authentic Greek music by Manos Hadjidakis.

But the historical recreation underpinned a Cold War epic. This time the 'evil empire' in the East is Persia and its ruler, the ruthless and tyrannical Xerxes (David Farrar) seeks to suppress the last surviving strongholds of freedom in the West, the Greek city states, to achieve his aim of 'one world, one ruler'. The Greeks are divided and Themistocles, the Athenian admiral, tells them that the power of the Persians lies in their unity and he offers to place the Athenian navy under the control of the Spartans, who have the finest army in Greece, in order to ensure unity. It is here that the casting has contemporary relevance. All casting has resonance, based on the image and previous performances of the stars. Here the American cowboy star Richard Egan, playing the rugged and determined King Leonidas, cements an alliance with the British actor Sir Ralph Richardson, shrewd and sagacious as Themistocles. Just as in classical Greece, so in the present, the American army and the British navy, joined together in NATO, will see off the Soviet Union, today's 'evil empire'. For American audiences the story has added resonance as Thermopylae can be seen as an ancient analogue of the Alamo, another mythic event in which a handful of soldiers defied the army of a dictator, and all died, but their sacrifice paved the way for eventual defeat for the dictator and the emergence of a new nation. As the epilogue of *The 300 Spartans* has it: 'It is a stirring example to free people throughout the world of what a few brave men can do when they refuse to submit to tyranny.'

Although the gods are central to Greek myth, the cinema has largely steered clear of them. A notable exception has been the two classic fantasy films of Ray Harryhausen, *Jason and the Argonauts* (1963) and *Clash of the Titans* (1981). He was doubtless drawn to classical mythology for the opportunity to create a series of mythical creatures by his dynamation process. *Jason and the Argonauts* was two years in the making and cost $3 million, though part of that was recouped when *Argo* (specially built at a cost of $250,000) was sold to Fox for *Cleopatra*. Columbia Pictures, who were backing it, insisted on two little-known contract players, Todd Armstrong and Nancy Kovack, for the star roles of Jason and Medea. But their American accents proved so far out of kilter with those of the largely British supporting cast that they were both dubbed by British actors to maintain linguistic consistency.

A literate script, a majestic score (Bernard Herrmann), effective direction (Don Chaffey) and visually impressive Italian location shooting all contributed to the evocation of a classical world of sunsets and seascapes, ruined temples and desert islands, and gold-painted priestesses dancing in barbaric temples. The narrative follows the quest of Jason and his companions aboard *Argo* to find the magical Golden Fleece. It is constructed around a series of imaginative and memorable special-effects set pieces, devised and executed by Ray Harryhausen in his stop-motion process, dynamation, in which models were slowly and painstakingly animated, a process now superseded by CGI (computer-generated imagery). These included encounters with the clanking giant bronze statue Talos, modelled on the Colossus of Rhodes; the trapping of the harpies, two satanic winged creatures tormenting a blind man; Jason fighting a seven-headed hydra; and the final battle with skeleton warriors, summoned from the ground by the King of Colchis.

The novelty was the inclusion of the gods on Olympus, querulous, capricious and impulsive, watching, commenting on and manipulating events. At the start of the film Jason does not believe in the gods but he soon comes to realize that they are real when he is transported to Olympus by Hermes and is thereafter aided at crucial points by Hera. The film ends with the winning of the Fleece and the union of Jason and Medea, the princess of Colchis who has aided him. At this point Zeus declares: 'For Jason there are other adventures. I have not yet finished with Jason. Let us continue the game another day.' This was perhaps fortunate, as later on in the story Medea kills and dismembers her two children by Jason, not quite the stuff of family films. The inclusion of the gods had been the idea of Raymond Bowers, the first of the three script-writers to work successively on the project (the others were Jan Read and Beverley Cross), though he ended up without a credit.[5]

Ray Harryhausen returned to the Greek myths and the gods of Olympus twenty years later in *Clash of the Titans* (1981). Telling the story of the hero Perseus, his destruction of the gorgon Medusa and his rescue of the beautiful Andromeda from a monster, this was a film which fulfilled the celebrated dictum of producer Sam Goldwyn: 'I want a story that begins with an earthquake and works up to a climax.' The film opens with Zeus, the king of the gods, ordering the fearsome Kraken to destroy Argos by a tidal wave after its king has cast Zeus' infant son Perseus and his mother Danaë into the sea in a box. Like Jason, Perseus, once grown up, encounters a memorable menagerie of Harryhausen creations in his quest to save Andromeda. There is Calibos, a hirsute half-lizard, half-man who lurks in the misty marshland with his ill-visaged, misshapen dwarfish attendants and covets the beautiful Andromeda. There is Pegasus, last of the winged horses, tamed by Perseus and flying to the rescue at key moments. There is the two-headed dog Dioskilos who guards the temple on the isle of the dead. There is the fearsome snake-haired gorgon Medusa whose look turns men to stone. There are three giant scorpions created from her poisoned blood. Finally there is the monstrous Kraken, standing in for the dragon of legend, which threatens to carry off the princess until defeated by Perseus with the aid of the gorgon's head.

As in *Jason and the Argonauts*, two relative unknowns were cast in the leading roles. Harry Hamlin made a splendidly athletic and quick-witted Perseus and Judi Bowker, a fragile, doll-like Andromeda. But they were surrounded by a host of veteran stars, with Burgess Meredith, in particular, stealing scenes as the whimsical poet Ammon. On Mount Olympus, its design inspired by the city in John Martin's apocalyptic painting *Joshua commanding the sun to stand still*, the gods manipulating characters and events were incarnated by Maggie Smith (Thetis), Claire Bloom (Hera), Ursula Andress (Aphrodite) and Laurence Olivier (a suitably majestic Zeus).

The film boasted an imaginative script (Beverley Cross), effective direction (Desmond Davis) and a thrillingly heroic score (Laurence Rosenthal), which evoked memories of the classic film music of Korngold, Waxman and Newman. Columbia Pictures, who had backed all but one of the fantasy films of Ray Harryhausen and producer Charles Schneer since 1956, balked at the expense involved in this one and backed out. But MGM stepped into the breach and provided a $16 million budget. The live-action scenes were filmed between 14 May and 1 September 1979 with exteriors shot in Spain, Italy and Malta and interiors at Pinewood Studios. Eighteen months were then taken up with creating the special effects and the film finally premiered in June 1981. It was generally well received by critics and public, Roger Ebert of the *Chicago Sun-Times* calling it 'a grand and glorious adventure'. But Harryhausen was particularly hurt by the review in *Variety* which comprehensively savaged the film, calling it 'an unbearable bore that will probably put to sleep the few adults stuck taking the kids to it', pronounced the special effects 'flat' and 'outdated', the direction 'tired' and the writing 'lackadaisical'.[6] These are the words of someone with no poetry in his soul and none of that sense of wonder that inspired Harryhausen to create his living myths.

When Harryhausen and Schneer failed to raise funding for the next project, *Force of the Trojans*, a version of the *Aeneid*, Harryhausen decided to retire. But he went out on a high for (*pace Variety*) *Clash of the Titans* is a deeply satisfying and visually engrossing fantasy film that pays respect not only to the myths but also to the Olympian gods.

In all the centuries' long history of Ancient Egypt, there are four episodes above all which have captured the popular imagination. There is the building of the pyramids, and in particular the Great Pyramid of Pharaoh Khufu, along with all the esoteric lore, much of it spurious, attached to the pyramids. There is the attempt of the 'heretic Pharaoh' Akhenaten and his beautiful wife Nefertiti to introduce monotheism, and the reversion to polytheism under his son (or perhaps brother) and successor Tutankhamun, the discovery of whose intact tomb made this hitherto obscure and short-lived ruler the most famous pharaoh of them all. There is the captivity of the Jews and the exodus under their leader Moses, dated by many scholars to the reign of Pharaoh Rameses II. Finally, there is the political and romantic career of Cleopatra VII, the last Ptolemaic ruler of Egypt, and her successive affairs with Julius Caesar and Mark Antony. Each of these episodes would inspire a major film in the 1950s and early 1960s.

The blockbusting success of *The Robe* inspired Darryl F. Zanuck to seek a follow-up in similar vein. He settled on *The Egyptian* as the ideal property. This was a 1949 bestselling novel by the Finnish writer Mika Waltari who, like Lloyd C. Douglas, author of *The Robe*, had exchanged a career in the ministry for the life of a writer of inspirational literature. Like *The Robe*, it provided an opportunity for spectacle and an uplifting message, involving as it did similar themes: one man's journey towards spiritual enlightenment and the persecution of a peace-loving, monotheistic sect by a polytheist, militarist dictatorship, both of them themes which had captured the imagination of the millions who turned out to see *The Robe*.

Zanuck assembled an impressive team to make the film, which would be in Cinemascope and De Luxe Colour. Michael Curtiz had just ended his 22-year-long association with Warner Brothers, for whom he had directed such classic historical spectacles as *The Charge of the Light Brigade*, *The Adventures of Robin Hood* and *The Sea Hawk*. He was signed as director and, to draft the script, another old Warner hand, Casey Robinson, a master of novel adaptation and author of among others the screen plays for *Dark Victory*, *King's Row* and *Now, Voyager*. Philip Dunne, who had provided the final version of *The Robe* script, was then brought in to revise Robinson's script. He was impressed by Waltari's novel because it had 'a love and feeling for ancient Egypt', and by Robinson's script, which he felt had made a good job of streamlining the novel and developing the various plot-lines.[7] But in Dunne's view, the film was then compromised by the casting.

Zanuck cast Marlon Brando as the leading figure Sinuhe, Victor Mature and Jean Simmons, both of whom had starred in *The Robe*, Peter Ustinov (who had starred in *Quo Vadis*) and contract star Gene Tierney. Dunne had wanted New York actor John Cassavetes cast as Akhnaton (*sic*), but Zanuck, who believed that all ancient rulers should be played by British actors, cast Michael Wilding. They ran into an immediate problem, however, when Brando withdrew. Dunne recalled that at the first script readthrough Brando had read the part 'absolutely beautifully. It was quite poetic.' But when it became clear to Brando that Curtiz did not understand the character, he threw up the part.[8] There was now a desperate search for a replacement and after Fox tried and failed to prise Dirk Bogarde from the grip of the Rank Organization, they settled for another English actor, the handsome but wooden Edmund Purdom, whose only previous starring role had been in MGM's *The Student Prince* in which he had replaced an overweight and recalcitrant Mario Lanza and mimed to Lanza's pre-recordings of the songs. Another major problem was Zanuck's insistence on casting his latest mistress, the heavily accented and cosmically talentless Bella Darvi as the Babylonian temptress Nefer. After six months of research, to ensure visual authenticity in costumes and settings, the creation of 167 major sets and the employment of 5,000 extras, the film was shot between 3 March and 7 May 1954. Nefertiti's headdress, Akhnaton's throne and the wall paintings and carvings were directly copied from ancient originals. The throne room alone cost $85,000 to recreate.[9] Zanuck had got wind of the fact that rival studios were also working on Egyptian stories and was anxious to get his film into release ahead of them, so there was a race on. Warner Brothers were producing *Land of the Pharaohs*, Paramount planning *The Ten Commandments* and MGM were filming *The Valley of the Kings* (an archaeological thriller about tomb robbing set in 1900). All three, unlike *The Egyptian*, would involve extensive location shooting in Egypt.

Over present-day footage of the ruins of Ancient Egypt, a narrator set up the film in a way which, echoing Bulwer-Lytton's introduction to his novel *The Last Days of Pompeii*, stressed both the exoticism of the world that was to be recreated on the screen and the similarity of the ancient people to us.

> Today the glory of Ancient Egypt is ruins and dust. And this greatest of the earth's early civilizations is a thing of darkness and mystery. These mighty monuments tell us of a people who were the rulers of the world and created a civilization never surpassed for beauty and splendour. The Egyptians were not only builders of monuments. They were human beings no different from ourselves.

The film is narrated by the now elderly Sinuhe (Edmund Purdom) from his place of exile near the Red Sea. He recalls in flashback how he was found abandoned floating in a reed boat on the Nile, like the infant Moses. Adopted by an idealistic physician dedicated to serving the poor, he grows up to follow the same career. Sinuhe and his old classmate, the humble-born soldier Horemheb (Victor Mature) save the new Pharaoh Akhnaton (Michael Wilding) from a marauding lion and are rewarded by being made court physician and member of the royal bodyguard respectively. Enslaved by desire for the Babylonian courtesan Nefer (Bella Darvi), Sinuhe sacrifices everything for her and ends up disgraced and exiled. Travelling the world, he makes a fortune by healing the rich. But he returns to warn Egypt about the danger from the Hittite kingdom which has developed a new secret weapon (iron swords). Pharaoh Akhnaton, who has introduced a new monotheistic religion, worship of the sun (Aton) dedicated to peace and love, prefers to negotiate with the enemy rather than crushing them as Horemheb, now commander-in-chief of the army, advocates. Horemheb, who believes in a strong and aggressive state, now allies with the priesthood of the old gods, to stage a coup. The army, under Horemheb's command, attacks and wipes out the gentle Aton-worshippers and destroys their temple. Among the dead is the tavern maid Merit (Jean Simmons), who had devotedly loved Sinuhe and borne him a son, Thoth. Blaming Akhnaton for the civil war engulfing Egypt, Sinuhe agrees to poison him. Dying, Akhnaton forgives Sinuhe and has a vision of the future. The Aton was only a symbol of the one true God, the creator of the world, before whom all men are equal. Akhnaton has only been a forerunner of this faith and one day it would gain its fulfilment (in, it is implied, Christianity). Sinuhe, who had planned in collusion with Akhnaton's ruthless sister Baketamun (Gene Tierney) to poison Horemheb at the same time and seize the throne for himself, now confesses the plot and declares his intention to preach the gospel just adumbrated by the dying Pharaoh. Horemheb, proclaimed Pharaoh and occupying the throne with Baketamun, sentences Sinuhe to lifelong exile. He dies after completing his memoirs and the endtitle, underlining the message, declares: 'This story happened 13 centuries before the birth of Jesus Christ.'

The film emerges as a proto-Christian morality tale, with an idealistic young humanitarian losing his ideals when in the grip of physical desire, realizing the search for wealth and revenge is empty and finding fulfilment in true love and a belief in the one true God. At the same time a compassionate and gentle Pharaoh, preaching peace and love, is overthrown by a new ruler who exterminates his followers, institutes military dictatorship and restores polytheism. It is another version of the age-old conflict between democratic Christianity and ruthless totalitarianism.

Desperate to ensure that he beat his rivals into cinemas, Zanuck took charge of editing the film while Curtiz was still shooting and the shortened post-production timescale necessitated the use of two composers to provide the score. Alfred Newman, the general musical director at 20th Century-Fox, was assigned to the score. But he was also engaged on *There's No Business like Showbusiness* and it was agreed he would need to divide the score with another composer. Bernard Herrmann was selected and Herrmann suggested that since there were three main strands to the script, the love story of Sinuhe and Merit, the love affair of Sinuhe and Nefer, and Pharaoh Akhnaton and his religious reforms, that Newman take the Merit and Akhnaton strands and Herrmann would take Nefer. They exchanged scores to ensure musical consistency. They agreed on a musical texture which involved pentatonic scale patterns, wordless chorus, and the use of authentic ancient Egyptian instruments (lute, harp, trumpets, tambourine percussion).[10] They collaborated harmoniously and creatively and produced one of the great symphonic scores of the golden age of the great studios: at once exotic, mystical and mysterious. Newman's love theme for Merit was exquisitely wistful, his Akhnaton music shimmeringly mystical, the Valley of the Kings' music haunting and mysterious. One of Newman's greatest contributions was giving a superb choral setting to the 2,000 year old words of the Hymn to the Aton. Herrmann ended up writing more than half the score, for not only did he do the Nefer theme, a dark-toned and fate-haunted piece, but much of the exciting action music (the chariot ride, the lion hunt, the massacre of the Atonists) and the prelude with its horns, brass, timpani, violins and wordless chorus. It all added up to a memorable musical achievement. But it was not enough to save the film.

As it finally emerged, the film failed to live up to Zanuck's expectations. It was ponderous, plodding and protracted, with none of the dynamism of Curtiz' best work, except in the massacre of the Atonists, a rare action highlight in the film, which was vividly and fluently shot and edited. It might have been even longer, as a visit to Minoan Crete by Sinuhe was filmed but cut. It was further handicapped by Edmund Purdom's uninspired and uninspiring Sinuhe and Bella Darvi's downright embarrassing, inept Nefer. Michael Wilding, himself an epileptic, played the epileptic visionary Pharaoh sensitively and movingly, although he considered himself miscast. Unfortunately the role was marginalized. Concentration on him and his Atonist revolution, inspiration later for a play by Agatha Christie and an opera by Philip Glass, would actually have made for a more interesting film. Neither Mature nor Tierney were great actors, more iconic presences, notable for being rather than acting. Peter Ustinov as Sinuhe's lovably rascally servant Kaptah spent his time sending the whole film up. He saw appearing in *The Egyptian* as 'like being on a monstrously huge set of *Aida* and not being able to find the way out'. He told Michael Wilding that in his white robes and conical Pharaonic crown he looked like a gigantic salt cellar, and thereafter Wilding could not keep a straight face and kept breaking up.[11] Wilding recalled in his autobiography his feeling that 'it would be a disaster from the word go, but another child was on the way and I could not allow myself the luxury of being put on suspension again for rejecting a role'. He found Ustinov the only saving grace on the film as, 'Both scornful of our roles and our absurd costumes', they amused themselves in mocking everything, not least the dictatorial Curtiz with his hilariously mangled English.[12]

The critics greeted the film without enthusiasm. In America, the *Saturday Review* (4 September 1954) said it was 'overlong, overtalky, underacted' and that it 'meanders for more than two hours through laboriously researched Egyptian throne rooms and side streets [...] all populated by such thoroughly twentieth-century types as Victor Mature, Gene Tierney, Jean Simmons and Michael Wilding'. *The New Yorker* (4 September 1954) said: '*The Egyptian* hardly qualifies as a movie. It barely moves at all, and when it does work up a bit of motion, it proceeds at the pace of a Spanish funeral [...] Mr Purdom as the Egyptian seems overcome to the point of paralysis by the magnitude of the enterprise on which he is engaged.'

The British critics were no more friendly. The *Daily Telegraph* (16 October 1954) called it 'frankly dull' and the *Daily Sketch* (15 October 1954), heading its review 'Corn in Egypt', called it 'This sorry epic'. The *Manchester Guardian* (16 October 1954) found it 'unbelievably tedious [...] childish and boring'. The *Daily Worker* (16 October 1954) complained about 'two hours nineteen minutes of almost stupefying boredom relieved here and there by the sight of old friends battling gamely against their scripts'. The *News Chronicle* (15 October 1954) found it 'ill-anchored to its cheap script and proportionately tawdry performance, the whole of this expensive spectacle goes adrift'. *The Times* (18 October 1954) found it a film to 'stun rather than stimulate'. The *Daily Mail* (15 October 1954) positively lambasted it:

> *The Egyptian* is another of those great tasteless mock-religious spectacles whose main purpose seems to be to fill the wide screen at any price and give regular employment to Victor Mature [...] the only emotion aroused is one of pity for capable performers, gallantly keeping their faces straight as they mouth the drivel that is Hollywood's idea of the noble lingo of antiquity.

There was a handful of critics who seemed to have been at a different film entirely. The *Sunday Dispatch* (17 October 1954) declared: 'Magnificent is the only word. The backgrounds are astonishing and the colour beautiful, while the action has a sweep that makes one hold one's breath.' The critic pronounced the cast 'perfect' and the dialogue 'exceptionally good'. The *Evening Standard* (14 October 1954) said: 'The picture is a constant delight on the eye. Pictorially and musically it is a triumph and there is some very good acting by Michael Wilding and Jean Simmons.' The *Daily Herald* (15 October 1954), finding the film so packed with the detail and colour of a forgotten civilization that 'you cannot fail to be absorbed', confidently predicted stardom for Purdom.

The film had been assigned a production budget of $4 million. Most reviewers quote a figure of $5 million, suggesting that post-production costs mounted. The film made only $4.25 million in domestic rentals, a far cry from the $17 million brought in by *The Robe*.[13] Zanuck's plans for a sequel to follow the careers of Horemheb and Baketamun were immediately abandoned.

Purdom returned to the period of *The Egyptian* in *Queen of the Nile* (produced in Italy as *Nefertiti, Regina del Nilo* in 1961 and released in a dubbed version in Britain as *Queen of the Nile* in 1963). This was one of a series of cut-price historical epics produced in Italy in the 1960s and featuring fading Hollywood stars, in this case Edmund Purdom, Jeanne Crain and Vincent Price. Despite colourful costumes and sets and an action-packed finale, this was a stilted and one-dimensional affair which overlaid the facts of the reign of Akhenaton and Nefertiti with a plethora of fictional subplots (forbidden love affairs; priestly intrigue against the throne). The inspiration for the script is clearly the celebrated bust of Nefertiti which showed her to be what critics called 'the most beautiful woman in the world'.

An innocent young girl, Tanit (Jeanne Crain) falls in love with the sculptor Tumos (Purdom). But her father, Benakon, High Priest of Amun (Vincent Price), marries her to the mentally unbalanced son of the Pharaoh, Amenophis. When his father dies, Amenophis ascends the throne as Amenophis IV and Tanit, renamed Nefertiti, becomes his Queen. Tumos is commissioned to do the bust of Nefertiti and she affirms her love for him but refuses to leave her vulnerable husband. He is converted by a Chaldean priest to the worship of Aton and tries to impose monotheism on the country. Benakon raises the priesthood and the enraged citizenry, kills Amenophis' confidant, the priest from Chaldea, and besieges the palace. Amenophis commits suicide but Tumos brings the army from the desert to relieve the siege and proclaims Nefertiti Queen. Benakon is killed by a gypsy girl in love with Tumos. In reality, Nefertiti predeceased her husband and the priesthood won and reinstated polytheism.

Jeanne Crain, who looks very like the famous bust, is an iconic presence, Purdom does a rerun of his Sinuhe and Vincent Price contributes a one-dimensional sneering villain. Amedeo Nazzari is totally miscast as Amenophis IV (who in this film never changes his name to Akhenaten), too virile, mature and assured for the sensitive, mystical and physically abnormal Pharaoh. Fernando Cerchio's direction is routine.

It was director Howard Hawks' idea to make a film about the building of the pyramids and Warner Brothers, anxious to emulate Fox's success with *The Robe*, agreed to back it, provided it could be filmed in Rome where the studio was also shooting *Helen of Troy* to utilize frozen funds. There was no script and so Hawks assembled a team of three writers to provide one: Nobel Prize-winning novelist William Faulkner, who had worked on the scripts of four earlier Hawks films, the sophisticated Harry Kurnitz, who in order to escape McCarthyism had retreated to Europe from Hollywood where his credits had included *The Thin Man Goes Home* and *What Next, Private Hargrove?* (for which he had been Oscar-nominated in 1945), and Harold Jack Bloom, a young writer Oscar-nominated for his first script, the western *The Naked Spur*. Hawks was really only interested in the story of the megalomaniac leader seeking immortality by building himself a monument that entailed a mammoth building programme. He was particularly intrigued by how the pyramid would be sealed when it was finished and it was art director Alexandre Trauner who researched this and came up with the solution. But there was not enough in this aspect for an entire script.

The eventual film, *Land of the Pharaohs*, fell into two parts. There was the semi-documentary account of the building of the pyramids and a melodramatic plot involving court intrigue, treachery and murder. The actual pyramid-building plot conformed to the anti-totalitarian propaganda of many 1950s' Ancient World epics. The central figure is Pharaoh Khufu (Jack Hawkins) an absolute ruler who has enslaved many races, whose will is law and who wants a pyramid to house his body and his treasures for eternity. In this, he could be seen to resemble Hitler and Stalin who both had monumental building programmes and delusions of architectural grandeur. To build the pyramid, a huge labour force is needed. It is drawn from the Egyptian people, who initially undertake the work joyously and voluntarily as an act of religious faith, and the captive races, notably the Kushites, whose leader, the architect Vashtar (James Robertson Justice) is put in charge of the project and predicts 'the stones of the pyramid will be cemented with blood and tears'. As the years drag on, the Egyptians have to be forced to continue. But Vashtar strikes a bargain with Pharaoh by which a proportion of the Kushites will be released at each stage of the completion of the pyramid. Vashtar's recurrent refrain 'Let my people go' turns him and his people into analogues of Moses and the Jews in the story of the exodus. The cruelty that is integral to Pharaoh's absolute rule is exemplified by his having those who showed cowardice in battle thrown to the crocodiles, Princess Nellifer flogged for defying him, and a group of priests having their tongues cut out so that they can assist Vashtar in the building without being able to reveal the secrets of the pyramid's inner workings.

The melodramatic plot has Pharaoh's scheming second wife, the Cypriot Princess Nellifer (Joan Collins) seduce the captain of the treasure chamber, murder Pharaoh's chief wife, Queen Nailla (Kerima), using a cobra, and despatch an assassin to kill Khufu. The mortally wounded Pharaoh dies. But Nellifer's plans to seize the throne and the treasure are foiled by the loyal High Priest Hamar, who allows her to accompany the sarcophagus to the centre of the pyramid and to order the sealing of the tomb, leading to her being buried alive with her husband.

This part of the film seems to be made up of ideas from other films rather than Egyptian history. The sequence of the ageing Khufu wrestling a bull to impress his young wife looks back to the wrestling scene in *The Private Life of Henry VIII* when King Henry tries something similar. The threat provided by a cobra summoned by the music of a flute recalls a similar scene in *The Lives of a*

Bengal Lancer. The idea of an upright young officer seduced by a scheming hussy comes from the actions of Milady de Winter in *The Three Musketeers*. The scene of a ruthless wife watching an incapacitated husband die is from *The Little Foxes*. The operatic finale of the film is a variation of the last act of *Aida*.

The making of the film was a gruelling business. It began with location shooting in Egypt between 1 April and 25 May 1954 (Russell Harlan as cameraman) and then a return to Rome where interiors were shot by Lee Garmes in two small and primitive studios, Scalera and Centro Sperimentale, finishing on 9 August. Dimitri Tiomkin was flown in to provide the score and produced a characteristically memorable one, dominated by thrilling brass and wordless choral singing, to emphasize the militarism and the mysticism which went hand in hand in Ancient Egypt. Hawks made excellent use of Cinemascope and Warnercolor, filling his screen with panoramic shots of pyramid-building and processions, triumphal and funerary. His casting conformed to the familiar aural paradigm with most of the leading parts played by British actors. Jack Hawkins gave a performance of power and authority and was wholly convincing as Pharaoh and Joan Collins made a sultry, sexy and scheming Nellifer. The only American in the cast, Dewey Martin, whose Brooklyn accent clashes incongruously with the British tones around him, played Vashtar's son Senta, occupying a very similar role in the narrative as he had previously in Hawks' fur-trapping movie *The Big Sky* (1952). The obligatory drive for authenticity included a recreation of the interior of the great Pyramid of Gizeh, complete with the funerary solar boat of Khufu, discovered as recently as 1954.[14]

The film opened in New York on 26 July 1955 and failed to meet Warner Brothers' high hopes of it. It had cost $5,716,210 to make and achieved worldwide receipts of only $4,181,909, leaving Warners with a whopping loss of $1,534,211.[15] When it opened in London, the critics fell on it like a pack of unforgiving wolves. 'Woeful' declared the *Observer* (6 May 1956); 'I didn't believe a word of it' thundered the *News of the World* (6 May 1956); 'ponderous' thought the *Daily Herald* (4 May 1956); 'The cinema's most monumental bore' pontificated the *Financial Times* (7 May 1956). 'Ineffably Hollow' reported the *News Chronicle* (4 May 1956). 'An expensive spectacular bore' pronounced the *Daily Express* (4 May 1956).

The film's two stars retrospectively damned it in their autobiographies. Joan Collins complained of the writers: 'Although they slaved away writing and rewriting daily, it was in spite of their efforts, a very hokey script with some impossible dialogue'.[16] Jack Hawkins called the film 'perfectly ridiculous' and said: 'some of the lines we were expected to speak were unspeakable'. When Hawkins was overheard complaining about one particular line, he was reassured by Hawks: '"Don't worry [...] I'll find you another. I have more used lines at my fingertips than anyone you know". He was quite serious about it. When he was short of dialogue, he would borrow lines from some old movie. I am quite sure that I ended up speaking words that Clark Gable had used in some quite different film.'[17]

Hawks himself subsequently disowned the film, requesting its omission from a retrospective of his work at the National Film Theatre in 1963. He said it failed because 'I didn't know how a Pharaoh talked'. This was taken seriously by his biographer Todd McCarthy, who wrote: 'Hawks' art was based on dialogue, gesture and behavioural exchanges' and that he could not deploy that aspect of his art in this case.[18] In his classic study of Hawks' work, Robin Wood consigned *Land of the Pharaohs* to an appendix headed 'Failures and Marginal Works', declaring 'The characters' interchange is so stilted as to make detailed commentary superfluous.'[19] However, he interestingly points out that the narrative does contain a series of classically Hawksian themes: the defined group engaged upon a specific task (the Kushites building the pyramid); a young man's development through experience to maturity (Senta in this case) and the instant sexual antagonism of the leading man and leading woman (here Khufu and Nellifer).

Actually the dialogue is no better and no worse than that in many Ancient World epics; the pyramid-building sequences are absorbing; the melodrama wickedly enjoyable; the two leading performances engaging; the score terrific; and the sets, costumes and recreated rituals fascinating. It has none of the longeurs of *The Egyptian* and remains throughout perversely watchable.

In contrast to the nineteenth-century stage, the twentieth-century British cinema almost never tackled the Ancient World. A notable exception was *Caesar and Cleopatra*. In 1935 a flamboyant but charming Hungarian chancer, Gabriel Pascal, had persuaded Bernard Shaw into giving him the rights to produce a film of *Pygmalion*. The resulting film, released in 1938 and co-directed by Leslie Howard and Anthony Asquith, was a worldwide success and brought Shaw an Oscar for best screenplay. Shaw and Pascal followed up *Pygmalion* with *Major Barbara* (1940), which Pascal directed as well as producing. It achieved a more modest success. But, on the basis of these two films, Pascal persuaded film tycoon J. Arthur Rank in 1943 to back a prestige Technicolor production of *Caesar and Cleopatra* with the enormous budget of £550,000, aimed in part at putting British films on the map in the USA. Pascal assembled a top team of production staff: costume designer Oliver Messel, art director John Bryan, composer Georges Auric and four of Britain's most accomplished cameramen, Freddie Young, Jack Cardiff, Jack Hilyard and Robert Krasker.[20] Shaw himself provided the script, streamlining his original play and adding new scenes and dialogue but retaining his distinctive take on the Caesar–Cleopatra relationship. He teaches her how to be a Queen and she yearns for the return of Mark Antony rather than embarking on a love affair with Caesar. Shaw took a keen interest in the costumes, make-up and pronunciation and Pascal called on him weekly with production stills to keep him informed on progress. Shaw had wanted John Gielgud for Caesar, regarding him as the natural successor to Sir Johnston Forbes Robertson, who had created the role on stage. But Gielgud was tied to a play and was unavailable. So Claude Rains was cast, with an eye to the American market, with Vivien Leigh (equally well known there, thanks to *Gone with the Wind*) as Cleopatra. Pascal surrounded them with a superb cast (Stewart Granger as Apollodorus the Sicilian, Flora Robson as Cleopatra's black handmaiden Ftatateeta, Francis L. Sullivan as the eunuch Pothinos, Cecil Parker as Caesar's secretary Britannus, Basil Sydney as his lieutenant Rufio) and in smaller roles Ernest Thesiger, Esmé Percy, Leo Genn, Stanley Holloway and Michael Rennie. Altogether there were a hundred named players and thousands of extras. Massive sets were constructed at Denham Studio: Cleopatra's Palace, the Pharos of Alexandria, the quayside, the Sphinx. Costumes and architecture were scrupulously copied from Egyptian originals. Pascal even consulted an astronomer to ascertain the precise pattern of the stars in the Egyptian sky at the time of the play. Given this galaxy of talent, the only problem was Pascal himself, who had virtually no experience of directing, had no idea how to use the camera creatively and tended just to photograph the action unimaginatively. On *Major Barbara* Pascal had been assisted by the experienced director Harold French who coached the actors and the brilliant editor David Lean who advised on the technical side. For *Caesar and Cleopatra* he engaged Brian Desmond Hurst as associate director but they soon quarrelled and he left. Pascal thereafter worked alone and his chief technique was to order endless retakes, needlessly prolonging the filming process. By the end of the shooting, neither Claude Rains nor Vivien Leigh was speaking to him. After shooting was completed, the technicians held a union meeting and voted never to work with him again.

Admittedly the production was plagued with unforeseen problems. Shooting began on 14 June 1944 and almost immediately V2 rocket attacks on London began, disrupting every aspect of production, in particular the costume-making as the dressmaking workshops were destroyed by a direct hit. Vivien Leigh became pregnant and subsequently had a miscarriage. Later she missed several weeks filming after succumbing to her manic depression. Her absences meant additional delays. The summer of 1944 proved disastrously overcast and sunless, making the shooting of exterior scenes difficult. Eventually it was decided to send a unit to Egypt to shoot exteriors and they departed, together with their Sphinx, which they later abandoned in the desert. The scrappy and unconvincing nature of the battle scenes filmed there suggests it was hardly worth all the effort. Shooting dragged on until the summer of 1945 and the film finally premiered on 13 December 1945, by which time the budget had risen to a staggering £1,278,000, making it the most expensive British film ever.[21]

The resulting film has impressive sets and fine colour photography. The acting is admirable, Claude Rains, quietly and good-naturedly underplaying, creates a Caesar who is wise, magnanimous, humane, shrewd and immensely good-humoured. Vivien Leigh manages the transition from naive teenager to politically aware and ruthless queen very effectively. Stewart Granger claimed to have been confused by his role: 'I think Shaw meant him to be queer, which was not exactly my scene.'[22] Shaw certainly meant him to be an aesthete. But Granger, bronzed, earringed and clad in a succession of eyecatchingly flamboyant outfits (tangerine tunic and pearl grey cloak, blue and silver tunic with yellow cloak) gives a mesmerizing performance of flashing-eyed virility. Indeed, C.A. Lejeune in the *Observer* asked why Cleopatra was asking Caesar to send her Mark Antony 'when such a stunning Sicilian gallant was at hand, ready and apt to drape his round, strong arms about her shoulders'.[23] But the direction never rose above the mediocre.

By the time the film was released, Pascal's profligacy had become notorious. Questions were being asked in the House of Commons about his extravagance and many critics determined not to like the film. Lord Beaverbrook, who viewed the film, liked it and ordered his newspapers to boost it and the *Daily Express* duly obliged: 'a tremendous achievement'. Elsewhere the *News Chronicle* (12 December 1945) pronounced it 'a dismal ordeal', *The Spectator* (21 December 1945) dismissed it as 'ordinary' and *The Times* (12 December 1945) thought it 'hollow at its heart'. C.A. Lejeune, heading her review 'Pshaw!' declared it 'cold'. The reviews in the United States were mixed – *Variety* thought the spectacle swamped the story – and, given the massive outlay on the production, it was never likely to make a profit and it is estimated that it made a loss of $3 million worldwide. Pascal never directed again and, seven year after the film was produced, dismissed it as 'a gorgeous bore'.[24]

Vivien Leigh returned to the role of Cleopatra in 1951 when, in a star attraction for Festival of Britain year, she and her husband Laurence Olivier starred in *Caesar and Cleopatra* and *Antony and Cleopatra* on alternate evenings at the St James's Theatre. Using the same cast for both plays, a revolving stage and spectacular sets, it was a bold venture. But it paid off. They ran from 10/11 May until September before transferring to New York. Both productions were highly praised and Barry Duncan recalled both Leigh and Olivier as 'magnificent'.[25] They strikingly contrasted, in Olivier's case, the weary, drily witty Caesar and the ageing sensualist Antony (whom privately Olivier considered to be 'an absolute twerp'), and in Leigh's, the teenage princess and the mature woman. But in retrospect they have been remembered for Kenneth Tynan's cruel comment on Leigh's Cleopatra ('She picks at the part with the daintiness of a debutante called upon to dismember a stag') and his suggestion that Olivier deliberately scaled down his performances to disguise his wife's dramatic limitations, something that was not apparent to other critics at the time but has entered theatrical folklore.[26]

If *Caesar and Cleopatra* became the most expensive film in British cinema history, Hollywood's *Cleopatra* (1963) matched it every step of the way for extravagance and behind the scenes turmoil. It was conceived, like *Ben-Hur*, as a solution to the growing financial problems of an ailing Hollywood giant – in this case 20th Century-Fox. The dynamic and autocratic head of Fox studios, Darryl F. Zanuck, had resigned in 1956 to pursue personal film-making projects. The divided and indecisive senior management who replaced him found itself unable to stem the rising losses being sustained by the studio. Eventually Spyros Skouras, whose background was in distribution and exhibition rather than production, emerged as the strongest figure at the studio and in 1959 he backed the suggestion of producer Walter Wanger that they make a new version of *Cleopatra*, previously filmed by Fox in 1917 and later by De Mille in 1934. The rights to Carlo Maria Franzero's book *The Life and Times of Cleopatra* were purchased to provide a basis for the script. Fox envisaged it as a comparatively inexpensive production, using contract stars such as Joan Collins and being filmed on the studio back lot in Hollywood. A budget of $2 million was allocated. But Wanger envisaged something altogether grander and he persuaded Fox to hire – for the then unprecedented fee of $1 million – Elizabeth Taylor. She was currently riding high in career terms (Oscar-nominated for her performance in *Cat on a Hot Tin Roof*) and had a notable public profile (spectacularly widowed by the death in a plane crash of her husband, producer Mike Todd, and then involved in a much publicized love triangle with singer Eddie Fisher and his then wife Debbie Reynolds). The great visual stylist Rouben Mamoulian, who had directed Garbo in *Queen Christina*, was hired as director, John De Cuir as production designer and Oliver Messel to devise the costumes as he had for *Caesar and Cleopatra*. Peter Finch was engaged to play Caesar, Stephen Boyd (fresh from *Ben-Hur*) as Antony and Keith Baxter as Octavian.

Wanger had a particular vision of Cleopatra, neither the femme fatale of Shakespeare nor the skittish teenager of Shaw. He saw her as:

> a fascinating, brilliant, irresistible young woman, admirably reared in rulership. She is a great administrator. She understands military tactics. Her sense of responsibility as a governing chief is enormous [...] She speaks seven languages and many dialects.

He envisaged the film as a political thriller rather than an epic spectacle:

> The entire picture is one of intrigue, conspiracy, suspense and adventure. It will not be presented – as historical films usually are – in a pompous manner, with endless pageantry, but rather in the speed and tempo and cliff-hanger excitement of an underworld picture.[27]

Although elements of both these conceptions remained, they were to be substantially diluted as the interpretations of Shaw and Shakespeare intruded into the script and the studio demanded a conventional historical spectacle.

It was decided in 1960 to shoot the film in England to take advantage of the government subsidies for film-makers available under the Eady Plan and the city of Alexandria began to be built on the back lot at Pinewood studios. Shooting began in September 1960 and very soon disaster struck. Persistent bad weather made outdoor shooting of the Alexandrian scenes impossible and Elizabeth Taylor was taken ill, an illness exacerbated by the English weather. Eventually, with only ten minutes of film footage completed, Mamoulian resigned and the studio decided to close down the production and relocate to Italy where the weather was better, the labour cheaper and there were frozen funds to be drawn on. So the sets at Pinewood were dismantled and Alexandria reappeared under De Cuir's supervision at Cinecittà studios in Rome. Joseph L. Mankiewicz was engaged as director. His success with *Julius Caesar* made him the ideal person to realize Wanger's conception of *Cleopatra* as political thriller and Taylor had confidence in him after he had directed her in *Suddenly Last Summer*. By now the budget had risen to $7 million. Mankiewicz, who was himself an accomplished scriptwriter, found the script, which had been through successive versions written by Nigel Balchin, Dale Wasserman and Laurence Durrell, wholly unsatisfactory and insisted on starting again from scratch. Two new scriptwriters were brought in to prepare drafts which Mankiewicz would then rewrite and rework. They were Sidney Buchman, who had co-written De Mille's *The Sign of the Cross* (1932) but had been blacklisted in the 1950s and moved to London, and Ranald MacDougall, who was an expert in 'women's pictures', having scripted the Joan Crawford vehicles *Mildred Pierce, Possessed* and *Queen Bee*. Meanwhile Elizabeth Taylor fell ill again with pneumonia and was near death when an emergency trachaeotomy had to be performed, leaving her with a permanent scar. She retreated to California to convalesce as the script was being rewritten and the budget rose steadily to $27 million. By now both Finch and Boyd, who had other film commitments, had withdrawn from the cast.

As costs mounted, Skouras insisted that filming begin in September 1961. So Mankiewicz began filming in Rome on 25 September 1961 with only half the script completed. He was to combine directing by day with rewriting the script by night for the next 18 months until, totally exhausted, he handed over to MacDougall to complete the final pages.

By now, Rex Harrison had been cast as Caesar, Richard Burton as Antony and Roddy McDowall as Octavian. Messel had been replaced as costume designer by Vittorio Nino Novarese. Filming was to drag on until 5 March 1963, with costs mounting steadily until the final total was $40 million.[28] This was the result of the wholly inadequate pre-production preparations, almost non-existent financial control and endless delays. During the course of the filming the producer Walter Wanger, blamed for the rising costs, was sacked and Spyros Skouras, who had continually battled against the board of directors' desire to close the production down and cut the losses, was forced to resign when the company recorded a record loss of $22,532,084 for 1961. Darryl F. Zanuck returned to take control of the company in July 1962.

Mankiewicz at this stage had a seven and a half hour film which he initially suggested be shown as two films, *Caesar and Cleopatra* and *Antony and Cleopatra*. When Zanuck vetoed that idea, Mankiewicz cut it to five hours and screened it for Zanuck. Zanuck's immediate reaction was 'where's the spectacle' and was told 'it's a love story'. Zanuck removed Mankiewicz from the production and with his favourite editor Elmo Williams cut the film further to four hours, only to find it was now full of loose ends and gaps in continuity. Mankiewicz was brought back to shoot extra footage to tidy up the continuity, and while so doing, contrived to restore some of the cut scenes. Meanwhile, Zanuck decreed that some of the action scenes looked scrappy and improvised and to expand the spectacle he brought back Andrew Marton, the experienced second-unit director who had shot the battle at the Moongate in Alexandria and the battle of Actium (using only three ships), to reshoot the aftermath of the battle of Pharsalia and the scene of Antony charging alone against Octavian's army. These scenes were shot at Almeria in Spain. The process of cutting reduced all but the three leading characters to one-dimensional ciphers.[29]

However, the film finally premiered in New York on 12 June 1963, in a four-hour version. Helped by the well-publicized romance of Burton and Taylor which had blossomed during the film, *Cleopatra* became the top box-office success of 1963, grossing $26 million in domestic rentals. But in order to fit in more showings of the film it was further cut to three hours and 14 minutes and this was the version premiered in London in August 1963. The film eventually broke even by the end of the 1960s, by which time Fox had been saved by the spectacular success of its production of *The Sound of Music*.

Whatever Wanger's original intentions for the film, it was publicized as 'the spectacle of spectacles' and Mankiewicz in his script followed the lead of Shaw in the first part and of Shakespeare in the second. In Part One, Caesar arrives in Alexandria, restores Cleopatra to the throne, falls in love with her and fathers her son Caesarion. It is to Caesar that she lays out her political blueprint for the creation of 'one world, one nation, one people, living in peace' to be achieved by the alliance of Rome and Egypt. But, returning to Rome to secure his control over the empire, Caesar is assassinated and Cleopatra is forced to retreat to Egypt. In Part Two, Antony, arriving in Egypt, falls totally under her spell, challenges Octavian for control of the empire, loses and commits suicide, followed to the grave by Cleopatra.

The film in the four-hour version, which is all that currently survives, remains one of the most sumptuous in Hollywood's history, deservedly winning Oscars for photography, art direction, costume design and special effects. The two great set pieces remain boldly and extravagantly memorable. The first is Cleopatra's ceremonial entry into Rome through the arch of Constantine (which was not in fact built until 350 years later). A tumult of colour and movement, it features dancers, tumblers, streamers, drummers, clouds of coloured smoke, a pyramid full of doves, a rain of gold leaf, and eventually Cleopatra herself and her son seated on an enormous Sphinx hauled by Nubian slaves. 'Nothing like this has come to Rome since Romulus and Remus' says Antony with some justice. The second sequence has Cleopatra's golden barge, wreathed in incense, sailing to Tarsus, and hosting a feast with a parade of exotic roasted birds and animals and a wild Bacchanalian dance. Mankiewicz ignored the aural paradigm, mingling Britons and Americans on both sides.

Elizabeth Taylor, though beautiful, is wholly inadequate vocally, emotionally and dramatically and this remains a continual drawback. But the first half of the film is saved by Rex Harrison's very Shaw-like Caesar, wise, witty and authorita-tive, and by Mankiewicz's literate and epigrammatic script which explores his political cunning and allows him to deliver with relish such lines as 'How dare you, the descendant of generations of inbred, incestuous mental defectives, call me a barbarian.' But there is also a vulnerable side to Caesar which is well developed (his epilepsy and fear of public humiliation, his consciousness of ageing and his desire for a son). Harrison was deservedly nominated for a best actor Oscar but lost out to Sidney Poitier.

Part Two is much less satisfying than Part One. Antony is an unattractive character, a self-pitying drunk, oppressed by feelings of inferiority to Caesar. Burton and Taylor were acting in two entirely different registers, she, a suburban American housewife, alternately simpering and shrewish; he strutting and ranting in best English stage melodrama style.

The British newspaper critics were divided on the film. Some remained stubbornly unimpressed: 'downright dull' (The Times, 31 July 1963), 'a total failure' (the Guardian, 31 July 1963), 'a ponderous vast artistic nullity' (The Spectator, 9 August 1963). Others, while agreeing that it was not a great film, found something to praise – the spectacle, the visuals, the set pieces – with the Daily Express (31 July 1963) calling it 'a must-see', the Daily Herald (31 July 1963) 'a great spectacle' and the People (4 August 1963) 'superbly exciting'.

Rex Harrison was almost universally praised and many thought that, when he died, so did the film. Both Taylor and Burton were found wanting. The Daily Herald thought her 'gorgeous [...] but shrill and monotonous', the Daily Mail (31 July 1963), 'a petulant Americanized impression of Vivien Leigh', the New Statesman (2 August 1963), 'monotony in a slit skirt', The Times, 'a mouse of a performance'. As for Burton, the *Sunday Telegraph* (4 August 1963) called his Antony 'a sad waste of a major talent', the *People* thought him 'quite ordinary', the *Sunday Express* (4 August 1963) 'largely window dressing' and the *Evening Standard* (31 July 1963) quite straightforwardly 'a bore'.

6

The Ancient World Revival

For 35 years, following the commercial disaster of *Fall of the Roman Empire*, Hollywood cinema steered clear of the Ancient World. The occasional attempt to revive the genre met with instant box-office failure. A 1970 remake of Shakespeare's *Julius Caesar*, shot in colour and featuring large-scale battle scenes (filmed in Spain), rioting mobs and flashy dream sequences, failed to match the definitive 1953 version. Directed by the experienced television director Stuart Burge, it starred Charlton Heston, who was a capable Mark Antony without effacing memories of Brando, and John Gielgud who was a much more successful Julius Caesar than Louis Calhern, stubborn, proud and dignified. But the film was sunk by a disastrously miscast Jason Robards as Brutus, barely turning in a performance at all, and an inexplicably bearded and neither 'lean' nor 'hungry' Cassius from Richard Johnson, enthusiastically hamming, perhaps to compensate for Robards' non-performance.

Julius Caesar was at least a serious effort. *Caligula* (1979) was a misbegotten pornographic farrago. In 1975 Gore Vidal signed a contract with Felix Cinematographica of Rome to write a biopic to be called *Gore Vidal's Caligula*. He intended it to be a warning to America as a modern empire of the danger it ran of succumbing to decadence and tyranny like imperial Rome. Suetonius' *Lives of the Caesars* was a favourite book of Vidal's and in 1961 he had published an essay on it, writing of Suetonius that 'in holding up a mirror to those Caesars of diverting legend, [he] reflects not only on them but on ourselves: half-tamed creatures whose great moral task is to hold in balance the angel and the monster within – for we are both – and to ignore this duality is to invite disaster'.[1] The film, however, turned out to be a gleeful celebration of decadence and tyranny, director Tinto Brass apparently intending a baroque extravaganza akin to Fellini's *Satyricon* (1969). Producer Bob Guccione, the proprietor of *Penthouse* magazine who was financing the film, insisted on more and more hardcore sex scenes and when Brass balked at this, he was removed from the film and Guccione shot them himself and inserted them into the film. Eventually both Vidal and Brass had their names taken off it. Two years in the making and shot at Dear Studios, Rome, it was eventually released in 1979. A dramatization of all the most scurrilous stories in Suetonius, it proved to be at 150 minutes a tediously prolonged and ultimately wearisome succession of sex scenes, orgies, rape, incest, buggery, necrophilia, fellatio and lesbian couplings. It said more about the relaxation of censorship rules after the permissive 1960s than about the Roman Empire. But it was leant a spurious respectability by a quartet of eminent British actors (Malcolm McDowell as Caligula, Peter O'Toole as Tiberius, Helen Mirren as Caesonia, John Gielgud as Nerva) who should have known better. McDowell capered around in a series of skimpy chiffon outfits alternately shouting and cackling. O'Toole, wearing what looked like a knitted tea-cosy, hammed it up shamelessly as the decrepit 77-year-old Tiberius and Gielgud's Nerva cut his wrists half an hour into the film. To add insult to injury, this tawdry effort had the effrontery to appropriate Prokofiev (*Romeo and Juliet*) and Khachaturian (*Spartacus*) scores for its soundtrack.[2]

Sian Phillips, who was at the time starring in the BBC television series *I, Claudius* which covered the same period as *Caligula*, visited her then husband, Peter O'Toole, on the set of the film and recalled the experience in her autobiography:

> John Gielgud stood there looking grand and pretending not to notice that the girls flanking him were bare-breasted and carrying dildos. In the trailer, Helen Mirren and Malcolm McDowell were beyond caring and very funny about their experiences. O'Toole was playing Tiberius and as I watched, he nearly drowned, swimming in a huge red robe, surrounded by up-to-no-good under-age boys […] It was so strange to leave the set of *I, Claudius* (which can't have cost much), which had been researched, old BBC-style, for a year before shooting began and to walk on to this huge set with all that *Penthouse* money behind it and where the actors were paid vastly more than any of us at home and to see it all going horribly wrong. The costumes and make-up and sets were a mess and as for the script […] I said nothing.[3]

An attempt to revive the Biblical epic came in 1985 with Paramount Pictures' *King David*, directed by Bruce Beresford and starring Richard Gere. It might better have been titled *Scenes from the Life of King David* as it essentially compressed material from several previous films (*David and Bathsheba*, *David and Goliath*, *Saul and David*) into two hours, requiring a narrator to bridge the gaps in the narrative. Handsomely photographed and effectively staged, it never cohered or developed satisfactorily. Contemporary critics ridiculed the scene in which David danced his way into Jerusalem and audiences were unenthusiastic, despite good work from Edward Woodward as a haunted, brooding Saul and a distinguished British supporting cast, among them Denis Quilley as the prophet Samuel, John Castle as Abner and Tim Woodward as Joab.

It was television which came to the aid of the Ancient World and two notable and successful series inaugurated a cycle of small-screen epics, *I, Claudius* and *Jesus of Nazareth*. An attempt to film *I, Claudius* in the 1930s had famously failed. There seems little doubt that Alexander Korda's *I, Claudius* would have been a notable addition to the ranks of the Roman epic if it had been completed. The story of its ill-fated progress was told in a notable BBC television documentary, *The Epic That Never Was* (1965), written and produced by Bill Duncalf and narrated by Dirk Bogarde. It combined interviews with the surviving participants and scenes from the surviving footage. Robert Graves, the poet and novelist revealed that he decided to tell the story of the Emperor Claudius in order to pay off his debts. Inspired by the works of Suetonius and Tacitus, he wrote two novels *I, Claudius* and *Claudius the God*, in the form of a memoir written by the Emperor himself. He made £8,000 from the venture, twice what he had hoped. Korda, in search of a new vehicle for his contract star Charles Laughton, purchased the film rights to the novels and Graves himself wrote a screenplay. But this was set aside and a script was put together in typical Hollywood fashion by three writers (Carl Zuckmayer, Lester Cohen and Lajos Biro). Korda assembled a notable production team: the ace cinematographer Georges Perinal, his brother Vincent Korda as set designer, Agnes de Mille as choreographer, and a cast, headed by Laughton as Claudius, Merle Oberon as Messalina, Flora Robson as the Empress Livia and Emlyn Williams as Caligula. Robson and Oberon were also under contract to Korda and Williams, who had recently been starring as a psychopathic killer in his own hit play *Night Must Fall*, must have seemed an ideal choice. Other roles were to be filled by other Korda regulars: John Clements (Valens), Robert Newton (Cassius Chaerea), Roy Emerton (Centurion), Allan Jeayes (Doctor) with F. Forbes Robertson as Tiberius and Bruce Winston as Asiaticus. For director, Korda selected and engaged Josef von Sternberg. Budgeted at £120,000, the film began shooting at Denham Studios on 15 February 1937. Sternberg was very happy with his sets: 'Thanks to the talents of Vincent Korda, a fine painter and superb artist, a Rome had been conjured out of pasteboard and plaster that was a joy to behold.'[4]

Sternberg, like so many film-makers tackling the Roman Empire, saw it not just as a recreation of history but as a commentary on the present. He recalled in his autobiography that he planned 'not only to bring to life an old empire and to depict the arrogance and decay of its civilization but to hold it up as a mirror to our own tottering values and to investigate the diseased roots of excessive ambition'.[5] Absolute historical authenticity was not a priority for Sternberg, a director with a notable visual sense which he applied to the imagery of Ancient Rome. Costume designer John Armstrong recalled in the BBC documentary that when he reported to Sternberg that in Ancient Rome there were six vestal virgins and they were chastely covered from head to toe, Sternberg replied: 'I want 60 and I want them naked'. The result was 60 beautiful maidens, scantily draped in diaphanous gauze and holding tapers. 'It looked lovely but it had nothing to do with Roman religion' commented Armstrong accurately.

The official synopsis of the film reveals that it was a merger of the two novels, with Claudius surviving Caligula's reign of terror, marrying Messalina, becoming emperor on Caligula's assassination, conquering Britain, uncovering evidence of Messalina's infidelity, signing her death warrant and being proclaimed a god in his own lifetime.[6]

The documentary revealed that Laughton had been deeply unhappy, unable to find the key to his character and causing long delays as he switched from one scene to another in order to achieve an interpretation. He got little help from his director. In the documentary Emlyn Williams recalled that what Laughton needed most was reassurance; 'he needed sun and all he got was frost'. Sternberg recorded his exasperation with the actor in his autobiography.[7] Eventually, after playing a record of the abdication speech of King Edward VIII, Laughton discovered the key he wanted and was able to begin to develop his performance. But then on 16 March 1937, a month into shooting, Merle Oberon was involved in a car accident and Korda took the opportunity to close down the production and to pocket £80,000 in insurance money. Emlyn Williams believed that the accident was a relief to Korda and he was anxious to be rid of the troubled production. He is almost certainly right. Two-thirds of the budget had been spent and less than a third of the film had been completed and Korda, who had had a succession of box-office failures and had other productions going over-budget, was in serious financial difficulties.[8]

But the film was even more troubled than was revealed in Duncalf's documentary. Sternberg, who had been seriously ill, was under considerable personal stress as, following the termination of his cinematic partnership with Marlene Dietrich and a string of box-office failures, his Hollywood career was in jeopardy. He had a nervous breakdown immediately after the cancellation of the film. Flora Robson, then in her thirties, was unhappy about being continually cast as old women. The 80-year-old Empress Livia followed on from her roles as the ageing Empress Elizabeth of Russia (*The Rise of Catherine the Great*) and Queen Elizabeth I of England (*Fire Over England*). Merle Oberon, who in the documentary claimed that Korda was building the film around her, was actually reluctant to return from Hollywood where she had enjoyed box-office success in *The Dark Angel* and wanted to develop her career with producer Sam Goldwyn. She was never happy with her role and, when Korda suggested closing the production until she recovered, she became hysterical and refused to continue. Her injuries were not as serious as the publicity suggested and she had actually shot comparatively few scenes and could easily have been replaced. Indeed Korda actually contacted Claudette Colbert (who had played Empress Poppaea in *Sign of the Cross*) about coming over from Hollywood to play Messalina. But she was not available and Korda decided on closure.[9]

The question remains: how good is the footage? About 20 minutes of completed footage remains: scenes including the deification of Augustus; Caligula in the Senate making his horse a consul; Claudius on his farm being arrested at

Caligula's orders; Claudius' interview with Caligula when Caligula announces he has become a god; Caligula condemning Claudius to marry Messalina; Claudius' speech to the Senate on accepting the throne. Scholars who have seen this footage (Simon Callow, Charles Drazin, Karol Kulik among them) believe that if completed it would have been a great film. Dirk Bogarde pronounced Claudius' Senate speech 'one of the most beautiful and powerful speeches I've ever seen on the screen'. John Baxter is a dissenting voice: 'none of the existing material indicates that *I, Claudius* would have been more than an interesting failure'.[10] My own judgement coincides with the majority. We have enough footage to regret that we were denied what would have been at least two memorable performances: Laughton's Claudius and Emlyn Williams' deliciously decadent Caligula, not to mention Vincent Korda's superb sets and Sternberg's memorable visuals. But the production's failure convinced Robert Graves that Claudius did not want to be seen on the screen and this gave rise to the legend of a curse, a curse that came to haunt the television production of *I, Claudius*.

When *I, Claudius* came to television in 1977, produced by the BBC in conjunction with London Films, who still held the rights to the novels, it did so in 13 episodes, adapted from the two Graves novels by Jack Pulman and covering the life of the Emperor Claudius from the cradle to the grave. Initially the actors were unsure of what was required of them as Herbert Wise, the director, told them he did not want the series to have the respectful, discreet BBC classic-serial style. He urged them to relish the villainy and not seek for psychological motivation. They soon got into the spirit of it when Pulman indicated that he saw it as a black comedy version of the Mafia, and Wise, pointing to the dominant and ambitious mothers, described it as 'a Jewish family comedy'. Christopher Biggins, who played Nero in the final episode, called it 'a Roman *Coronation Street*'.

There are certainly elements of soap opera in it. As Hilary Kingsley wrote on the soap-opera genre:

> Problems, of course, are soap's lifeblood. All drama is conflict; conflict causes problems. In soap the problems must be something like we have experienced ourselves, or problems we can imagine having.[11]

She defined the themes of soap opera as 'infidelity, money problems, paternity uncertainty, childlessness, loneliness, betrayal, worry about loved ones who have gone off to some other part of the world'. All these themes appeared in *I, Claudius*. But it was principally about sex and power. In succession, Livia schemes to gain power for her son Tiberius, Sejanus power for himself, Caligula to gain not only political power but divine power, Agrippinilla to gain the throne for her son Nero. They were prepared to eliminate anyone who stood in their way. On the other hand, a procession of promiscuous hussies (Julia, Livilla, Messalina) betray their husbands and indulge in a succession of flagrant adulteries. In classic soap-opera manner, the series was dominated by strong-willed matriarchs often in conflict with each other and this led in particular to notable performances from Sian Phillips as the ruthlessly manipulative Livia and Margaret Tyzack as the severely moralistic Antonia. Among the men, George Baker scored as the gloweringly resentful Tiberius, John Hurt as the dissolute Caligula and in particular Derek Jacobi as the lame and stammering Claudius who beneath a shambling, apparently half-witted exterior concealed a shrewd mind and a principled integrity. The performance earned Jacobi a British Academy award. The filming schedule was demanding, ten days' rehearsal and two days' shooting for each episode. Several of the continuing characters (notably Livia, Tiberius and Claudius) had to age during the course of the series by some 60 years. They ended up swathed in layers of latex to give them an elderly appearance, necessitating eventually nine hours in the make-up chair. The style adopted was totally opposite to the expansiveness of the Hollywood epic. The series was shot entirely in the studio, making much use of close-ups. Scenes set in the arena, for example, focused on the imperial box with sound effects representing the crowd and the gladiatorial conflicts. Art director Tim Harvey constructed his sets in sections which could be moved round and combined into different formations and only a handful of extras was used. But audiences were riveted by the plotting and scheming, the sexual shenanigans and the vivid interpersonal relationships. When the series first aired on television, the critics were lukewarm, but when it became a hit with the public, they re-evaluated it and began praising it. The production team congratulated themselves that they had apparently avoided the curse that Graves believed Claudius had placed on the book. But they were given pause for thought when the producer Martin Lisemore was killed in a car crash soon after the series was shown and the writer Jack Pulman died of a heart attack at the early age of 52.[12]

I, Claudius' blend of melodrama, gossip and soap opera was so successful that it banished the memory of the historically superior and far more accurate six-part series *The Caesars*, produced by Granada in black and white and covering the period from the last years of Augustus to the accession of Claudius. Scripted by Philip Mackie and directed by Derek Bennett, it was originally transmitted between 22 September and 27 October 1968 to critical acclaim. Bennett pioneered the technique repeated in *I, Claudius* of eschewing spectacle, shooting entirely in the studio and depending much on close-ups to explore the inter-personal relationships. Mackie's script, intelligent, literate and sinewy, was an impressive study of realpolitik which explored the dangers of absolute monarchy from the police state of Tiberius to Caligula's reign of terror. He outlined the manoeuvrings and machinations of imperial power plays with impressive clarity and understanding. As such, it was part of the fascination of 1960s' and 1970s' television with power politics, whether in the contemporary board room (*The*

Power Game, The Troubleshooters) or in British history (*The First Churchills, The Pallisers*). The multi-episode format permitted the detailed exploration of the ruthless and labyrinthine dynamics of politics. Long unseen, its recent revival on DVD proves it to be every bit as good as was claimed at the time.

Among the cast of *The Caesars*, André Morell and Freddie Jones gave two of the most outstanding performances in the history of television drama. Morell's brooding, sardonic, austere and mistrustful Tiberius was portrayed as an emperor reluctantly shouldering the burden of empire and endeavouring to secure the succession to ensure political stability and to maintain the peace without entanglement in foreign wars. It was an altogether richer and more complex reading of Tiberius than George Baker's admittedly more vivid but essentially single note Gravesian caricature in *I, Claudius*. Freddie Jones' stammering, crippled, shrewd Claudius, who inherits the throne in the end, matched Jacobi's performance and like Jacobi was recognized by an award (at the 1969 Monte Carlo Television Festival). But these two notable performances were surrounded by a galaxy of good acting, both male and female. Among the men, Ralph Bates' deranged Caligula, Barrie Ingham's scheming Sejanus, Jerome Willis' power-hungry Macro and Gerald Harper's canny Lucius Vitellius all scored. They were matched by a series of strong, calculating, power-hungry female characters, notably Sonia Dresdel's Livia, Caroline Blakiston's Agrippina, Nicola Pagett's Messalina and Barbara Murray's Caesonia.

The idea of a television life of Christ originated with three Italian producers. But for such a huge undertaking they needed a co-production partner and approached British television mogul Lew Grade of ITC. Lew Grade had previously entered into a co-production deal with RAI, the Italian television network, to produce a six-hour television mini-series, *Moses the Lawgiver*. It was assigned a $6 million budget and secured the services of Burt Lancaster for his first major television role. His son William Lancaster played the younger Moses in the first episode. Lancaster, who had hitherto resisted the lure of television, was intrigued by the Anthony Burgess script, which depicted Moses as someone who questioned and battled with God rather than heroically carrying out his instructions. Director Gianfranco de Bosio eschewed De Mille-style spectacle and the customary trappings of the epic, opting instead for semi-documentary realism. But the result, shot on location in Israel and completed at Cinecittà Studios in Rome, emerged as drab, lifeless and ultimately boring. Nevertheless, when shown on Italian television, it secured the largest-ever audience (23 million viewers) and when shown in America between 21 June and 2 August 1975 it secured an average audience of 25 million for each episode, but there was a drastic falling off in numbers after the initial episodes as audiences understandably lost interest. Cut down to a 141-minute feature, it was released to British cinemas, a decision which enraged both Burgess and Lancaster. Even in the reduced form, it left one longing for De Mille. Officially, however, it had been a success and Grade eagerly accepted the idea of participating in the production of a life of Christ.

Jesus of Nazareth was to become a television 'event'. Running six and a half hours and first shown over Easter 1977, Part One on 3 April and Part Two on 10 April, it had cost $18 million to produce, making it the most expensive television film to date. Rerun in 1979, it was divided into four parts and subsequently cut down to four and a half hours to make a single feature, eliminating in the process the entire performances of Claudia Cardinale and Ralph Richardson.

The Italian producers' initial idea of hiring Ingmar Bergman to direct the film collapsed when his proposed treatment included Jesus and Mary Magdalene becoming lovers. Grade pressed for Franco Zeffirelli who was a devout Catholic ('I believe totally in the teachings of the Church') and had recently directed a film on the life of St Francis of Assissi.[13] Initially reluctant, Zeffirelli was completely won over by Grade, a Jew, 'talking persuasively of the need to reaffirm Christian values in a time of moral laxity'. Grade's only condition was that the film should be acceptable to all Christian denominations. Where Zeffirelli's approach was to be novel was in his stress on Jesus' Jewishness. He wrote in his autobiography:

> If there was to be any interpretation it would be more backward-looking than fashionably contemporary [...] The point I wanted to make most evident was that Christ was a Jew, a prophet who grew out of the cultural, social and historical background of the Israel of his time, with its farms and small villages, each with its cramped little synagogue; an Israel occupied by an arrogant enemy and always smouldering on the edge of civil disorder. More than that, Christ's words had to be seen as a continuation and fulfilment of centuries of Jewish religious teaching.[14]

Zeffirelli had been inspired by the declaration in 1965 of Pope Paul VI, *Nostra Aetate*, acquitting the Jews as a race of responsibility for the death of Christ ('what happened in His Passion cannot be charged against all of the Jews, without distinction, then alive, nor against the Jews of today').[15]

For visual inspiration, Zeffirelli turned regularly to Old Master paintings of the Gospel stories. Cinematically, he turned not to Hollywood epics but to the 1936 film *Golgotha*, 'the spare, beautiful film by the French director Julien Duvivier, shot [...] entirely on location in Provence'.[16] This confirmed for him the vital importance of location and having scouted and rejected Israel, he found what he wanted in the form of villages, ancient buildings and landscape in Morocco and Tunisia, where the film was eventually shot. For one important sequence he drew on his own experience. The Crucifixion was not inspired by the work of Renaissance artists, as so often in films, but his own wartime memory of seeing the bodies of young Italian partisans hanged on trees by the Nazis and the reactions of their relatives to the sight.[17]

Zeffirelli had decided, like George Stevens, to recruit a cast of well-known stars to play character parts. The agreement of Laurence Olivier, whom Zeffirelli had directed on stage, to play the comparatively small role of Nicodemus, for a comparatively small fee, was the signal for many major stars to join the project. It was agreed that all would be paid the same $30,000 a week with no exceptions or variations. The result was some memorable cameos from Anne Bancroft (Mary Magdalene), Michael York (John the Baptist), Christopher Plummer (Herod Antipas), Peter Ustinov (Herod the Great), James Mason (Joseph of Arimathea), Ralph Richardson (Simeon) and Olivier himself. Zeffirelli reversed the 'aural paradigm' by having the leading Romans played by American actors (Rod Steiger as Pilate, Ernest Borgnine as the Centurion, Tony Lo Bianco as Quintilius).

As Christ, Zeffirelli cast Robert Powell. Powell was being screen-tested for Judas (a part eventually capably played by Ian McShane). But Zeffirelli saw in him the quality he wanted in his Christ. Powell was a blue-eyed, Pre-Raphaelite Christ in the tradition of H.B. Warner and Jeffrey Hunter. But he gave an inspired and inspiring performance. This can be seen, for example, in the conviction with which he preaches the Sermon on the Mount and the parable of the Prodigal Son, delivered in the house of a despised tax collector Matthew (later an apostle) and pointedly directed at those disapproving of his presence there. Zeffirelli recorded:

> I shall never tire of saying how wonderful Robert Powell was. How rewarding it was to work with someone so determined to ensure that every inflection was true to what must surely be the most terrifying role any actor could play. It became clear that something more than acting was required: a deeper personal commitment was needed, and Robert gave it.[18]

This commitment stretched to his insisting on carrying a heavy wooden beam for the cross rather than a fake one and his genuine suffering when strapped to the cross.

The script was provided by Anthony Burgess. Zeffirelli called it 'a tour de force. Anthony has an amazing, almost sponge-like capacity to absorb what he reads and he had obviously drawn on a wealth of sources, Biblical and Rabbinical, to weld the sometimes patchy history that the apostles have left us into a homogeneous story.'[19] But Zeffirelli disliked the vernacular dialogue that Burgess had given to Jesus and the disciples. So with Suso Cecchi d'Amico and Emilio Gennarini he reworked the dialogue, often using paraphrases of the Authorized Version of the Bible which will have awoken many echoes in the minds of his English-speaking viewers.

The result of Zeffirelli's labours was an absorbing and compelling six hours of television, visually, intellectually and emotionally gripping. It fully emphasized Jesus' Jewish background with the depiction of the betrothal and marriage of Mary and Joseph, the circumcision of Jesus, his bar mitzvah, the sermons in the synagogue and the rituals in the Temple. But Catholicism was also present in the idealization of the Virgin Mary and the prominence accorded to Peter. Many of the familiar Gospel stories were recreated but, despite the six and a half hours, some important episodes were omitted (Jesus walking on the water, the Temptation in the wilderness, the wedding at Cana, the encounters with the lepers). There are also inventions. Judas is tricked into betraying Christ by the fictitious Zerah, a temple scribe anxious to stamp out a movement that challenges the supremacy of the Priesthood. Barabbas is made a member of the Zealots, the Jewish Resistance movement, who wants to kill Herod Antipas and to rise up against the Romans, his gospel of violence being explicitly rejected by Jesus. But it is Barabbas' followers in the crowd who intimidate them into calling for Barabbas when Pilate offers them the choice of Jesus or Barabbas as a freed prisoner.[20]

When the film was shown on television, it was praised by the Pope and watched by 80 per cent of the Italian population. In America, 50 per cent of television viewers watched it.[21] How are we to account for the success of a religious epic on television compared to the failure of religious epics in the cinema? The answer lies in the nature of the audience. Where cinema films were now aimed mainly at an audience of under-30s, television was geared to a cross-class all-age audience. In 1988, pollster George Gallup reported that his surveys revealed that 'levels of religious belief and practice in the US are extraordinarily high. For example, the large majority of Americans believe in a personal God [...] believe their prayers are answered and say that religion is either "very" or "fairly" important in their lives. In fact, only four per cent of Americans are totally "nonreligious".'[22] Whereas by the last decades of the twentieth century, only 10 per cent of the British population were regular churchgoers, in America the figure was nearer to 50 per cent. These constituted the core of the viewership for *Jesus of Nazareth*.

But the success of both *Jesus of Nazareth* and *I, Claudius*, a hit on the American Public Broadcasting System, led producers to embark on a series of three-, four- and five-hour Ancient World epics made specifically for television. Many of the great cinema epics were remade for the small screen. But almost none of them came near to eclipsing the achievements of their big-screen predecessors.

Many of these made-for-television Ancient World films were shot in Europe, often with beautiful but bland and forgettable American leads, supporting casts of reliable British character actors, but none of the gusto or visual distinction of their cinema predecessors. Visually bland, dramatically insert, tediously protracted, it was as if the extra length afforded to film-makers in these six-hour-plus extravaganzas had the effect of deadening the imagination.

Another weakness of many of these films was the language. Howard Hawks had famously claimed that his film *Land of the Pharaoh* failed because he did not know how a Pharaoh spoke. As L.P. Hartley wrote: 'The past is a foreign country. They do things differently there.' That included the way they spoke. In the nineteenth century, historical novelists used a consciously archaic form of speech to convey a sense of distance from the present. For example, the villainous priest Arbaces in Bulwer-Lytton's *The Last Days of Pompeii* tells the heroine Ione: 'Maiden, thy suit hath touched me – I will minister to thy will. Listen to me [...] At the base of Vesuvius, less than a league from the city, there dwells a powerful witch; beneath the rank dews of the new moon, she has gathered the herbs which possess the virtue to chain Love in eternal fetters. Her art can bring thy lover to thy feet.' Needless to say not a line from the original novel survived into the 1984 television adaptation. Although it had the virtue of conveying a sense of otherness, by the late twentieth century it was simply too strange to preserve. Historical novelists of the 1950s and 1960s, however, remained conscious of the problem and the best of them – Mary Renault, Rosemary Sutcliff, Henry Treece, Mary Ray – wrote in an English that avoided clichés and modern slang and conveyed otherness while remaining comprehensible and not alienating the reader. The writers of television adaptations frequently did not bother, with the result that, whatever the era and whatever the culture, characters tended to talk like late-twentieth-century Californians. The worst offenders in this regard were the popular 1990s' television series, *Hercules: the Legendary Journeys* and *Xena: Warrior Princess*, extraordinary mélanges of martial arts, mythology and monsters, filmed in New Zealand. The introductory statement in the *Hercules* series: 'This is a story of a long time ago, a time of myth and legend' is rather negated by the absolutely contemporary language of the characters, with Hercules asking Jason after the Golden Fleece has been recovered: 'Is everything okay, Jason?' or an Amazon warrior explaining having hit the target with a javelin, 'Just lucky, I guess' or Hercules replying to the god Zeus sending him on a dangerous mission 'You've got to be kidding'. In *Xena*, where the heroine is given a sidekick with the ludicrously unclassical name of Gabrielle, characters say things like 'Get off my back', 'I feel your pain', 'I will always be there for you', 'She's crazy about me', 'You look great', and 'Why don't you stick around'. This is pure and unforgivable laziness: scriptwriters who cannot be bothered to find an idiom that is both comprehensible to a present-day audience and able to convey a sense of pastness. It has the effect of convincing audiences that historical or mythological characters are merely contemporary Americans in fancy dress.

A good example of how language could be used to convey meaning without resorting to modern slang or colloquialisms is the excellent series of Biblical films, produced for the Turner network by a consortium of film and television companies, principally Italian. They frequently drew directly on the Authorized Version of the Bible, simplifying and paraphrasing where necessary in the interests of clarity and ease of communication with a modern audience. In this way, we are spared such potential horrors as 'Have a nice day, Jacob', 'Listen up, Israelites' and 'No way, Moses'.

These films, among them *Abraham* (1993), *Jacob* (1994), *Joseph* (1995), *Moses* (1995), *Samson and Delilah* (1997), *David* (1997), *Solomon* (1997), *Jeremiah* (1998) and *Esther* (1998), largely eschewed the trappings of the Hollywood Ancient World epic: large-scale battles, hordes of extras, melodramatic plots and special effects; a notable exception to this being the spectacular destruction of the temple of Dagon by Samson. They opted instead for naturalism in settings and acting and absolute fidelity to the Old Testament texts. Shot on location at Ourzazate in Morocco, they made full use of the desert wastes, the barren hills, the fast-flowing rivers and the fertile oases to provide a visually appropriate setting for the stories. They also at times had the feel of ethnographic documentaries as they depicted Oriental religious rituals, markets, weddings, funerals, banquets, desert encampments, sheepherding and the rigours of the nomadic life. They were bound together by the running themes of the struggle between monotheism and polytheism, the nature of the relationship between the individual and God and the emergence of the people and later the state of Israel. They boasted a succession of stellar performances from major Hollywood actors (Richard Harris as Abraham, Ben Kingsley as Moses, Matthew Modine as Jacob, F. Murray Abraham as Mordecai, Ben Cross as Solomon), backed by a contingent of internationally known continental stars (Max von Sydow, Klaus Maria Brandauer, Maximilian Schell, Franco Nero, Irene Papas, Anouk Aimée, Jürgen Prochnow) and a raft of top British actors (Michael Gambon, Diana Rigg, Daniel Massey, David Suchet, Jonathan Pryce, Oliver Reed, Sean Bean, Christopher Lee and Sir John Gielgud as the voice of God). The series also attracted some notable directors, among them Nicolas Roeg, Peter Hall and Roger Young, who succeeded in producing some of the most faithful adaptations of the key stories from the Bible ever made.

Anyone who doubts the magnitude of the achievement of the 1951 film *Quo Vadis* needs only to look at the 1985 made-for-television mini-series remake. Produced by the Italian television company RAI, in association with television stations in France, Germany, Spain and Britain, it is an interminable, slow and dreary six and a half hour ordeal. It is also hopelessly miscast, with Klaus Maria Brandauer far too sane and intelligent to persuade as the deluded and posturing Nero, Frederick Forrest a wan and unconvincing Petronius, completely lacking the elegance and wit of Leo Genn, and Francesco Quinn (son of Anthony) an implausibly wimpish Marcus Vinicius who makes you regret the absence of Robert Taylor.

Similarly the 1984 made-for-television *Samson and Delilah*, shot on location in Mexico, wholly lacks the scale, style and magnificence of De Mille's version. Newcomer Antony Hamilton portrays Samson as a muscle-bound American college athlete and Belinda Bauer is a very twentieth-century all-American temptress. It is notable only for a guest appearance by the original Samson, Victor Mature, understandably scowling throughout, in the role of Samson's father Manoah.

Something altogether different was being attempted in the six-hour Universal Pictures' mini-series *Masada* (1980), which was filmed on location in Israel. Recounting the story of the siege and eventual capture in AD 73 of Masada, the last remaining Jewish stronghold resisting the Roman occupation of Judaea, it emerged as slow, talky, portentous Zionist propaganda. The Jewish War was recast at one level as an analogue of Zionist resistance to the British mandate in Palestine and at another of the current status of Israel, surrounded on all sides by enemies. The Jews, all played by Americans, were sanctimonious, one-dimensionally heroic freedom-fighters, their leader Eleazar Ben Yair (Peter Strauss), echoing Ben-Hur when he declared: 'We want our freedom back. We want our country back.' Jewish guerrillas, ambushing Roman patrols and poisoning wells, came over as equivalents of the Irgun and Stern gangs who fought the British troops in Palestine. The Romans, all played by British actors, veered between negotiation and aggression as they sought to solve the Jewish problem. It solved itself when the defenders of Masada committed mass suicide. The contemporary parallels were underlined by the fact that the Zealot Messiah calling for all-out war with the Romans was named Menachem and the opposition spokesman within Masada, who called for negotiation with the enemy rather than conflict, was named Shimon, allusions surely to the hardline right-wing Israeli leader Menachem Begin and his more moderate left-wing opposite number Shimon Peres.

The Romans were considerably more complex and interesting than their Jewish opponents. Peter O'Toole dominated proceedings with a barnstorming performance as the war-weary, battle-scarred, larger than life Roman commander Flavius Silva. There was excellent support from Timothy West as the canny Emperor Vespasian, walking a political tightrope as he tried to negotiate factional rivalries in Rome and Anthony Quayle, looking and sounding exactly right as the veteran siegemaster Rubrius Gallus. They all deserved to be in a better film than this one with its anachronistic dialogue, scrappily staged action scenes and anonymous direction (Boris Sagal). In 1981 it was cut from six hours to two and released as a feature film to British cinemas under the title *The Antagonists*. Even then it still seemed too long.

Andrei Konchalovsky's *The Odyssey* (1997), shot on photogenic locations in Turkey and Malta, was a respectful but on the whole uninspired three-hour retelling of the principal episodes from Homer. Armand Assante as Odysseus headed a cast of mixed British, American, Greek and Italian actors. It was enlivened by a visit to the underworld, though one critic disapprovingly likened the sequence to 'a theme-park boat-ride through a fiery Christian hellish inferno' rather than 'the sobering gloom of the Homeric Land of the Dead'.[23]

Rather better than any of these productions was the 1984 television version of *The Last Days of Pompeii*, directed by Peter Hunt. It returned for the first time since the nineteenth century to Bulwer-Lytton's narrative. The Victorian multiplot novel was ideal material for extended television adaptation. Screenwriter Carmen Culver took the central themes of Lytton (the Arbaces/Glaucus/Ione triangle, the love of the blind girl Nydia, the fate of Apaecides (here renamed Antonius)), and added several more. Lydon the gladiator, a minor character killed off in the book, became a major character, in love with Nydia the flowergirl (and they both survive the eruption). Marcus the arena-manager was borrowed from the 1935 film version. Greater prominence, in line with Hollywood epic conventions, was accorded to gladiators and Christians than in Lytton's novel. Handsome sets, good special effects, satisfying spectacle and an all-star cast (Nicholas Clay as a dashing Glaucus, Franco Nero as a sinister Arbaces, Ernest Borgnine as a grizzled gladiator, Laurence Olivier and Anthony Quayle as noble Romans and Benedict Taylor as the idealistic young priest who turns Christian) combined to make this one of the more acceptable television Ancient World epics.

In 2000 a three-hour television epic, *Attila the Hun*, was produced for American cable television. Directed by Dick Lowry and written by Robert Cochran, it charted the rise to power of Attila, who unites the Huns and eventually confronts the Roman Empire, intercutting it with the career of the Roman general Aetius who sought by all means possible to counter the threat from the Huns. Their careers run in parallel until they eventually face each other in battle. Aetius is victorious and Attila and his horde withdraw. But Attila is then poisoned on his wedding night by a vengeful captive Ildico with whom he has become obsessed and Aetius, now no longer needed by the Empire, is murdered by the Emperor Valentinian.

Attila differed in several respects from the two 1950s' versions of his career, *Attila the Hun* and *Sign of the Pagan*. In the earlier film, Attila was an anti-hero. But in 2000 he was undoubtedly the hero and, as played by Gerard Butler, emerged as a courageous, visionary, virile and just figure. Evidently embarrassed by the Christian element of the story, the film-makers omitted the famous meeting with Pope Leo the Great who persuaded the superstitious Attila to turn back from the gates of Rome. This had formed the dramatic climax of the two previous films. The whole motif of Attila's attacks on churches which had earned him the sinister sobriquet 'the scourge of God' is also omitted. Instead the story is thoroughly paganized, with a prominent role accorded to a diminutive witch prophetess Galen whose powers are genuine and Attila's decision to turn back is prompted by his talisman, the sword of the war god, breaking in battle.

The film displays a cynicism about the power politics of the so-called civilized states. The Western Roman Emperor Valentinian (Reg Rogers) and the Eastern Roman Emperor Theodosius (Tim Curry) are both treacherous and corrupt. There is felt to be something more healthy, honest and straightforward about the Huns, a kind of 'barbarian chic'.

Handsome to look at and taking full advantage of the sweeping Lithuanian landscape, where it was shot, the film boasted excellent battle scenes. But it was seriously flawed by the woeful miscasting of Powers Boothe as Aetius, hopelessly unconvincing and uncharismatic in a role that called out for an actor of equal presence to Butler. It also unforgivably contrived to waste such able British actors as Sian Phillips and Jonathan Hyde in bit parts.

A 2000 television remake of *Jason and Argonauts*, directed by Nick Willing, retold the story of the 1963 film at twice the length and with less than half the charm. It managed to fit in more monsters and – in a sign of the times – a politically correct crew, which included a black Orpheus and a feisty female archer Atalanta. Historian Gideon Nisbet dismissed it as 'notoriously feeble'.[24] That may be an overly harsh judgement but it certainly succeeded in making you nostalgic for the earlier version with its unique Ray Harryhausen creatures.

The most idiotic of these made-for-television Ancient World epics was *Noah's Ark* (1999), directed by John Irvin, scripted by Peter Barnes, and filmed in Australia. Finding the Biblical narrative too short for a three-hour film, Barnes grafted onto the familiar story elements from two other films, *Sodom and Gomorrah* and *Waterworld*. So Noah, his wife and sons, who came across as a typical middle-class American sitcom family, join Lot as the only survivors when God rains down thunderbolts on Sodom and Gomorrah. Later when the ark is afloat on the flooded world, they encounter a cheerful water-borne pedlar who sells them luxury goods and later survive an attack by pirates, led by Lot. The good special effects hardly compensate for the absurdity of the whole venture, which wasted the undoubted talents of two Oscar-winning actors, Jon Voight (as Noah) and F. Murray Abraham (as Lot).

While television catered for churchgoers with *Jesus of Nazareth*, the cinema courted controversy in a new version of the life of Christ. *The Last Temptation of Christ* (1988) was based not on the Gospels but on a 1955 novel by Nikos Kazantzakis. It was scripted by Paul Schrader for director Martin Scorsese and was planned for production in 1983 by Paramount Pictures. Scorsese's idea was not to go 'the traditional route of the American or Italian epic, but to go the other way, and make it intimate, make a character study'. But the religious right in America got wind of the planned film and began to bombard Martin Davis, chairman of Gulf and Western, Paramount's parent company, with letters denouncing the project. Typical of them was this:

> I wish to express my disgust with the upcoming film called *The Last Temptation of Christ*. The material it contains is straight from the pit of hell. We may as well destroy our country with the nuclear bomb as show this film. It's as destructive. If you have any concern for your own peace of mind and the welfare of Gulf and Western industries, you will destroy this film at the earliest possible moment. Such smut is not American.

Davis, concerned to avoid controversy, put pressure on the Paramount studio head, Barry Diller, to drop the film and, when Scorsese requested the addition of $2 million to the proposed budget of $14 million, Diller cancelled the project. After six years of trying to raise the funding elsewhere, and reducing the budget to $7 million, Scorsese secured a distribution deal with Universal and shot the film entirely in Morocco, whose landscape and villages looked more authentically first-century than the originally planned locations in Israel.[25]

A far cry from the serenity of H.B. Warner, Jeffrey Hunter and Robert Powell, Willem Dafoe's Jesus is frankly neurotic. Tormented, self-questioning, hearing voices he cannot interpret, unsure of his mission, he is also torn between the demands of the spirit and the desires of the flesh. He is first seen making crosses for the Romans to use in crucifying their opponents, as a bid to make God hate him. He preaches, performs miracles, drives the money-changers from the temple, is arrested and crucified. It is on the cross that he experiences his last temptation, as he appeals to God to be spared death. A female angel appears, leads him from the cross and allows him to experience a long and full life. He marries Mary Magdalene, has sex with her and after she dies in childbirth, co-habits polygamously with Martha and Mary, the sisters of Lazarus, and fathers children. It was these scenes that most offended the Christian fundamentalists. But when he is on his death bed, Jesus is denounced by Judas for betraying his mission, realizes that the angel was in fact the Devil and prays to be returned to the cross where he does finally die, fulfilling his mission.

The film rings many changes in the Gospel narrative. Lazarus, having been raised from the dead, is murdered by the zealot Saul (Harry Dean Stanton) to undermine Christ's credibility. Later having been converted and renamed Paul, he encounters Jesus who tells him he did not die on the cross and therefore was not resurrected. Paul tells him that this does not matter. He will continue to preach about the death and resurrection of Christ as this is necessary to inspire his followers. Pontius Pilate, played by David Bowie, his English accent conforming to the 'aural paradigm', condemns Jesus to death, saying he is more dangerous than the zealots because of the ideas he is preaching. The most startling transformation is in Judas (Harvey Keitel), who is Jesus' conscience, keeps him true to his mission, reluctantly agrees to betray him to fulfil his destiny and later by denouncing him causes him to return to the cross. Universal Studios were picketed, the businesses of its parent company, MCA, boycotted and there were protests at showings of the film, as the Christian right mobilized against the picture. The result of the controversy, perhaps inevitably, was that the film broke box-office records in Los Angeles during the first weekend of its release.[26] But interest rapidly waned and the domestic gross of $7 million barely covered the cost of promotion and distribution. Universal made an estimated loss of $10 million on the project.[27]

Controversy of a different kind attended the next cinematic interpretation of Jesus, *The Passion of the Christ*. *The Passion of the Christ* (2004) was a personal project of Mel Gibson. He told *The New Yorker*: 'I wanted to bring you there and I wanted to be true to the Gospels. That has never been done. The Holy Ghost was working through me.' Gibson, a devout traditionalist Catholic, put up $30 million of his own money to produce the film when the studios shied away from the idea of a film which was to be entirely spoken in Aramaic, Latin and Hebrew with subtitles. He enlisted another devout Catholic, Jim Caviezel, to play Christ. Gibson directed, co-wrote and co-produced the film, which was shot in Italy at Matera, Rome and at Cinecittà Studios. What emerged was a technically accomplished but hideous and virtually unwatchable sado-masochistic fantasy covering the last twelve hours of the life of Christ, from his arrest in the Garden of Gethsemane through his trial, scourging, the Way of the Cross, the Crucifixion and, in a final single shot, the Resurrection.

Apart from extremely brief flashbacks to key events in Christ's life (the Sermon on the Mount, the defence of the woman taken in adultery, Palm Sunday, the Last Supper), this is a prolonged, unrelenting, gratuitous wallow in graphic violence. The cumulative effect of the numbingly repetitive action leaves you feeling as if you have been repeatedly hit over the head with a mallet for two hours. Indeed there is little to distinguish it, apart from the Latin and Aramaic, from the currently popular genre of exploitation gore-fests like *Hostel* and *Saw* in which groups of hapless American teenagers are captured and tortured non-stop for the duration of the film.

In *The Passion*, Christ is scourged to a bloody pulp in a long, lingeringly shot sequence; he is kicked and punched and flogged as he drags himself agonizedly to Golgotha; nails are driven into his hands in close-up; and he suffers agonies of pain on the cross. For good measure, Gibson throws in an invented scene in which a raven pecks out the eyes of the 'bad thief' after he has mocked Christ.

The film demonstrated its Catholic credentials by according a prominent role to Mary, the Mother of Christ, who is present at every stage of the ordeal and is intercut with Christ's suffering as a symbol of concern and compassion. The film acquits Pontius Pilate of any guilt for the death of Christ. For all the gleeful brutality of the ordinary Roman soldiers, Gibson places the guilt for the death squarely on the Jews. The priestly establishment under Caiaphas arrange the arrest of Christ, demand his trial and crucifixion, pay the crowd to bay for blood and attend every stage of the process. In an untranslated piece of dialogue, the Jewish crowd cry: 'His blood be upon ourselves and upon our children', after Pilate washes his hands of the matter. God punishes them by wrecking the Temple with an earthquake after Christ dies. Although a shaven-headed Satan floats about in the background of the action, he is not made responsible as is the analogous figure in *The Greatest Story Ever Told* for stirring up the crowd.

The film provoked an angry response from Jewish organizations which with some justification accused the film of anti-Semitism. It was already known that Gibson's ultra right-wing father was a holocaust-denier and had said that the Vatican II reforms were 'a Masonic plot backed by the Jews'. Further substance was given to the charge when Gibson, arrested for drunken driving, launched into a much-publicized anti-Semitic rant. Despite all this, and despite the fact that, as critic Nick James put it, the film substituted 'gore and bombast' for the 'richness and complexity' of the true story of the death of Christ, the film was a huge box-office success worldwide. The film made $370 million at the American box office and $609 million worldwide. This was in part because coachloads of devout Catholics turned up to see it as an affirmation of their faith.[28]

The Ancient World made a decisive and triumphant return to the big screen in 2000 with *Gladiator*. *Gladiator* was a remarkable and unexpected worldwide success, single-handedly reviving the genre which had languished in cinema since the box-office failure of *Fall of the Roman Empire* in 1965. Costing $103 million to produce, it made $456 million worldwide.[29] Fittingly, perhaps, *Gladiator* chose to tell the same story as *Fall of the Roman Empire*, and to show how it should have been done to achieve maximum audience satisfaction. In Ridley Scott the film had a director who, like Anthony Mann, was a supreme visual stylist but could also handle large-scale action scenes for maximum impact.

The plot of *Gladiator* is simple and straightforward. In AD 180, Spanish general Maximus leads the armies of the Emperor Marcus Aurelius to a final victory over the German tribes. Marcus Aurelius wants to name Maximus as his successor and to restore power to the people. Maximus, anxious to return home to his family, is doubtful. When Marcus Aurelius informs his unstable son Commodus that he is to be disinherited, Commodus strangles him and is proclaimed Emperor. He orders Maximus and his family killed. Maximus escapes but finds his wife and son crucified and his villa burned. Captured by slave traders, Maximus is sold to the *lanista* Proximo, is trained as a gladiator and becomes a star in the arenas of North Africa. When Proximo brings his troupe to Rome, Maximus triumphs in the Colosseum and identifies himself to Commodus. Maximus now plots with Commodus' sister Lucilla and the republican senator Gracchus to overthrow Commodus, but Commodus, forcing Lucilla to reveal details of the plot by threatening the life of her son, Lucius Verus, rounds up the plotters. Proximo is killed helping Maximus to escape but Maximus is then also captured. Surviving several attempts to have him killed in the arena, and becoming more and more popular, Maximus eventually fights Commodus himself, after Commodus has taken the precaution of stabbing him in the side. Maximus kills Commodus and dies himself, but before doing so he proclaims the restoration of the republic according to the wish of the Emperor Marcus Aurelius.

This is not really an attempt to tell an accurate story from Roman history. It is full of provable errors. Lucilla was executed by her brother for plotting and did not therefore survive him as she does in the film. Her son Lucius Verus died in infancy. There is no evidence that Marcus Aurelius was murdered. No one contemplated restoring the Republic. After a brief hiatus, the Severan dynasty was installed on the throne and restored order. According to historian Allen M. Ward, 'the depiction of gladiatorial armor, weapons, and combat in *Gladiator* is riddled with inaccuracies'.[30]

The inspirations for *Gladiator* were the Hollywood Roman epics of the 1950s and 1960s and nineteenth-century paintings of the Roman World, which had done so much to shape the popular cultural image of the Roman Empire and thus conditioned audience expectations. The characters of Marcus Aurelius, Commodus and Lucilla derived as much from Anthony Mann's *Fall of the Roman Empire* as they did from history. They were joined by characters inspired by *Spartacus*. The Numidian, Juba, in *Gladiator* is the counterpart of the African, Draba, in *Spartacus*. Proximo, the ruthless businessman who becomes a 'good guy' at the end, recalls Batiatus in *Spartacus* and the republican senator Gracchus is lifted directly, even to his name, from *Spartacus*. Maximus is a composite of Livius in *Fall of the Roman Empire* and Spartacus. His death, like that of Spartacus, turns him into a legend. The murder of Marcus Aurelius and the romance with Lucilla are taken from *Fall of the Roman Empire*. But the anti-climactic ending of *Fall*, in which Livius walks away, allowing the Empire to decline, is replaced by the much more satisfying finale of *Gladiator* in which Maximus ensures the implementation of the dying wish of Marcus Aurelius – restoration of the republic.

The film's powerful visuals were inspired directly by Victorian painting. Ridley Scott was persuaded to take on the project when producer Douglas Wick showed him a print of Jean-Léon Gérôme's 1872 painting *Pollice Verso* (Thumbs Down), in which a gladiator straddles a fallen opponent in the arena and waits for the crowd's verdict of thumbs up or down. This moment is reproduced in the film. So too are scenes inspired by other Gérôme paintings, *Ave Caesar, Morituri te Salutant* (1859) in which the gladiators salute the imperial box, and *The Christian Martyrs' Last Prayer* (1883) in which lions emerge from underground tunnels and advance towards a huddled group of Christians. In *Gladiator* it is tigers. Similarly, costume designer Janty Yates declared that the inspiration for the fashions she created was the paintings of Alma-Tadema. The combination of a narrative structure derived from two earlier Hollywood epics and the visual inspiration provided by nineteenth-century painters was supplemented by the latest technology, as CGI was deployed to recreate the Colosseum in awe-inspiring detail.

Filmed on location in Malta, Morocco and Farnham, Surrey (standing in for Germania), *Gladiator*, like all good epics, had its memorable action set pieces. It opens with the pyrotechnic battle between the Roman legions and the German tribesmen, initiated by Maximus' unforgettable command: 'Unleash hell'. There are the bone-crunching battles in the arena in North Africa and Rome. One highlight is the restaging of the battle of Zama with the gladiators playing the army of Hannibal and fighting Roman soldiers who have chariots with scythes attached to their wheels. Maximus so organizes the gladiators that they beat the Romans, reversing the actual historical outcome of Zama. Another is the single combat between Maximus and the Gaul Tigris amid a ring of menacing tigers. Finally, there is the duel between Maximus and Commodus.

But there is more to it than just spectacle. The characters and the story have greater depth than they might have done. This is because the script went through three distinct versions. The original screenplay was by David Franzoni and in that version the hero was called Narcissus (after the wrestler who actually strangled Commodus) and he and his family survived at the end. The playwright John Logan was then brought in to provide a three-act structure, fleshing out the characters, deepening the relationships and polishing the dialogue. He it was who renamed the hero Maximus, a more virile name than Narcissus, and had him killed at the end. But producer and director felt there was still something missing after the preliminary script read-through and brought in English playwright William Nicholson. He shifted the emphasis from the hero's search for revenge to his desire to be reunited with his family in the afterlife, a desire regularly reiterated throughout the film, and achieved at the end. He also simplified the rather confused plotting of the second half of the film.

However, an additional and unexpected problem presented itself when Oliver Reed, playing Proximo, died of a heart attack three weeks before the end of shooting. Rather than re-shoot his entire performance, which they had all admired, director and producer completed the film using a body double, out-takes from earlier scenes and computer-generated imagery. The script had to be changed to include Proximo being killed as it was originally intended that he should survive.

The politics of the film were not Roman at all but contemporary American. David Franzoni said: 'The movie is about us. It is not about Ancient Rome; it's about America.'[31] Producer Douglas Wick thought the Roman obsession with the games in the arena had a direct parallel in present-day America: 'The whole population distracted by entertainment from the serious issues – like today.' Ridley Scott believed that, while dress and weapons might be different, people do not change and his characters were recognizable human beings motivated by the same emotions in the second century as they are in the twenty-first century.

In the light of such comments, *Gladiator* can fairly be seen as a critique of Clintonian America. It is now America and not Britain or Russia that is 'the evil empire', though the film maintained the familiar 'aural paradigm'. Richard Harris (Marcus Aurelius), David Hemmings (Cassius) and Derek Jacobi (Gracchus) were all British actors. Joaquin Phoenix essayed a nicely understated British accent as Commodus and Russell Crowe's (Maximus) Australian twang served to identify him as a provincial, a Spaniard who had never been to Rome.

The film was made at a time when the American government was mired in financial and sexual scandals and embroiled in overseas adventures (the Balkans, Somalia) while the public was immersed in a culture of sports, entertainments and celebrity. *Gladiator* opens with Rome engaged in a costly high-tech war, defeating the last enemy to become the sole global superpower. The Emperor wants peace, denounces the corruption that has crept into public life, urges the restoration of power to the people and the re-energizing of the supine Senate. The republic that Marcus Aurelius wants restored is not so much the Roman Republic as the Republic of Jeffersonian America, the eighteenth-century construct led by honest men and devoted to democratic ideals. However, when Commodus seizes the throne, he institutes what is, in effect, a Fascist regime. This is indicated visually by Scott when he stages Commodus' triumphal entry into Rome exactly like Hitler's arrival in Nuremberg in Leni Riefenstahl's classic documentary *The Triumph of the Will*, complete with eagles, drums and geometric patterns of humanity, and with the colour muted to black and silver. Commodus then distracts the people with games, presided over by a bloated, bewigged and almost unrecognizable David Hemmings as Cassius, the ancient equivalent of a twentieth-century sports commentator. The mob gather to watch people killed as their modern equivalent gather to cheer on their sports teams. When Commodus and Maximus finally face each other, they embody rival visions of Rome, Commodus' of a totalitarian Empire and Maximus' of a democratic Republic and Maximus' vision triumphs. Maximus, who once fought for the glory of Rome, ritually scrapes off his SPQR (*Senatus Populusque Romanus*, 'Senate and People of Rome') tattoo when he becomes a gladiator but throughout longs for his family and his farm like a good eighteenth-century American yeoman.

The film is superbly directed by Ridley Scott and contains fine performances from Russell Crowe as the general turned gladiator, longing for home and family but willing to fight for a better Rome, from Joaquin Phoenix as the autocratic, unstable and incestuous Commodus and Oliver Reed (to whom the film is dedicated) as the former gladiator turned *lanista* who eventually sacrifices his life to help Maximus. In 2001 it deservedly won five Academy Awards for best picture, best actor, best costume design, best sound and best visual effects.[32]

The critical and popular success of *Gladiator* sparked a full-scale revival of the Ancient World epic. Undeterred by the box-office failure of their production of *Helen of Troy* in 1955, Warner Brothers returned to the subject in *Troy* (2004), spending $175 million on a new epic treatment, directed by Wolfgang Petersen. *Troy* emulated *Gladiator* by filming in Malta and opening with a battle, in this

case a David and Goliath confrontation between Achilles and Boagrius to settle
the fate of Thessaly, the last state in Greece to hold out against the overlordship
of King Agamemnon.

The writer David Benioff insisted that his *Troy* was not an adaptation of
Homer but it was based on a variety of retellings of the Trojan War myths, his
own being yet another variation. It includes the familiar elements – Paris eloping
with Helen, the Greeks besieging Troy, Hector killing Patroclus, Achilles killing
Hector, Odysseus devising the Wooden Horse, Troy being captured and burned
and Paris killing Achilles.

Benioff, however, made considerable alterations in detail which reduced the
richness and complexity of the original myth. He omitted completely the gods
and their interaction with the human characters, removing a vital element of the
Homeric original. The elimination of the sacrifice of Iphigenia, the prophecies of
Cassandra and the grief and defiance of Hecuba removed an important human
dimension. The unhappy ending is mitigated by major narrative changes. The
villains Agamemnon and Menelaus, who both survive in the myth, are killed
in the film to satisfy the audience desire for justice. Helen, Paris, Andromache,
Astyanax and Briseis all escape through a secret tunnel where, traditionally, Paris
is killed, Helen returned to Sparta, Astyanax thrown from the walls of Troy and
Andromache reduced to slavery by the Greeks. This may help to rectify the usual
bleak ending in which all the 'good guys' die while the 'bad guys' survive. But
there is a touch of bathos in the scene in which Paris casually hands the symbol
of eternal Troy, a sword (instead of the Palladium, the statue of Pallas which
was the mythic symbol of the city) to a passing youth who identifies himself as
Aeneas and promises to save the Trojans. In 1955 Aeneas, as a cousin of Paris,
had been present throughout the action, making sense of his role as the leader
of the Trojan survivors.

The film looks handsome in terms of costumes and sets. It credits no historical
adviser, but J. Lesley Fitton, curator of Greek and Roman antiquities at the British
Museum, was consulted about rituals and customs after the designs for sets and
costumes had been completed.[33] The film-makers aimed at a late Bronze Age
setting *c.*1200 BC based on the excavations at Troy VI. But anachronisms, such
as classical Greek statues and coins on the eyes of the dead, inevitably crept in.
However, alterations and anachronisms were not the problem. It was neither
as well written nor as well acted as *Gladiator*. Only Peter O'Toole rises to the
appropriate level of tragic grandeur, genuinely moving when as Priam he visits
the Greek camp to beg for the body of his son Hector from Achilles and later as
he views his burning city. A buffed and burnished Brad Pitt and a muscular Eric
Bana make little dramatic impact as Achilles and Hector. Orlando Bloom's callow
juvenile lead does little to endear Paris to audiences. The relationship between
Achilles and Patroclus is heterosexualized, so that Patroclus becomes Achilles'

cousin rather than his lover. His love object is the Trojan captive Briseis, a merger of the original Briseis with Cassandra, turning Briseis into a priestess of Apollo and the cousin of Paris. It is Briseis who kills Agamemnon and, when Achilles is killed, she is spirited away to safety.

The topical resonance for the film-makers was attested by Wolfgang Petersen, who had had a classical education in Hamburg, learning both Latin and Greek. He said:

> Look at the present! What the *Iliad* says about humans and wars is, simply, still true. Power-hungry Agamemnons who want to create a new world order – that is absolutely current. Of course we didn't start saying: Let's make a movie about American politics [...] But while we were working on it we realized that the parallels to the things that were happening out there were obvious.[34]

The 'new world order' was a phrase of George Bush Sr and, when Petersen was making his film, George Bush Jr was president and engaged in his 'war on terror'; if *Gladiator* was a comment on Clinton's America then *Troy* looks to have been one on Bush's America. *Troy* adopts a stance of opposition to aggressive, imperialistic wars, making it clear that Agamemnon was only using Helen's abduction as a pretext to engage in a war of conquest. The two heroes of the film are Achilles and Hector and neither actually want a war. Achilles has no time for Agamemnon and his schemes, thinks Priam a better king than Agamemnon, wants to take his troops home, prefers romance with Briseis to fighting but enters the fray when his cousin is killed. Hector, devoted husband and father, has a personal creed of honour ('Honour the gods, love your woman, defend your country'). He never wanted war, opposes counter-attacks on the Greeks but is forced by his sense of honour to fight Achilles. Three times personal combat is invoked to settle disputes rather than full-scale battle.

It was savaged critically but cleaned up at the box office, taking $481 million worldwide. This can probably be attributed to the presence of two popular heart-throbs (Brad Pitt and Orlando Bloom), whatever their thespic inadequacies, and to the spectacularly staged action set pieces (Achilles storming the beach at Troy; the two armies clashing; the single combats of Hector and Achilles and Paris and Menelaus; the fireball attack on the Greeks and the final sack of Troy).

The success of *Gladiator* led directly to plans being announced for four different productions devoted to the life of Alexander the Great. The putative directors of these rival versions were Baz Luhrmann, Martin Scorsese, Mel Gibson and Oliver Stone. It was Stone, both writer and director of *Alexander* (2004), who won the race to produce a script and secure financing and the other three projects were dropped. Stone had in his film career been fascinated by war (*Platoon, Born on the Fourth of July*), cultural icons (Jim Morrison in *The Doors*) and flawed leaders

(*Nixon*). *Alexander* brought all these interests together. Stone set out his vision of Alexander in the foreword he wrote to the official guide to the epic, *The Making of 'Alexander'*, written by the film's historical adviser, Oxford historian Robin Lane-Fox. Admitting that he had loved the earlier cycle of Ancient World epics such as *Alexander the Great, Helen of Troy* and *300 Spartans*, and he had studied Greek mythology at New York university, Stone said:

> The story is beautiful – a heroic young man, a dynamic prince, then a king in his time who struggled mightily with his two strong parents, succeeded them, and achieved many of his dreams on earth. I would say he was the world's greatest idealist and as a result he took the world's greatest fall. A brilliant military commander who never suffered defeat in battle, he risked his life numerous times, yet remained a visionary of remarkable and generous spirit, who sought to live a life modelled on the great mythological Greek figures of Herakles, Dionysus, Achilles, and, to my mind, Prometheus. From these beliefs grew his monumental drive and destiny. He was clearly a man of his time, or some might say, a new definition of man. His vision of reconciling barbarian and Greek races was too much for many Greeks, and made his last years particularly painful. He lost many friends; there were betrayals; his love life was fascinating, as well as heartbreaking; he could be extraordinarily gentle and extravagantly savage. His failures, in the end, towered over most men's achievements [...] Such men are the great invigorators of history.[35]

The film was shot over a 915-day period in Morocco, Thailand and Britain, and is throughout visually striking. Interestingly, Stone ran D.W. Griffith's *Intolerance* for production designer Jan Roelfs and his staff to give them an idea of the Babylon he envisaged and a Bollywood epic on the life of King Asoka as a guide for the Indian scenes. Cinematographer Rodrigo Prieto utilized a series of different camera filters and film types to secure the colour-coding that Stone had devised for the film. Lane-Fox summarizes it:

> In Macedonia, the whites and primary colours were not filtered at all, whereas a polarising filter brought out the blue of the sky. At Gaugamela golden filtration brilliantly enhanced the desert dust. For the triumphal entry into Babylon, golden filtrations gave the right tone again, with a finer grain of film than was seen in the preceding battle scenes. In the Bactrian fort, chocolate filters brought out the reds and earth tones of the costumes. The colouring of the Indian battle, of course, is the masterpiece: it was sharpened by film which retained the silvering. By this 'by-pass technique', the light becomes bright and the shadows much more black. When Alexander is wounded the camera work is then slowed for the first time, until each second takes fifteen. The Macedonian army surge forwards, but as Alexander lies wounded, he and the Macedonians appear to see with fresh eyes. The cameras use an infra-red film: the green leaves shade into magenta, their skin into white and their ears into a hint of yellow.[36]

The two battle sequences were particularly impressive: Gaugamela, which mingled dizzying aerial shots and claustrophobic close-quarters fighting sequences, and the battle in India with elephants crashing through a forest, Alexander injured and the screen suffused in crimson.

But the film had serious structural problems. It is narrated by the elderly Ptolemy (Anthony Hopkins), pacing up and down in the great library of Alexandria, dictating his memoirs and indulging in long passages of exposition which slow down the action and could have been delivered more succinctly in voice-over. He comes across merely as a rambling old bore.

Stone had decided on a flashback structure in which, while concentrating on the adult Alexander's Asiatic campaigns, he would flash back to important episodes of his youth, when he was torn between the demands of his mutually hostile and perpetually quarrelling parents, Philip (Val Kilmer) and Olympias (Angelina Jolie), while seeking to fulfil his destiny. But it is too cumbersome and simply does not work. It is further slowed down by a long, clunking and portentous sequence in which Philip expatiates on the cruelty of the Greek gods and the Greek myths. Philip's second marriage to Eurydice, which estranged him from Alexander, and Philip's murder, which are key events in Alexander's life, come much too late in the narrative to have a proper impact which they did in Robert Rossen's linear narrative, *Alexander the Great*.

A third issue which was to cause Stone unanticipated problems was the subject of Alexander's sexuality. Unlike Robert Rossen, Stone frankly acknowledged his hero's bisexuality, which became a running theme in the film. The Greek attitude is expounded early on by Aristotle (Christopher Plummer) as he explains to a group of boys that if two men lie together in lust, it is evil; if they lie together and seek to bring out the best in each other, it is good. Therefore, in contrast to the film *Troy*, male lovers Achilles and Patroclus are held up as exemplars and taken as a model by Alexander. Alexander's great love is for Hephaestion (Jared Leto) and they have three big scenes declaring their love for each other, but it is a love expressed only in intense gazes and manly hugs. Later, Alexander's love of the beautiful Persian eunuch Bagoas is developed entirely without dialogue. The camera, representing Alexander's gaze, picks him out when the Macedonians visit the Persian harem. Later Bagoas is ever-present at his side and when he performs an erotic dance in India, Alexander kisses him full on the lips. The only scene of vigorous physical sex in the film is between Alexander and the Bactrian princess, Roxane, whom he marries as part of his project for uniting the Greeks and the Asiatics.

A further problem is Colin Farrell as Alexander who comes across alternately as surly and self-pitying, never as charismatic or lovable. He is no more convincing an Alexander than Richard Burton in *Alexander the Great*. Connor Paolo as the boy Alexander, however, gives a memorable performance conveying precisely the qualities that both Farrell and Burton missed.

When *Alexander* was released in America, it was a critical and box-office disaster. A shell-shocked Stone brokenly recalled the American reviews in a newspaper interview: 'Puerile writing ... confused plotting ... limp acting ... weak script ... shockingly off-note performances ... disjointed narrative ... acted at a laughably hysterical pitch ... it has wonderful highlights, but most of them are in Colin Farrell's hair'. He took full responsibility for the failure which was all the more devastating both because it was unexpected and because the film had been for him a labour of love.

> I didn't see this coming, this utter trashing of the movie. I should have. I got bloody battered for acknowledging Alexander's bisexuality. That hug between him and his lover, Hephaestion – it wasn't even a kiss, for fuck's sake – got slated. The gays lambasted me for not making Alexander openly homosexual and, in the Bible belt, pastors were up in the pulpit saying that to watch this film was to be tempted by Satan. The criticism has been ball-breaking. I was devastated, Colin Farrell was devastated.

But it was not just the gay angle that alienated audiences. 'The audiences, they didn't know the story, and they were confused by it. I did that wrong. That was my fault.'[37] The removal of an hour of running time during final editing to get the film down to manageable length also contributed to lack of coherence in the narrative development.[38]

The British critics were marginally less dismissive than their American counterparts, Philip French in the *Observer* (9 January 2005) typically arguing: 'Unlike most big-scale historical movies, *Alexander* is never truly risible. Colin Farrell's tousled blond locks, for instance, are no odder than Brad Pitt's in *Troy*, and his Irish accent is unextraordinary and supposedly intended to suggest a people regarded by Greeks as their inferiors. It is well designed, plausible and has two superbly staged battle sequences [...] The real problem is that the picture is plodding, unvaried in its pace and repetitive.' Costing $155 million, the box-office take at $167 million barely broke even and *Alexander* joined the list of famous big-budget failures.

But Stone was unable to leave *Alexander* alone. In 2005 he issued a director's cut on DVD, which removed eight minutes of running time and reduced the older Ptolemy's scenes which had slowed down the original. But in 2007, again on DVD, came *Alexander Revisited: the Final Cut* in which he put back 30 minutes of previously unseen footage and radically recut and restructured it. This version opens spectacularly with the great battle of Gaugamela set piece. Stone's aim was to simplify and clarify the narrative and to deepen the characters and motivations. So there is more, for instance, on Alexander's love of Bagoas, a defiant rejection of homophobic attacks on the film. The flashback structure, which Stone retains, now makes more sense. This 205-minute version, complete with intermission, is undeniably more coherent and more satisfying than the two previous versions. But it remains a flawed film, partly due to the absence of any notable or memorable performance in the central roles.

David Franzoni followed up his success with *Gladiator* with the script for *King Arthur* (2004), in which he reworked some of the ideas from the earlier film. Uniquely, but with firm historical justification, Franzoni set the story of King Arthur and his knights where it belonged, not in the high Middle Ages but in Dark Age Britain at the end of the Roman occupation of the island in the early fifth century. As his basic plot-line, Franzoni took a theme familiar in westerns – the lone cavalry patrol despatched into hostile Indian territory to rescue a settler family. But filmed in Ireland and directed by Antoine Fuqua, it emerged as a vigorous, fast-moving and visually impressive action film.

Arthur is Artorius Castus, British-born commander of the Sarmatian cavalry, stationed at Hadrian's Wall, who are his knights. They are engaged in perpetual warfare with the pagan Pictish tribes north of the wall who they call 'the woads'. Artorius, like Maximus in *Gladiator*, believes that the Roman Empire equals civilization, a belief reinforced by his faith. He is a Christian but follows the teachings of Pelagius who believed that all men were created equal and had free will. The knights sit at a round table to symbolize that equality. His belief in the Roman Empire and the Roman Church is shattered, however, when he learns that the church has executed Pelagius as a heretic and the Empire is withdrawing its legions from Britain, leaving the people defenceless. He is further disillusioned when he discovers a Roman patrician ill-treating free peasants in the name of God and fundamentalist Christian monks walling up pagan villagers and Pictish prisoners alive. He frees the surviving prisoners and orders the monks walled up. Instructed by the duplicitous Bishop Germanus to undertake a final mission before his knights can be released from their service and enabled to return to Sarmatia, Artorius is sent to rescue a godson of the Pope who lives in a villa far to the north of the Wall. They fulfil the mission but are confronted by a horde of invading Saxons who are racist (ordered not to mate with the Britons for fear of weakening the race) and ruthless (destroying every settlement and every peasant they encounter). The Saxons pursue them back to the Wall, from which the Romans withdraw, taking the Pope's godson to safety. Artorius and his Sarmatians now join forces with the Picts, with whom they actually have much more in common than with the Romans. Picts and Sarmatians are both pagan, talk constantly about freedom and are characterized by nobility, courage and loyalty. They defeat and destroy the Saxons. Artorius now unites Britons, Picts and Sarmatians in a new kingdom of Britain, founded on equality and freedom. He is crowned King and cements the alliance by marrying the Pictish female warrior Guinevere, whom he had rescued from the monks' prison. So, just as Maximus had restored the republic at the end of *Gladiator*, Arthur (as he is now called) creates a multicultural melting-pot state with democratic values, a prototype United States.

The film boasts some excellent action scenes: a bloody and visceral opening Pictish ambush on a Roman patrol; a battle on the ice between the Saxons and the knights, inspired by Eisenstein's *Alexander Nevsky* but none the less effective for that, and at the end the 'unleash hell' pitched battle in which the Saxons are wiped out and which is the equivalent to the opening sequence of *Gladiator*. But Clive Owen is a colourless Arthur and the film has no performances to equal those of Russell Crowe and Joaquin Phoenix in *Gladiator*. The script is also marred by implausibilities. The idea of the Pope's godson living in a villa deep in Pictish territory north of Hadrian's Wall is ludicrous. So is the idea of the Saxons invading Britain from the north of Scotland. They presumably landed there having lost their way to the isle of Thanet, where the first Anglo-Saxon invasion actually took place. Also Cerdic and Cynric, the leaders of the Saxons who are both killed in the final battle, actually founded the kingdom of Wessex a hundred years after the Roman withdrawal. None of this would have mattered to the average viewer, but what did disorientate some was the absence of most of the familiar elements of Arthurian cinema. As one critic observed the film was 'an Arthurian tale minus everything the average person knows or cares about Arthur and his knights'.[39] Costing $90 million to make, it achieved a worldwide gross of $203 million, achieving greater popularity in Europe than in the USA.

The film *300* (2007) is probably the most Fascistic film to come out in cinemas since the fall of the Third Reich. Purporting to tell the historical story of the heroic stand of King Leonidas of Sparta and his 300 bodyguard warriors at Thermopylae against the army of the Persian king Xerxes, which allowed the rest of Greece to mobilize and eventually defeat the Persians and secure the future of freedom and democracy, this is a comprehensive celebration of Fascist ideology. It exalts a Sparta where weak and blemished children are hurled to their deaths on a heap of skulls, a policy emulated by Hitler with his programme for the elimination of the mentally and physically unfit in Nazi Germany. In Sparta, boys are taken from their families at seven and trained for war, like the Hitler Youth. Leonidas (Gerard Butler) articulates the Spartan creed: 'Only the hard and the strong can call themselves Spartans'; 'There is no room for softness, weakness'; and in battle 'No prisoners, no mercy.' Heavily muscled, naked except for leather jockstraps and red cloaks, the Spartans resemble the naked Aryan supermen sculpted for the Reich by Hitler's favourite sculptor Arno Breker or the naked athletes celebrated in the eulogy to Ancient Greece that forms the prologue to Leni Riefenstahl's *Olympia*. Intoning the mantra 'honour, duty, glory', they look forward to a 'beautiful death' and are duly all killed in a climactic *Heldentod*. Their 'ho-ho' chant is delivered as if it were *Sieg Heil*. The last stand of the

Spartans at Thermoplylae becomes the ultimate 'triumph of the will', the death Hitler ordered for his besieged army in Stalingrad. Much of the film consists of an orgy of slaughter and bloodletting. The film is based on a graphic novel by Frank Miller and all the settings and many of the effects have recreated the panels of the novel by the use of CGI.

It is not enough for the Spartans to intone the word 'freedom' periodically as if they were the warriors of democratic America or for the film to hint that the Persians represent the modern-day 'axis of evil', Iran. There is no freedom in this Sparta for anyone different. The Athenians are contemptuously dismissed as 'philosophers and boy lovers' and the villain Ephialtes is an embittered hunchback who narrowly escaped being exterminated because of his deformity. But, more significantly, and explicable only in racial terms, the Spartans are all played by macho white actors, shouting their lines, hurling envoys into a well and indulging in locker-room banter in between bouts of slaughter, and the Persians are all played by non-white actors.

The author Frank Miller claims to have been inspired by a boyhood visit to see Rudolph Maté's *The 300 Spartans* (1962). Watching *300*, one longs for the classical purity and Homeric nobility of the earlier film. But *300* even has added monsters who seem to have strayed in from *The Lord of the Rings*. The 'Immortals', the historically attested bodyguard of the Persian King, are here literally immortal, a hideously decaying zombie army like the Black Riders of Mordor, and Ephialtes is a clone of Gollum.

The critics were divided on the film. Philip French in the *Observer* (25 March 2007) thought the film 'ridiculous' with the Persians 'got up to resemble the doormen at an upmarket body-piercing salon' and the Greeks apparently 'responding to an invitation to a fancy-dress party at a gay New York club'. Jenny McCartney in the *Sunday Telegraph* (25 March 2007) thought it 'historically one-dimensional, ethically distasteful, and frequently ludicrous [...] however, hardly ever boring'. Sukhdev Sandhu in the *Daily Telegraph* (23 March 2007) was unimpressed by the CGI effects which seemed to him 'cheap and nasty, transparently pixellated and lacking dynamics. Many shots appeared to be based on Athena posters and old Guinness ad-campaigns'. Depressingly, some critics liked it, with Nigel Andrews in the *Financial Times* (23 March 2007) saying it was 'the kind of movie that gives Hollywood a good populist name. Pshaw to history and political correctness', and Anthony Quinn in the *Independent* (23 March 2007) praising its 'fatuous magnificence'. Even more depressingly, it is reported to have been a surprise box-office success in America.

The *Gladiator* effect ensured that the cycle of made-for-television Ancient World epics continued. *Spartacus* (2004), an entirely superfluous remake for American cable television, shot in Bulgaria during 2003, came nowhere near to matching Kubrick's magnificent 1960 epic. The Croatian-born American television star Goran Visnjic played Spartacus with a supporting cast mainly of British television actors such as Ross Kemp, doing his familiar East End thug act in the role of a brutal gladiator trainer. It is notable only for the final screen appearance of Sir Alan Bates, eloquent and moving as the democratic senator Antonius Agrippa, the equivalent role to that taken by Charles Laughton in 1960. As Bates' biographer, Donald Spoto, concluded:

> His presence in the film was the only reason for viewers to tune in when *Spartacus* was broadcast the following year; otherwise this was the sort of witless television fare that required talented actors to say remarkably silly lines […] In at least one scene an actor blithely chews gum as another speaks further inanities. And in the absence of a compelling narrative and reasonably intelligent discourse, the producers simply chose to offer an escalating assortment of bloody, brutal and sadistic sequences that appealed to viewers' worst instincts.[40]

The year before the cinema blockbuster *Troy*, American cable television produced a two and a half hour television film *Helen of Troy* (2003). Although lacking the global superstars, expensive CGI effects and any performance of the tragic stature of Peter O'Toole's Priam, this was actually more entertaining than *Troy*. It included the influence of the gods and the importance of prophecy, giving it more of a feel of the ancient world and, by including episodes not usually featured in Trojan War films (the exposure of the baby Paris on Mount Idah; the judgement of Paris on the beauty of three goddesses Hera, Aphrodite and Athena; Helen's abduction by Theseus, King of Athens, and her rescue by her brother; the sacrifice of Iphigenia to the goddess Artemis to ensure favourable winds for the Greek fleet), it had a novelty and a freshness lacking in Wolfgang Petersen's one-dimensional epic.

The film's sympathies are firmly with the Trojans. The Greeks are for the most part vicious brutes, apart from Menelaus, a decent man who genuinely loves Helen and the wily and diplomatic Odysseus. Agamemnon is a ruthless aggressor. Achilles is a shaven-headed thug. Paris' denunciation of the Greeks as mindlessly militaristic and brutally anti-feminist is endorsed by the narrative. The love of Paris and Helen is shown as entirely innocent. It is willed by the gods and Helen is continually trying to give herself up to the Greeks to end the bloodshed. But it is made clear that Agamemnon does not want her back. He wants only to sack and loot Troy. After two hours, the story is wrapped up very quickly. Achilles kills Hector. Paris kills Achilles. Agamemnon kills Paris and rapes Helen. Then Agamemnon's wife Clytemnestra turns up and slaughters Agamemnon in his bath in revenge for the sacrifice of their daughter Iphigenia. Helen returns sadly to Sparta with an understanding Menelaus. Paris and Helen were played by a pair of beautiful but little-known British actors (Matthew Marsden and Sienna Guillory) with a strong supporting cast of British character actors (Rufus Sewell as Agamemnon, John Rhys-Davies as Priam, James Callis as Menelaus, Emilia Fox as Cassandra).

However, a triumphal highpoint in the televisual Ancient World revival that followed the success of *Gladiator* has been the two series of *Rome* (2005–7). Co-produced at a cost of £60 million by the American company HBO and the BBC, which was very much the junior partner, contributing £9 million to the overall budget, it provoked howls of outrage in the quality press. The columnist Simon Jenkins in the *Guardian* (11 November 2005) used its highly praised serialization of *Bleak House* as a stick with which to beat the BBC: 'How can one institution, the BBC, make something as good as *Bleak House* and as bad as *Rome* [...] is a mystery. A rambling plot, weighed down by *Troy*-like dialogue, is interrupted – as if by commercial breaks – by inserts of copulation and throat-slitting.' The writer Robert Harris, author of the bestselling historical novel *Pompeii*, in an article in the *Sunday Telegraph* (6 November 2005) headed 'The decline and fall of the BBC', declared *Rome* 'historically, morally and artistically worthless', though he had the good grace to pronounce 'The sets are alluring. The acting is accomplished.' He was particularly exercised by the historical inaccuracies and the obsession with sex, his two concerns coinciding in his disapproval of the characterization of Atia, in reality a morally upright and respectably married Roman matron, as a cunning, sexually voracious and amoral intriguer.

Rome's historical adviser Jonathan Stamp hit back in a letter to the *Sunday Telegraph* (13 November 2005) in which he admitted that dramatic licence had been taken with the historical record, but 'it is after all a drama'. He argued that the production had done 'everything we could to make the world we had recreated historically authentic [...] From the costumes, to the set, to the battle sequences, to gestures used by the public crier in Rome's Forum, or the rituals practised in its temples, we took the greatest pains to present the city as it really was.'

Harris, however, was unwise enough to compare *Rome* unfavourably with *I, Claudius*, which 'showed that it was possible to be both accurate and entertaining, and to convey (justifiably, in its case) extremes of sexual perversity without degenerating into a *Penthouse*-style bonkathon'. But *I, Claudius*, based as it was largely on Suetonian gossip, was no more accurate than *Rome*, and in fact *Rome* effectively adopted and refurbished the *I, Claudius* formula of blending high politics and soap opera. It also had the courage to do so at length, twelve episodes in Series One and ten episodes in Series Two, which enabled the team of writers to explore and explicate in detail the complicated tangle of political faction, power plays, plots and betrayals and to develop the personal stories, deepening the characters and conveying something of the complexity, ambivalence and unpredictability of human relationships. It was also enabled by its parallel narratives of aristocratic intrigue and plebeian domestic drama to portray a society in the round, focusing as much on brothels and back streets as on the Senate and the villas of the mighty.

Opening with a *Gladiator*-style battle between the Romans and the Gauls, it retells the story of the fall of the Roman Republic and the establishment of the Empire from Caesar's Gallic Wars through the Civil Wars, the assassination of Caesar, the establishment of the triumvirate of Antony, Octavian and Lepidus to the final victory of Octavian over Antony and Cleopatra.

But politics and war were balanced by the domestic soap-opera plots. One strand centred on the deadly rivalry of two aristocratic matriarchs, Atia (the mother of Octavian) and Servilia (the mother of Brutus), continually plotting to upstage, outdo and humiliate each other. They are the classic 'bitches' of soap opera. As Hilary Kingsley writes:

> The bitch is a perennial soap figure. She provides a focus of dislike for the viewer, a chance for wilful wickedness for the producers and an outlet for wild sexuality. Heroines can have sex, can even be involved […] in extra-marital hanky panky, but heroines have to *suffer*. Bitches do not. They enjoy it […] Bitches dive right into bad behaviour, eyes glittering, cloven bosoms heaving. They *gloat* as they plot a rival's downfall. They *sneer* as the heroine is metaphorically tied to the railway lines. They *laugh exultantly* when one of their schemes succeeds. They *screw* any man they fancy, without thinking about it.[41]

That is a perfect description of Atia and Servilia.

The second continuing strand centres on two of Caesar's soldiers, Lucius Vorenus and Titus Pullo. They were real historical characters, each mentioned once in Caesar's *Gallic Wars*, rival centurions who constantly argued about who was the better soldier, but each saving the life of the other in battle. Nothing else is known about them. But the scriptwriters develop lives for them which run the gamut of the soap themes listed by Hilary Kingsley as essential elements of the soaps: infidelity, money problems, paternity uncertainty, childlessness, loneliness, betrayal, worry about loved ones who have gone off to some other part of the world. During the course of the two series, Vorenus' wife is revealed to have been unfaithful and kills herself; the child Vorenus believes is his grandson is actually the love child of his wife; Vorenus loses all his money when a slave-trading venture fails and he has to turn assassin to earn money; he believes his children murdered but, on learning they are alive, rescues them from a slave camp; he is betrayed by his daughter to a rival gang leader after he becomes one of the political bosses of the Aventine district.

At the heart of this strand is the relationship of Vorenus and Pullo as fellow soldiers in Caesar's legions. Vorenus is stern, principled, duty-loving, moralistic and republican, unable to articulate his feelings but clinging unshakeably to his beliefs. Pullo is violent, profane, hedonistic, cheerfully insubordinate. They are initially antagonistic but over the course of the series a warm comradeship and mutual loyalty develops between them. In Series Two, Pullo's character is softened by his love for the slave girl Eirene whom he marries. Vorenus, deranged by the infidelity and death of his wife, himself becomes temporarily savage and profane. They quarrel and part but are reunited before the end. What is fascinating is how the lives of these two ordinary citizens impinge continually on the great events of the age. It is Pullo who executes Cicero and fathers the child of Cleopatra, Caesarion, that Caesar believes is his. It is Vorenus who helps Antony commit suicide after his defeat.

An important character in the whole drama is Rome itself. The decision was taken to film in Rome at Cinecittà studios to get the quality of the light right and to utilize real Roman extras. The production designer, Joseph Bennett, in building his five-acre set of Rome wanted to create, not a stylized nineteenth-century image, but a living, organic city like modern Bombay or Mexico City and he succeeded magnificently. His Rome is not a shining, monumental marble construct, it is a noisy, dirty, violent, vibrant metropolis, seething and teeming with life.

This was what Jonathan Stamp meant by authenticity. Similarly, throughout the series the practices of pagan religion – rituals, curses, sacrifices, auguries, prophecies – are ever-present. So is a vigorously expressed sexuality which takes the form not just of energetic heterosexual couplings, which in the upper class mansions often take place in the presence of silent, immobile slaves, who are regarded as part of the furniture, but also episodes of incest, rape, buggery, lesbian sex, prostitution and drug-fuelled orgies, which are seen as all part of life's rich pageant.

The two series were graced with some outstanding performances by the largely British cast. Ciaran Hinds was completely convincing as the cunning, calculating Julius Caesar, as were James Purefoy as a tough-minded, priapic, vulgarian Antony, David Bamber as a slippery, scheming Cicero and Tobias Menzies as a youthful Brutus, torn between his political ideals and his loyalty to Caesar. The two actors who played Octavian, Max Pirkis and Simon Woods, created a memorable portrait of Octavian both as a boy and a man, watchful, shrewd, cold and manipulative. There were outstanding performances from Polly Walker and Lindsay Duncan as Atia and Servilia, and Kevin McKidd and Ray Stevenson as Vorenus and Pullo, all of them positive landmarks in television acting.

No one can know how long the *Gladiator*-inspired cycle will last. But each Ancient World cycle has produced enduring masterworks: *Ben-Hur* (1926), *King of Kings* (1927), *Sign of the Cross* (1932), *Quo Vadis* (1951), *The Ten Commandments*

(1956), *Ben-Hur* (1959), *Spartacus* (1960), *Jesus of Nazareth* (1977), *Gladiator* (2000) and *Rome* (2005–7). Each of them used the Ancient World as a vehicle to comment on the ideas and values of its own age. That probably guarantees that, in some form or other, the Ancient World will be back on the screen in due course. That combination of spectacle, action, conflict, inspiration and larger than life characters will simply be too potent and appealing for future film-makers to resist.

Notes

Notes to Chapter 1: The Ancient World: the Nineteenth-Century Context

1. Kathleen M. Coleman, 'The pedant goes to Hollywood: the role of the academic consultant' in Martin M. Winkler (ed.), *Gladiator: Film and History* (Oxford: Blackwell, 2004), pp. 45–52.
2. P.M. Pasinetti, '*Julius Caesar*: the role of the technical adviser', *The Quarterly of Film, Radio and Television* 8 (Winter 1953), p. 132.
3. Robin Lane-Fox, *The Making of 'Alexander'* (Oxford: Rowman and Littlefield., 2004), pp. 157–8.
4. Martin M. Winkler (ed.), *Troy: from Homer's 'Iliad' to Hollywood Epic* (Oxford: Blackwell, 2007), p. 105
5. William Vance, *America's Rome*, Volume 1 (New Haven and London: Yale University Press, 1989), p. 2.
6. On the Victorians and Ancient Greece, see Frank M. Turner, *The Greek Heritage in Victorian Britain* (New Haven and London: Yale University Press, 1981); Richard Jenkyns, *The Victorians and Ancient Greece* (Oxford: Blackwell, 1981); Richard Jenkyns, *Dignity and Decadence: Victorian Art and the Classical Inheritance* (London: HarperCollins, 1991); G.W. Clarke (ed.), *Rediscovering Hellenism: The Hellenic Inheritance and the English Imagination* (Cambridge: Cambridge University Press, 1989).
7. Norman Vance, *The Victorians and Ancient Rome* (Oxford: Blackwell, 1997), p. 197.
8. On the Victorians and Ancient Rome, see Vance, *The Victorians and Ancient Rome*; Catharine Edwards (ed.), *Roman Presences: Receptions of Rome in European Culture, 1789–1945* (Cambridge: Cambridge University Press, 1999); R.F. Betts, 'The allusion to Rome in British imperialist thought of the late nineteenth and early twentieth centuries', *Victorian Studies* 15 (1971), pp. 149–59.
9. Charles Kingsley, *The Roman and the Teuton* (London: Macmillan, 1906), pp. 17, 18, 19.
10. Frank M. Turner, 'Christians and pagans in Victorian novels' in Edwards (ed.), *Roman Presences*, p. 174.
11. On these novels see Turner, 'Christians and pagans in Victorian novels' in Edwards (ed.), *Roman Presences* pp. 173–87 and Royal Rhodes, *The Lion and the Cross: Early Christianity in Victorian Novels* (Columbus, Ohio: Ohio University Press, 1995).
12. Richard Hingley, *Roman Officers and English Gentlemen* (London and New York: Routledge, 2000), pp. 30–2.

13. Lord Lytton, *The Last Days of Pompeii* (London: Routledge, 1873), pp. v–x. See also Wolfgang Leppmann, *Pompeii in Fact and Fiction* (London: Elek, 1968).

14. Lord Lytton, *The Life of Edward Bulwer, first Lord Lytton by his grandson*, Volume 1 (London: Macmillan, 1913), p. 440.

15. Edward Lytton Bulwer, *England and the English* (Chicago: University of Chicago Press, 1970), pp. 343–4.

16. Richard Altick, *Paintings from Books* (Columbus, Ohio: Ohio State University Press, 1985), pp. 461–3; Michael Liversidge and Catharine Edwards (eds), *Imagining Rome: British Artists and Rome in the Nineteenth Century* (London: Merrell Holberton, 1996), pp. 116–17.

17. The latest evidence is reviewed in Michael Wood, *In Search of the Trojan War* (London: BBC Books, 2005) and Bettany Hughes, *Helen of Troy* (London: Jonathan Cape, 2005).

18. William Feaver, *The Art of John Martin* (Oxford: Clarendon Press, 1975) pp. 40–1.

19. Gerald M. Ackerman, *The Life and Work of Jean-Léon Gérôme* (London: Philip Wilson, 1986).

20. Christopher Wood, *Olympian Dreamers* (London: Constable, 1983), p. 16.

21. Mrs Russell Barrington, *The Life, Letters and Work of Frederic Leighton*, Volume 1 (London: George Allen, 1906), p. 24.

22. Frederick Dolman, 'Illustrated interviews 68: Sir Lawrence Alma-Tadema', *Strand Magazine* 18 (1899), p. 607.

23. Vern G. Swanson, *Sir Lawrence Alma-Tadema* (London: Ash and Grant, 1977), p. 44.

24. Christopher Frayling, *The Face of Tutankhamun* (London: Faber, 1992).

25. David Jeffreys (ed.), *Views of Ancient Egypt since Napoleon Bonaparte* (London: UCL Press, 2003), p. 84.

26. Jeffreys (ed.), *Views of Ancient Egypt*, p. 19.

27. Richard Altick, *The Shows of London* (Cambridge, Mass. and London: The Belknap Press, 1978), pp. 234–52.

28. James Stevens Curl, *The Egyptian Revival* (London: Routledge, 2005).

29. Patrick and Viviane Berko (eds), *Ancient Egypt in Nineteenth Century Painting* (Knokke-Zoute: Berko, 1992).

30. Charles Keith Maisels, *The Near East: Archaeology in the 'Cradle of Civilization'* (London: Routledge, 1998), p. 6.

31. On Middle Eastern archaeology, see Maisels, *The Near East*; Seton Lloyd, *Foundations in the Dust: The Story of Mesopotamian Exploration* (London: Thames and Hudson, 1980); Lesley Adkins, *Empires of the Plain* (London: HarperCollins, 2003).

32. Michaela Giebelhausen, *Painting the Bible: Representation and Belief in Mid-Victorian Britain* (Aldershot: Ashgate, 2006), p. 31.

33. Giebelhausen, *Painting the Bible*, p. 2

34. Giebelhausen, *Painting the Bible*, pp. 189–90.

35. Joanna Richardson, *Gustave Doré* (London: Cassell, 1980), pp. 72–3.

36. Richardson, *Gustave Doré*, p. 127.

37. Michael Wentworth, *James Tissot* (Oxford: Clarendon Press, 1984), p. 191.

38. Richard Schoch, *Shakespeare's Victorian Stage* (Cambridge: Cambridge University Press, 1998), p. 2.

39. On stage censorship, see John Russell Stephens, *The Censorship of English Drama 1824–1901*

(Cambridge: Cambridge University Press, 1981) and L.W. Conolly, *The Censorship of English Drama 1737–1824* (San Marino: Huntington Library, 1976).

40. Stephens, *The Censorship of English Drama*, p. 93.
41. On spectacle, see Altick, *The Shows of London*; Michael Booth, *Victorian Spectacular Theatre* (London: Routledge, 1981); Martin Meisel, *Realizations* (Princeton: Princeton University Press, 1983).
42. David Mayer, *Playing out the Empire* (Oxford: Clarendon Press, 1994), p. 20.
43. Full details of the productions can be found in Jeffrey Richards, *Sir Henry Irving: a Victorian Actor and his World* (London: Hambledon, 2005).
44. On the toga play genre, see Mayer, *Playing out the Empire* and Jeffrey Richards, *The Ancient World on the Victorian and Edwardian Stage* (forthcoming).
45. Oscar Wilde, 'The truth of masks' in *The Works of Oscar Wilde* (London: Spring Books, 1965), pp. 905–6.
46. Bernard Shaw, *Prefaces* (London: Constable, 1934), p. 717.

Notes to Chapter 2: The Birth of the Ancient World Epic in the Cinema

1. On the Italian silent-screen epics see Pierre Leprohon, *The Italian Cinema* (London: Secker and Warburg, 1972), pp. 7–46 and Maria Wyke, *Projecting the Past: Ancient Rome, Cinema and History* (London: Routledge, 1997).
2. On *Cabiria*, see in particular Maria Wyke, 'Screening ancient Rome in the new Italy' in Catharine Edwards (ed.), *Roman Presences* (Cambridge: Cambridge University Press, 1999), pp. 188–204.
3. Kevin Brownlow, *The Parade's Gone By* (London: Secker and Warburg, 1968), p. 92.
4. Edward Wagenknecht and Anthony Slide, *The Films of D.W. Griffith* (New York: Crown, 1975), p. 29.
5. William K. Everson, *American Silent Film* (New York: Oxford University Press, 1978), pp. 72–4.
6. Brownlow, *The Parade's Gone By*, pp. 51–64 for Joseph Henabery's memories of filming *Intolerance*.
7. Bernard Henson, 'D.W. Griffith: some sources', *Art Bulletin* 54 (1972), p. 499.
8. Henson, 'D.W. Griffith: some sources', p. 498.
9. Henson, 'D.W. Griffith: some sources', pp. 493–515
10. Everson, *American Silent Film*, p. 92.
11. Lillian Gish, *The Movies, Mr Griffith and Me* (New York: Avon Books, 1970), p. 177.
12. Gish, *The Movies, Mr Griffith and Me*, p. 175. There is a full account of the filming of *Intolerance* in Gish, pp. 165–83.
13. Details of the creation of *The Mother and the Law* and *The Fall of Babylon* are given in Wagenknecht and Slide, *The Films of D.W. Griffith*, pp. 88–9.
14. 'Delightful' is Kevin Brownlow's verdict on *Male and Female* in Brownlow, *The Parade's Gone By*, p. 180. The recreation of 'The Lion's Bride' is reported by Robert Birchard, *Cecil B. De Mille's Hollywood* (Lexington: University Press of Kentucky, 2004), pp. 146–7. I am grateful to Stephen Wildman for identifying the artist whose name is not mentioned in Birchard.

15. Charles Higham, *Cecil B. De Mille* (New York: Dell, 1976), p. 79 on De Mille's research; Brownlow, *The Parade's Gone By*, p. 184 for his verdict on the film.
16. Higham, *Cecil B. De Mille*, p. 82.
17. Phil Koury, *Yes, Mr De Mille* (New York: G.P. Putnam's Sons, 1959), p. 90.
18. Higham, *Cecil B. De Mille*, pp. 99–100, explains how the parting of the Red Sea was filmed.
19. Birchard, *Cecil B. De Mille's Hollywood*, p. 178.
20. Sumiko Higashi, *Cecil B. De Mille and American Culture: The Silent Era* (Berkeley and London: University of California Press, 1994), p. 190.
21. Birchard, *Cecil B. De Mille's Hollywood*, pp. 216–26.
22. Cecil B. De Mille, *Autobiography* (London: W.H. Allen, 1960), p. 252.
23. Father Daniel A. Lord SJ, *Played by Ear* (Chicago: Loyola University Press, 1956), p. 279.
24. Higham, *Cecil B. De Mille*, pp. 126–7.
25. Higham, *Cecil B. De Mille*, pp. 127–9.
26. De Mille, *Autobiography*, p. 255.
27. De Mille, *Autobiography*, p. 253.
28. De Mille, *Autobiography*, p. 254.
29. De Mille, *Autobiography*, p. 256.
30. Lord, *Played by Ear*, p. 279. Contrary to Lord's assertion, De Mille had had many more than one box-office failure.
31. Lord, *Played by Ear*, pp. 281–2.
32. Koury, *Yes, Mr De Mille*, p. 128.
33. Higham, *Cecil B. De Mille*, p. 128.
34. Lord, *Played by Ear*, pp. 281–2.
35. Stephenson Humphries-Brooks, *Cinematic Savior* (Westport, Connecticut: Praeger, 2006), p. 9.
36. De Mille, *Autobiography*, p. 252.
37. De Mille, *Autobiography*, p. 259–61.
38. Humphries-Brooks, *Cinematic Savior*, pp. 10–12.
39. De Mille, *Autobiography*, p. 259.
40. Humphries-Brooks, *Cinematic Savior*, p. 16.
41. Birchard, *Cecil B. De Mille's Hollywood*, pp. 225–7.
42. For a full discussion of *The King of Kings* see Higham, *Cecil B. De Mille*, pp. 125–38; Birchard, *Cecil B. De Mille's Hollywood*, pp. 216–26; Humphries-Brooks, *Cinematic Savior*, pp. 9–19; Bruce Babington and Peter William Evans, *Biblical Epics* (Manchester: Manchester University Press, 1993), pp. 110–26.
43. James C. Robertson, *The Hidden Cinema* (London: Routledge, 1989), pp. 31–3.
44. Betty Blythe recounted her memories of the film in Kevin Brownlow, *The Parade's Gone By*, pp. 378–85.
45. Ivan Butler, *Religion in the Cinema* (London: Zwemmer, 1969), p. 16.
46. James C. Robertson, *The Casablanca Man: The Cinema of Michael Curtiz* (London: Routledge, 1993) pp. 15–16.
47. Robert Tanitch, *Oscar Wilde on Stage and Screen* (London: Methuen, 1999), pp. 134–59.
48. Michael Morris, *Madam Valentino* (New York: Abbeville Press, 1991), pp. 83–93.

49. Brownlow, *The Parade's Gone By*, p. 394.

50. Eason's account of the filming of the chariot race is in Ezra Goodman, *The Fifty Year Decline and Fall of Hollywood* (New York: Simon and Schuster, 1961), pp. 298–303.

51. Robert E. and Katharine M. Morsberger, *Lew Wallace: Militant Romantic* (New York: McGraw Hill, 1980), p. 495.

52. Brownlow, *The Parade's Gone By*, p. 411.

53. David Chierichetti, *Hollywood Director: the career of Mitchell Leisen* (New York: Curtis Books, 1973), pp. 48–50. For production costs and box-office returns, see Birchard, *Cecil B. De Mille's Hollywood*, p. 251.

54. De Mille, *Autobiography*, p. 280.

55. Maria Wyke, *Projecting the Past*, p. 95.

56. Lucy Hughes-Hallett, *Cleopatra: Histories, Dreams and Distortions* (London: Bloomsbury, 1990), p. 284.

57. Henry Wilcoxon with Katherine Orrison, *Lionheart in Hollywood* (Metuchen, New Jersey and London: Scarecrow Press, 1991), p. 39. See Wyke, *Projecting the Past*, pp. 90–100 and Hughes-Hallett, *Cleopatra*, pp. 269–71, 274, 284, 288, 292–3, for insightful comments on the film.

58. An account of how Willis O'Brien created the sequence can be found in Don Shay, 'Willis O'Brien: creator of the impossible', *Focus on Film* 16 (1973), pp. 36–8.

59. Richard Jewell with Vernon Harbin, *The RKO Story* (London: Octopus, 1982), p. 89. There are extended analyses of the film in Wyke, *Projecting the Past*, pp. 171–80 and Gerald Forshey, *American Religious and Biblical Spectaculars* (Westport, Connecticut: Praeger, 1992), pp. 22–5.

Notes to Chapter 3: The 1950s and 1960s: The Roman Empire

1. Michael Wood, *America in the Movies* (London: Secker and Warburg, 1975), p. 169.

2. The *Daily Express*, 17 September 1953; John Spraos, *The Decline of the Cinema* (London: Allen and Unwin, 1962), pp. 14, 34.

3. Rudy Behlmer (ed.), *Memo from Darryl F. Zanuck* (New York: Grove Press, 1993), pp. 233–4.

4. John Ellis, 'Art, culture and quality', *Screen* 19 (Autumn 1978), pp. 9–49.

5. Christopher Cook (ed.), *The Dilys Powell Film Reader* (Oxford: Oxford University Press, 1992), p. 307.

6. Wood, *America in the Movies*, p. 169.

7. The phrase was coined by Maria Wyke, in *Projecting the Past* (London: Routledge, 1997), p. 71.

8. Jay Robinson, *The Comeback* (Lincoln, Virginia: Chosen Books, 1979), p. 41.

9. Charlton Heston, *The Actor's Life: Journals 1956–1976* (New York: Pocket Books, 1979), p. 71.

10. Kirk Douglas, *The Ragman's Son* (London: Pan Books, 1989), p. 314.

11. Stephen Whitfield, *The Culture of the Cold War* (Baltimore: Johns Hopkins University Press, 1996), p. 77.

12. Whitfield, *The Culture of the Cold War*, p. 78.

13. Whitfield, *The Culture of the Cold War*, p. 83.
14. John Huston, *An Open Book* (London: Columbus Books, 1998), pp. 174–6. On Hugh Gray, see Colin Eldridge, *Hollywood's History Films* (London: I.B. Tauris, 2006), pp. 138–45.
15. Huston, *An Open Book*, p. 175.
16. Huston, *An Open Book*, pp. 174–6; Laurence Grobel, *The Hustons* (London: Bloomsbury, 1990), pp. 330–1.
17. Mervyn LeRoy, *Take One* (London: W.H. Allen, 1974), p. 169.
18. *Continental Daily Mail*, 8 July 1950.
19. Jas Elsner and Jamie Masters (eds.), *Reflections of Nero* (London: Duckworth, 1994), p. 27.
20. Derek Elley, *The Epic Film: Myth and History* (London: Routledge, 1984), p. 126.
21. Christopher Palmer, *The Composer in Hollywood* (London: Marion Boyars, 1993), pp. 212–16; Miklos Rosza, *Double Life* (Tunbridge Wells: The Baton Press, 1982), pp. 146–7.
22. *Daily Telegraph*, 20 January 1952.
23. Peter Ustinov, *Dear Me* (Harmondsworth: Penguin, 1978), pp. 225–6.
24. John Houseman, *Runthrough* (New York: Touchstone, 1980), p. 298.
25. On the play see John Ripley, *'Julius Caesar' on Stage in England and America 1599–1973* (Cambridge: Cambridge University Press, 1980), pp. 222–32; Houseman, *Runthrough*, pp. 285–333; Simon Callow, *Orson Welles: The Road to Xanadu* (London: Vintage Books, 1996), pp. 322–43.
26. Kenneth Geist, *Pictures Will Talk: the Life and Films of Joseph L. Mankiewicz* (New York: Charles Scribner's Sons, 1978), p. 224.
27. John Houseman, *Front and Center* (New York: Touchstone, 1980), pp. 392–3.
28. Geist, *Pictures Will Talk*, p. 224.
29. Palmer, *The Composer in Hollywood*, pp. 217–19; P.M. Pasinetti, 'Julius Caesar: the role of the technical adviser', *The Quarterly of Film, Radio and Television* 8 (Winter 1953), pp. 137–8.
30. Houseman, *Front and Center*, pp. 406–9.
31. James Mason, *Before I Forget* (London: Hamish Hamilton, 1981), p. 231; Geist, *Pictures Will Talk*, p. 227.
32. Kenneth Rothwell, *Shakespeare on Screen* (Cambridge: Cambridge University Press, 1999), p. 41.
33. Geist, *Pictures Will Talk*, p. 228.
34. Henry Koster with Irene Kahn Atkins, *Henry Koster* (Metuchen, New Jersey and London: Scarecrow Press, 1987), pp. 127–53.
35. George Custen, *Twentieth Century's Fox* (New York: Basic Books, 1997), pp. 324–5.
36. Philip Dunne, *Take Two* (New York: Limelight Editions, 1992), pp. 253–4.
37. Report in the *Daily Herald*, 18 September 1953.
38. Derek Elley (ed.), *Variety Movie Guide* (London: Hamlyn, 1991), p. 509.
39. Aubrey Solomon, *Twentieth Century-Fox* (Metuchen, New Jersey and London: Scarecrow Press, 1988), pp. 225, 248; Monica Silveira Cyrino, *Big Screen Rome* (Oxford: Blackwell, 2005), p. 54.
40. Palmer, *The Composer in Hollywood*, pp. 84–5.
41. Dunne, *Take Two*, pp. 255–6.

42. Solomon, *Twentieth Century-Fox*, pp. 221, 249.

43. Roy Moseley, *Evergreen: Victor Saville in His Own Words* (Carbondale and Edwardsville: Southern Illinois University Press, 2000), pp. 197–200.

44. Richard B. Jewell, with Vernon Harbin, *The RKO Story* (London: Octopus, 1982), p. 217.

45. Jesse Lasky Jr, *Whatever Happened to Hollywood?* (London: W.H. Allen, 1973), p. 251.

46. James Robert Parish and Don E. Stanke, *The Glamour Girls* (Carlstadt, New Jersey: Rainbow Books, 1977), p. 269.

47. Jon Halliday (ed.), *Sirk on Sirk* (London: Faber, 1971), pp. 115–16.

48. Axel Madsen, *William Wyler* (New York: Thomas Y. Crowell, 1973), p. 339.

49. Fry's comments are recorded in Heston, *The Actor's Life*, pp. 78–9. Vidal's interpretation is in Vito Russo, *The Celluloid Closet* (New York: Harper and Row, 1981), pp. 76–7 and Heston's response in the *Independent*, 27 July 1996.

50. On the filming of the chariot race, see Andrew Marton with Joanne D'Antonio, *Andrew Marton* (Metuchen, New Jersey and London: Scarecrow Press, 1991), pp. 279–319. Most of the reviews report that it took three months to film but this may include the editing process after the shooting was completed.

51. Madsen, *William Wyler*, p. 353. For the box-office returns, see Madsen, *William Wyler*, p.354.

52. Rosza, *Double Life*, p. 178.

53. For an excellent analysis of the score see Palmer, *The Composer in Hollywood*, pp. 218–23.

54. Elley, *The Epic Film*, p. 135.

55. Elley, *The Epic Film*, p. 109.

56. On the pre-cinematic and early cinematic history of Spartacus see Maria Wyke, *Projecting the Past*, pp. 34–72 and Alison Futrell, 'Seeing red: Spartacus as domestic economist', in Sandra R. Joshel, Margaret Malamud and Donald T. McGuire Jr (eds), *Imperial Projections Ancient Rome in Modern Popular Culture* (Baltimore: The Johns Hopkins University Press, 2001), pp. 77–118.

57. Futrell, 'Seeing red', p. 89.

58. Douglas, *The Ragman's Son*, p. 304

59. Douglas, *The Ragman's Son*, p. 316.

60. Tony Curtis and Barry Paris, *Tony Curtis: the Autobiography* (London: Heinemann, 1994), pp. 180–1, 184.

61. On the filming, see Douglas, *The Ragman's Son*, pp. 303–34; Curtis and Paris, *Tony Curtis*, pp. 180–8; Ustinov, *Dear Me*, pp. 273–8. Bruce Cook, *Dalton Trumbo* (New York: Charles Scribner's Sons, 1977), p. 271 says Mann and Douglas quarrelled violently about the rushes.

62. Elley, *The Epic Film*, p. 110.

63. The censors cut this scene before the film's general release but it was restored for the 1991 DVD version, the lost soundtrack recreated with Anthony Hopkins impersonating Olivier and Curtis speaking his own lines.

64. On Bronston's method of financing his films, see Bernard Gordon, *Hollywood Exile* (Austin, Texas: University of Texas Press, 1999), pp. 98–100 and Neal Moses Rosendorf, "Hollywood in Madrid': American film producers and the Franco regime, 1950–1970', *Historical Journal of Film, Radio and Television* 27 (March 2007), pp. 77–109.

65. Marton, *Andrew Marton*, pp. 423–4.

66. Bronston Studio publicity handout, BFI microfiche *Fall of the Roman Empire*.

67.   *Films and Filming* 10 (March 1964), pp. 7–8.

68.   *Monthly Film Bulletin* 31 (May 1964), p. 69.

Notes to Chapter 4: The 1950s and 1960s: The Bible

1.   George Custen, *Twentieth Century's Fox* (New York: Basic Books, 1997), pp. 293–9; Dore Schary, *Heyday* (Boston: Little, Brown, 1979), pp. 156–7.

2.   Stephen Whitfield, *The Culture of the Cold War* (Baltimore: Johns Hopkins University Press, 1996), pp. 184–6.

3.   Jonathan Gathorne-Hardy, *Love, Sex, Marriage and Divorce* (London: Triad Paladin, 1983), p. 52.

4.   Phil Koury, *Yes, Mr De Mille* (New York: G.P. Putnam's Sons, 1959), p. 242.

5.   Cecil B. De Mille, *Autobiography* (London: W.H. Allen, 1960), p. 364–5.

6.   Koury, *Yes, Mr De Mille*, p. 206.

7.   Robert Birchard, *Cecil B. De Mille's Hollywood* (Lexington: The University Press of Kentucky, 2004), p. 335.

8.   De Mille, *Autobiography*, p. 365.

9.   Henry Wilcoxon with Katherine Orrison, *Lionheart in Hollywood* (Metuchen, New Jersey and London: Scarecrow Press, 1991), p. 172; Birchard, *Cecil B. De Mille's Hollywood*, p. 340.

10.   Wilcoxon, *Lionheart in Hollywood*, p. 176.

11.   Philip Dunne, *Take Two* (New York: Limelight Editions, 1992), pp. 250–3.

12.   Dunne, *Take Two*, p. 252.

13.   Dunne, *Take Two*, p. 252

14.   Aubrey Solomon, *Twentieth Century-Fox* (Metuchen, New Jersey and London: Scarecrow Press, 1988), pp. 223, 246.

15.   De Mille, *Autobiography*, p. 376.

16.   De Mille, *Autobiography*, p. 377.

17.   De Mille's address is contained on the BFI *Ten Commandments* microfiche.

18.   Wilcoxon, *Lionheart in Hollywood*, pp. 226–8.

19.   On Noerdlinger, see David Eldridge, *Hollywood's History Films* (London: I.B. Tauris, 2006), pp. 145–51.

20.   Koury, *Yes, Mr De Mille*, pp. 55–6.

21.   Koury, *Yes, Mr De Mille*, p. 235.

22.   Koury, *Yes, Mr De Mille*, pp. 229–42, 255.

23.   Gerald Forshey, *American Religious and Biblical Spectaculars* (Westport, Connecticut: Praeger, 1992), pp. 128, 136.

24.   Jesse Lasky Jr, *Whatever Happened to Hollywood?* (London: W.H. Allen, 1973), p. 258.

25.   Lasky Jr, *Whatever Happened to Hollywood?* on Frank (p. 213), on Mackenzie (p. 260) and on Gariss (p. 260).

26.   De Mille, *Autobiography*, p. 379.

27.   Sir Cedric Hardwicke, *A Victorian in Orbit* (London: Methuen, 1961), p. 241.

28.   Edward G. Robinson with Leonard Spigelgass, *All My Yesterdays* (New York: Hawthorn Books, 1973), p. 272.

29. Wilcoxon, *Lionheart in Hollywood*, pp. 274–5.

30. Wilcoxon, *Lionheart in Hollywood*, p. 262.

31. Koury, *Yes, Mr De Mille*, p. 126.

32. Paramount Publicity Press Release, 1960, BFI *Ten Commandments* microfiche.

33. Birchard, *Cecil B. De Mille's Hollywood*, p. 351.

34. Wilcoxon, *Lionheart in Hollywood*, pp. 285–7.

35. Elmer Bernstein, 'The De Mille legend' in Gabe Essoe and Raymond Lee, *De Mille: The Man and His Pictures* (Cranbury, New Jersey: A.S. Barnes, 1970), pp. 277–82.

36. Joan Collins, *Past Imperfect* (London: Coronet, 1979), pp. 188–9.

37. Stuart Kaminsky, *John Huston: Maker of Magic* (London: Angus and Robertson, 1978), p. 163.

38. On the making of the film see Kaminsky, John Huston, pp. 161–70; Forshey, *American Religious and Biblical Spectaculars*, pp. 144–61; John Huston, *An Open Book* (London: Columbus Books, 1988), pp. 317–29.

39. Kaminsky, *John Huston*, pp. 169–70.

40. Richard Combs (ed.), *Robert Aldrich* (London: BFI, 1978), p. 44.

41. Christopher Frayling, *Sergio Leone: Something To Do With Death* (London: Faber, 2000), pp. 110–16.

42. Miklos Rozsa, *Double Life* (Tunbridge Wells: The Baton Press, 1982), pp. 184–5.

43. Patrick McGilligan and Paul Buhle (eds), *Tender Comrades* (New York: St Martin's Press, 1997), p. 173.

44. Christopher Frayling, *Ken Adam and the Art of Production Design* (London: Faber, 2005), pp. 89–92.

45. Michael Munn, *The Stories Behind the Scenes of the Great Epics* (Watford: Argus Books, 1982), p. 35.

46. *Movie* 6 (January 1963), p. 19.

47. The British censor cut the three scenes that hint at lesbianism, incest and homosexuality, but they were restored in the video release.

48. Tony Williams, *Body and Soul: The Cinematic Vision of Robert Aldrich* (Lanham, Maryland: Scarecrow Press, 2004) pp. 335–47 has a full discussion of the film.

49. Munn, *The Stories Behind the Scenes of the Great Epics*, p. 41.

50. *Movie* 9 (May 1963), p. 24.

51. There are sympathetic appreciations of the film in Geoff Andrew, *The Films of Nicholas Ray* (London: Charles Letts, 1991), pp. 179–84 and Bruce Babington and Peter William Evans, *Biblical Epics* (Manchester: Manchester University Press, 1993), pp. 127–38.

52. *Movie* 9 (May 1963), p. 24.

53. *Movie* 9 (May 1963), p. 23.

54. Rosza, *Double Life*, pp. 178–80.

55. On Rosza's score see Derek Elley, *The Epic Film: Myth and History* (London: Routledge, 1984), p. 47 and Christopher Palmer, *The Composer in Hollywood* (London: Marion Boyars, 1993), pp. 222–5.

56. All the quotes, including those following, relating to *Barabbas* come from the film's souvenir booklet.

57. Munn, *The Stories Behind the Scenes of the Great Epics*, p. 47.

58. On Newman's score, see Elley, *The Epic Film*, p. 51 and Palmer, *The Composer in Hollywood*, pp. 85–7. The full story is told in Ken Darby, *Hollywood Holyland: The Filming and Scoring of 'The Greatest Story Ever Told'* (Metuchen, New Jersey and London: Scarecrow Press, 1992).

59. The reviews are summarized in Darby, *Hollywood Holyland*, pp. 256–8 and Marilyn Ann Moss, *Giant: George Stevens, a Life on Film* (Madison, Wisconsin: University of Wisconsin Press, 2004), pp. 287–8.

60. For a full analysis of the film see Babington and Evans, *Biblical Epics*, pp. 139–48 and Forshey, *American Religious and Biblical Spectaculars*, pp. 95–104.

61. Moss, *Giant*, p. 286.

Notes to Chapter 5: The 1950s and 1960s: Greece and Egypt:

1. On Rattigan's play, see B.A. Young, *The Rattigan Version* (London: Hamish Hamilton, 1986), pp. 82–9; Geoffrey Wansell, *Terence Rattigan* (London: Fourth Estate, 1995), pp. 182–93; Michael Darlow, *Terence Rattigan: The Man and His Work* (London: Quartet, 2000), pp. 229–43.

2. Alan Casty, *The Films of Robert Rossen* (New York: Museum of Modern Art, 1969), p. 33.

3. Casty, *Robert Rossen*, p. 33.

4. *Monthly Film Bulletin* 22 (July 1955), pp. 103–4. There is a notably more positive evaluation of the film in Derek Elley, *The Epic Film: Myth and History* (London: Routledge, 1984), pp. 64–6 and Jon Solomon, *The Ancient World in the Cinema* (New Haven and London: Yale University Press, 2001), pp. 108–11.

5. On the making of *Jason and the Argonauts*, see Jan Read, *Young Man in Movieland* (Lanham, Maryland: Scarecrow Press, 2004), pp. 121–4 and Ray Harryhausen and Tony Dalton, *Ray Harryhausen: an animated life* (London: Aurum, 2003), pp. 151–74.

6. On the making of *Clash of the Titans*, see Harryhausen and Dalton, *Ray Harryhausen*, pp. 261–82.

7. Patrick McGilligan, *Back Story* (Berkeley and London: University of California Press, 1986), p. 164.

8. McGilligan, *Back Story*, p. 164.

9. Solomon, *The Ancient World in the Cinema*, pp. 243–4.

10. Steven C. Smith, *A Heart at Fire's Center* (Berkeley and London: University of California Press, 2002), pp. 181–3.

11. Tony Thomas, *Ustinov in Focus* (London: Zwemmer, 1971), pp. 97–9.

12. Michael Wilding and Pamela Wilcox, *Apple Sauce* (London: Allen and Unwin, 1982), pp. 106–7).

13. Aubrey Solomon, *Twentieth Century-Fox* (Metuchen, New Jersey and London: Scarecrow Press, 1988), pp. 225, 248)

14. Solomon, *Ancient World in the Cinema*, p. 249.

15. Todd McCarthy, *Howard Hawks: The Grey Fox of Hollywood* (New York: Grove Press, 1997), p. 520. McCarthy recounts the full story of the filming, pp. 512–38.

16. Joan Collins, *Past Imperfect* (London: Coronet, 1979), p. 16.

17. Jack Hawkins, *Anything for a Quiet Life* (London: Coronet, 1975), pp. 148–9.

18. McCarthy, *Howard Hawks*, p. 520.

19. Robin Wood, *Howard Hawks* (London: Secker and Warburg, 1968), p. 164.

20. Young's and Cardiff's accounts of the experience are to be found in their respective autobiographies: Freddie Young, *Seventy Light Years* (London: Faber, 1999), pp. 58–63 and Jack Cardiff, *Magic Hour* (London: Faber, 1996), p. 86.

21. On the filming of *Caesar and Cleopatra*, see Alan Wood, *Mr Rank* (London: Hodder and Stoughton, 1952), pp. 162–9; Geoffrey Macnab, *J. Arthur Rank and the British Film Industry* (London: Routledge, 1993), pp. 99–104; Valerie Pascal, *The Disciple and his Devil* (London: Michael Joseph, 1971), pp. 103–10. The script editor Marjorie Dean published an account of the filming in *Meeting at the Sphinx* (London: Macdonald, n.d.). There are detailed analyses of the film, comparisons with the play and assessments in Donald P. Costello, *The Serpent's Eye: Shaw and the Cinema* (Notre Dame, Indiana: University of Notre Dame Press, 1965), pp. 113–46 and Bernard Dukore (ed.), *The Collected Screenplays of Bernard Shaw* (London: George Prior, 1980), pp. 125–47.) According to Wood, p. 167, the film cost £1,278,000, but *Film Daily* and *Motion Picture Daily* put it at £1,500,000 (Dukore, p. 136).

22. Stewart Granger, *Sparks Fly Upwards* (London: Granada, 1982), p. 82.

23. C.A. Lejeune, *Chestnuts in her Lap* (London: Phoenix House, 1947), p. 167.

24. Dukore, *Collected Screenplays of Shaw*, pp. 146, 143.

25. Barry Duncan, *The St James's Theatre* (London: Barrie and Rockliff, 1964), p. 339.

26. Alexander Walker, *Vivien* (London: Weidenfeld and Nicolson, 1987), pp. 204–6; Margaret Lamb, *Antony and Cleopatra on the English Stage* (London and Toronto: Associated University Presses, 1980), pp. 138–44.

27. Matthew Bernstein, *Walter Wanger, Hollywood Independent* (Minneapolis and London: Minnesota University Press, 2000), pp. 349–50.

28. Solomon, *Twentieth Century-Fox*, pp. 253. He gives the domestic rental figures on p. 229.

29. For an account of the filming of *Cleopatra*, see Bernstein, *Walter Wanger*, pp. 343–86; Kenneth L. Geist, *Pictures Will Talk: The Life and Films of Joseph L. Mankiewicz* (New York: Charles Scribner's Sons, 1978), pp. 302–45; Andrew Marton with Joanne D'Antonio, *Andrew Marton* (Metuchen, New Jersey and London: Scarecrow Press, 1991), pp. 395–412.

Notes to Chapter 6: The Ancient World Revival

1. Fred Kaplan, *Gore Vidal* (London: Bloomsbury, 1999), p. 491.

2. Kaplan, *Gore Vidal*, pp. 690–1.

3. Sian Phillips, *Public Places* (London: Sceptre, 2001), p. 319.

4. Josef von Sternberg, *Fun in a Chinese Laundry* (San Francisco: Mercury House, 1988), p. 179.

5. Sternberg, *Fun in a Chinese Laundry*, p. 172.

6. John Baxter, *The Cinema of Josef von Sternberg* (London: Zwemmer, 1971), pp. 136–7.

7. Sternberg, *Fun in a Chinese Laundry*, pp. 174–89

8. Baxter, *The Cinema of Josef von Sternberg*, p. 140.

9. The full story of the production is told in Simon Callow, *Charles Laughton: a difficult actor* (London: Methuen, 1987), pp. 111–21; Charles Drazin, *Alexander Korda: Britain's Only Movie Mogul* (London: Sidgwick and Jackson, 2002), pp. 180–6; Karol Kulik, *Alexander*

Korda: the man who could work miracles (London: W.H. Allen, 1975), pp. 191–8; Charles Higham and Roy Moseley, *Merle* (Sevenoaks: New English Library, 1983), pp. 61–4; Sternberg, *Fun in a Chinese Laundry*, pp. 171–89.

10.   Baxter, *The Cinema of Josef von Sternberg*, p. 142.

11.   Hilary Kingsley, *Soap Box* (London: Papermac, 1988), pp. 2–3.

12.   For the story of the filming of *I, Claudius*, see Sian Phillips, *Public Places*, pp. 313–20; George Baker, *The Way to Wexford* (London: Headline, 2002), pp. 267–9; Documentary 'I, Claudius – a television epic' on the DVD box set of *I, Claudius*.

13.   Franco Zeffirelli, *Zeffirelli* (London: Weidenfeld and Nicolson, 1986), p. 241.

14.   Zeffirelli, *Zeffirelli*, p. 274

15.   Gerald Forshey, *American Religious and Biblical Spectaculars* (Westport, Connecticut: Praeger, 1992), p. 165

16.   Zeffirelli, *Zeffirelli*, p. 275.

17.   Zeffirelli, *Zeffirelli*, p. 34.

18.   Zeffirelli, *Zeffirelli*, p. 282.

19.   Zeffirelli, *Zeffirelli*, p. 277.

20.   For analyses of the series see Stephenson Humphries-Brooks, *Cinematic Savior* (Westport, Connecticut: Praeger, 2006), pp. 70–82; Forshey, *American Religious and Biblical Spectaculars*, pp. 164–71.

21.   The figures are given in Zeffirelli, *Zeffirelli*, p. 296 and Humphries-Brooks, *Cinematic Savior*, p. 77.

22.   Michael Medved, *Hollywood vs. America: Popular Culture and the War on Traditional Values* (New York: HarperCollins, 1992), p. 70.

23.   Jon Solomon, *The Ancient World in the Cinema* (New Haven and London: Yale University Press, 2001), p. 111.

24.   Gideon Nisbet, *Ancient Greece in Film and Popular Culture* (Exeter: Bristol Phoenix Press, 2006), p. 62.

25.   The making of the film is recounted in Steve Jenkins, 'From the pit of Hell', *Monthly Film Bulletin* 55 (December 1988), pp. 352–3.

26.   For detailed analysis of the film, see Humphries-Brooks, *Cinematic Savior*, pp. 83–99 and Bruce Babington and Peter William Evans, *Biblical Epics* (Manchester: Manchester University Press, 1993), pp. 149–68.

27.   Medved, *Hollywood vs. America*, p. 49.

28.   For an extended consideration of the film, see Nick James, 'Hell in Jerusalem', *Sight and Sound* 14 (new series) (April 2004), pp. 15–18. The box-office returns are reported in the *Observer*, 2 January 2005.

29.   *Observer*, 28 January 2007.

30.   Martin M. Winkler (ed.), *Gladiator: Film and History* (Oxford: Blackwell, 2004), p.39.

31.   Winkler, *Gladiator*, p. 125.

32.   On the making of the film and for detailed analysis see Winkler, *Gladiator: Film and History*; Monica Silveira Cyrino, *Big Screen Rome* (Oxford: Blackwell, 2005), pp. 207–56; documentary 'Strength and Honour' on the DVD Special Edition of the film.

33.   Martin M. Winkler (ed.), *Troy: from Homer's 'Iliad' to Hollywood Epic* (Oxford: Blackwell, 2007), p. 105.

34. Winkler, *Troy*, p. 7

35. Robin Lane-Fox, *The Making of 'Alexander'* (Oxford: Rowman and Littlefield, 2004) Foreword.

36. Lane-Fox, *The Making of Alexander*, p. 150.

37. Oliver Stone interview, *Sunday Telegraph*, 2 January 2005.

38. *Observer*, 9 January 2005.

39. *Observer*, 2 January 2005.

40. Donald Spoto, *Otherwise Engaged* (London: Hutchinson, 2007), pp. 265–6.

41. Kingsley, *Soap Box*, p. 38.

Select Bibliography

Ackerman, Gerald M., *The Life and Work of Jean-Léon Gérôme*, London: Philip Wilson, 1986.

Adkins, Lesley, *Empires of the Plain*, London: HarperCollins, 2003.

Altick, Richard, *Paintings from Books*, Columbus, Ohio: Ohio State University Press, 1985.

Altick, Richard, *The Shows of London*, Cambridge, Mass. and London: the Belknap Press, 1978.

Andrew, Geoff, *The Films of Nicholas Ray*, London: Charles Letts, 1991.

Babington, Bruce and Evans, Peter William, *Biblical Epics*, Manchester: Manchester University Press, 1993.

Baker, George, *The Way to Wexford*, London: Headline, 2002.

Baxter, John *The Cinema of Josef von Sternberg*, London: Zwemmer, 1971.

Behlmer, Rudy (ed.), *Memo from Darryl F. Zanuck*, New York: Grove Press, 1993.

Berko, Patrick and Viviane (eds), *Ancient Egypt in Nineteenth Century Painting*, Knokke-Zoute: Berko, 1992.

Bernstein, Matthew, *Walter Wanger, Hollywood Independent*, Minneapolis and London: Minnesota University Press, 2000.

Betts, R.F., 'The allusion to Rome in British imperialist thought of the late nineteenth and early twentieth centuries', *Victorian Studies* 15 (1971), pp. 149–59.

Birchard, Robert, *Cecil B. De Mille's Hollywood*, Lexington: University Press of Kentucky, 2004.

Booth, Michael, *Victorian Spectacular Theatre*, London: Routledge, 1981.

Brownlow, Kevin, *The Parade's Gone By*, London: Secker and Warburg, 1968.

Butler, Ivan, *Religion in the Cinema*, London: Zwemmer, 1969.

Callow, Simon, *Charles Laughton: a difficult actor*, London: Methuen, 1987.

Callow, Simon, *Orson Welles: the Road to Xanadu*, London: Vintage Books, 1996.

Cardiff, Jack, *Magic Hour*, London: Faber, 1996.

Casty, Alan, *The Films of Robert Rossen*, New York: Museum of Modern Art, 1969.

Chierichetti, David, *Hollywood Director: the Career of Mitchell Leisen*, New York: Curtis Books, 1973.

Clarke, G.W. (ed.), *Rediscovering Hellenism: the Hellenic Inheritance and the English Imagination*, Cambridge: Cambridge University Press, 1989.

Collins, Joan, *Past Imperfect*, London: Coronet, 1979.

Combs, Richard (ed.), *Robert Aldrich*, London: BFI, 1978.

Cook, Bruce, *Dalton Trumbo*, New York: Charles Scribner's Sons, 1977.

Cook, Christopher (ed.), *The Dilys Powell Film Reader*, Oxford: Oxford University Press, 1992.

Costello, Donald P., *The Serpent's Eye: Shaw and the Cinema*, Notre Dame, Indiana: University of Notre Dame Press, 1965.

Curl, James Stevens, *The Egyptian Revival*, London: Routledge, 2005.

Curtis, Tony and Paris, Barry, *Tony Curtis: the Autobiography*, London: Heinemann, 1994.

Custen, George, *Twentieth Century's Fox*, New York: Basic Books, 1997.

Cyrino, Monica Silveira, *Big Screen Rome*, Oxford: Blackwell, 2005.

Darby, Ken, *Hollywood Holyland: The Filming and Scoring of 'The Greatest Story Ever Told'*, Metuchen, New Jersey: Scarecrow, 1992.

Darlow, Michael, *Terence Rattigan: The Man and His Work*, London: Quartet, 2000.

De Mille, Cecil B., *Autobiography*, London: W.H. Allen, 1960.

Dean, Marjorie, *Meeting at the Sphinx*, London: Macdonald, n.d.

Douglas, Kirk, *The Ragman's Son*, London: Pan, 1989.

Drazin, Charles, *Alexander Korda: Britain's Only Movie Mogul*, London: Sidgwick and Jackson, 2002.

Dukore, Bernard (ed.), *The Collected Screenplays of Bernard Shaw*, London: George Prior, 1980.

Duncan, Barry, *The St James's Theatre*, London: Barrie and Rockliff, 1964.

Dunne, Philip, *Take Two*, New York: Limelight Editions, 1992.

Edwards, Catharine (ed.), *Roman Presences: Receptions of Rome in European Culture, 1789–1945*, Cambridge: Cambridge University Press, 1999.

Eldridge, Colin, *Hollywood's History Films*, London: I.B. Tauris, 2006.

Elley, Derek, *The Epic Film: Myth and History*, London: Routledge, 1984.

Elley, Derek (ed.), *Variety Movie Guide*, London: Hamlyn, 1991.

Ellis, John, 'Art, culture and quality', *Screen* 19 (1978), pp. 9–49.

Elsner, Jas and Masters, James (eds), *Reflections of Nero*, London: Duckworth, 1994.

Essoe, Gabe and Lee, Raymond, *De Mille: The Man and His Pictures*, Cranbury, New Jersey: A.S. Barnes, 1970.

Everson, William K., *American Silent Film*, New York: Oxford University Press, 1978.

Feaver, William, *The Art of John Martin*, Oxford: Clarendon Press, 1975.

Forshey, Gerald, *American Religious and Biblical Spectaculars*, Westport, Connecticut: Praeger, 1992.

Frayling, Christopher, *The Face of Tutankhamun*, London: Faber, 1992.

Frayling, Christopher, *Ken Adam and the Art of Production Design*, London: Faber, 2005.

Frayling, Christopher, *Sergio Leone: Something To Do With Death*, London: Faber, 2000.

Gathorne-Hardy, Jonathan, *Love, Sex, Marriage and Divorce*, London: Triad Paladin, 1983.

Geist, Kenneth, *Pictures Will Talk: The Life and Films of Joseph L. Mankiewicz*, New York: Charles Scribner's Sons, 1978.

Giebelhausen, Michaela, *Painting the Bible: Representation and Belief in Mid-Victorian Britain*, Aldershot: Ashgate, 2006.

Gish, Lillian, *The Movies, Mr Griffith and Me*, New York: Avon Books, 1970.

Goodman, Ezra, *The Fifty Year Decline and Fall of Hollywood*, New York: Simon and Schuster, 1961.

Gordon, Bernard, *Hollywood Exile*, Austin, Texas: University of Texas Press, 1999.

Granger, Stewart, *Sparks Fly Upwards*, London: Granada, 1982.

Grobel, Laurence, *The Hustons*, London: Bloomsbury, 1990.

Halliday, Jon (ed.), *Sirk on Sirk*, London: Faber, 1971.

Hardwicke, Sir Cedric, *A Victorian in Orbit*, London: Methuen, 1961.

Harryhausen, Ray and Dalton, Tony, *Ray Harryhausen: an animated life*, London: Aurum, 2003.

Hawkins, Jack, *Anything for a Quiet Life*, London: Coronet, 1975.

Henson, Bernard, 'D.W. Griffith: some sources', *Art Bulletin* 54 (1972), pp. 493–515.

Heston, Charlton, *An Actor's Life: Journals 1956–76*, New York: Pocket Books, 1979.

Higashi, Sumiko, *Cecil B. De Mille and American Culture: the Silent Era*, Berkeley and London: University of California Press, 1994.

Higham, Charles, *Cecil B. De Mille*, New York: Dell, 1976.

Higham, Charles and Moseley, Roy, *Merle*, Sevenoaks: New English Library, 1983.

Hingley, Richard, *Roman Officers and English Gentlemen*, London and New York: Routledge, 2000.

Houseman, John, *Front and Center*, New York: Touchstone, 1980.

Houseman, John, *Runthrough*, New York: Touchstone, 1980.

Hughes, Bettany, *Helen of Troy*, London: Jonathan Cape, 2005.

Hughes-Hallett, Lucy, *Cleopatra: Histories, Dreams and Distortions*, London: Bloomsbury, 1990.

Humphries-Brooks, Stephenson, *Cinematic Savior*, Westport, Connecticut: Praeger, 2006.

Huston, John, *An Open Book*, London: Columbus Books, 1998.

James, Nick, 'Hell in Jerusalem', *Sight and Sound* 14 (April 2004), pp. 15–18.

Jeffreys, David (ed.), *Visions of Ancient Egypt since Napoleon Bonaparte*, London: UCL Press, 2003.

Jenkins, Steve, 'From the pit of Hell', *Monthly Film Bulletin* 55 (December 1988), pp. 352–3.

Jenkyns, Richard, *The Victorians and Ancient Greece*, Oxford: Blackwell, 1981.

Jenkyns, Richard, *Dignity and Decadence: Victorian Art and the Classical Inheritance*, London: HarperCollins, 1991.

Jewell, Richard B. with Harbin, Vernon, *The RKO Story*, London: Octopus, 1982.

Joshel, Sandra R., Malamud, Margaret and McGuire, David T., Jr, *Imperial Projections: Ancient Rome in Modern Popular Culture*, Baltimore: Johns Hopkins University Press, 2001.

Kaminsky, Stuart, *John Huston: Maker of Magic*, London: Angus and Robertson, 1978.

Kaplan, Fred, *Gore Vidal*, London: Bloomsbury, 1999.

Kingsley, Charles, *The Roman and the Teuton*, London, Macmillan, 1906.

Kingsley, Hilary, *Soap Box*, London: Papermac, 1988.

Koster, Henry with Irene Kahn Atkins, *Henry Koster*, Metuchen, New Jersey and London: Scarecrow, 1987.

Koury, Phil, *Yes, Mr De Mille*, New York: G.P. Putnam's Sons, 1959.

Kulik, Karol, *Alexander Korda: the man who could work miracles*, London: W.H. Allen, 1975.

Lamb, Margaret, *'Antony and Cleopatra' on the English Stage*, London and Toronto: Associated University Presses, 1980.

Lane-Fox, Robin, *The Making of 'Alexander'*, Oxford: Rowman and Littlefield, 2004.

Lasky, Jesse, Jr, *Whatever Happened to Hollywood?* London: W.H. Allen, 1973.

Lejeune, C.A., *Chestnuts in Her Lap*, London: Phoenix House, 1947.

Leppmann, Wolfgang, *Pompeii in Fact and Fiction*, London: Elek, 1968.

Leprohon, Pierre, *The Italian Cinema*, London: Secker and Warburg, 1972.

Leroy, Mervyn, *Take One*, London: W.H. Allen, 1974.

Liversidge, Michael and Edwards, Catharine (eds), *Imagining Rome: British Artists and Rome in the Nineteenth Century*, London: Merrell Holberton, 1996.

Lloyd, Seton, *Foundations in the Dust: The Story of Mesopotamian Exploration*, London: Thames and Hudson, 1980.

Lord, Father Daniel A., *Played by Ear*, Chicago: Loyola University Press, 1956.

McCarthy, Todd, *Howard Hawks: The Grey Fox of Hollywood*, New York: Grove Press, 1997.

McGilligan, Patrick, *Back Story*, Berkeley and London: University of California Press, 1986.

McGilligan, Patrick and Buhle, Paul (eds), *Tender Comrades*, New York: St Martin's Press, 1997.

Macnab, Geoffrey, *J. Arthur Rank and the British Film Industry*, London: Routledge, 1993.

Madsen, Axel, *William Wyler*, New York: Thomas Y. Crowell, 1973.

Maisels, Charles Keith, *The Near East: Archaeology in the 'Cradle of Civilization'*, London: Routledge, 1998.

Mann, Anthony, 'Empire demolition', *Films and Filming* 10 (March 1964), pp. 7–8.

Marton, Andrew with D'Antonio, Joanne, *Andrew Marton*, Metuchen, New Jersey and London: Scarecrow, 1991.

Mason, James, *Before I Forget*, London: Hamish Hamilton, 1981.

Mayer, David, *Playing Out the Empire*, Oxford: Clarendon Press, 1994.

Medved, Michael, *Hollywood vs. America: Popular Culture and the War on Traditional Values*, London: HarperCollins, 1992.

Meisel, Martin, *Realizations*, Princeton: Princeton University Press, 1983.

Morris, Michael, *Madam Valentino*, New York: Abbeville Press, 1991.

Morsberger, Robert E. and Katharine M., *Lew Wallace: Militant Romantic*, New York: McGraw Hill, 1980.

Moseley, Roy, *Evergreen: Victor Saville in His Own Words*, Carbondale and Edwardsville: Southern Illinois University Press, 2000.

Moss, Marilyn Ann, *Giant: George Stevens, a Life on Film*, Madison, Wisconsin: University of Wisconsin Press, 2004.

Munn, Michael, *The Stories Behind the Scenes of the Great Epics*, Watford: Argus Books, 1982.

Nisbet, Gideon, *Ancient Greece in Film and Popular Culture*, Exeter: Bristol Phoenix Press, 2006.

Palmer, Christopher, *The Composer in Hollywood*, London: Marion Boyars, 1993.

Parish, James Robert and Stanke, Don E., *The Glamour Girls*, Carlstadt, New York: Rainbow Books, 1977.

Pascal, Valerie, *The Disciple and his Devil*, London: Michael Joseph, 1971.

Pasinetti, P.M., 'Julius Caesar: the role of the technical adviser', *The Quarterly of Film, Radio and Television* 8 (Winter 1953), pp. 131–8.

Phillips, Sian, *Public Places*, London: Sceptre, 2001.

Read, Jan, *Young Man in Movieland*, Lanham, Maryland: Scarecrow, 2004.

Rhodes, Royal, *The Lion and the Cross: Early Christianity in Victorian Novels*, Columbus, Ohio: Ohio University Press, 1995.

Richards, Jeffrey, *Sir Henry Irving: a Victorian Actor and his World*, London: Hambledon, 2005.

Richardson, Joanna, *Gustave Doré*, London: Cassell, 1980.

Ripley, John, '*Julius Caesar' on Stage in England and America 1599–1973*, Cambridge: Cambridge University Press, 1980.

Robertson, James C., *The Hidden Cinema*, London: Routledge, 1989.

Robertson, James C., *The Casablanca Man: The Cinema of Michael Curtiz*, London: Routledge, 1993.

Robinson, Edward G. with Spigelgass, Leonard, *All My Yesterdays*, New York: Hawthorn Books, 1973.

Robinson, Jay, *The Comeback*, Lincoln, Virginia: Chosen Books, 1979.

Rosendorf, Neal Moses, '"Hollywood in Madrid": American film producers and the Franco regime, 1950–1970', *Historical Journal of Film, Radio and Television* 27 (March 2007), pp. 77–109.

Rozsa, Miklos, *Double Life*, Tunbridge Wells: The Baton Press, 1982.

Rothwell, Kenneth, *Shakespeare on Screen*, Cambridge: Cambridge University Press, 1999.

Russo, Vito, *The Celluloid Closet*, New York: Harper and Row, 1981.

Schary, Dore, *Heyday*, Boston: Little, Brown, 1979.

Schoch, Richard, *Shakespeare's Victorian Stage*, Cambridge: Cambridge University Press, 1998.

Shay, Don, 'Willis O'Brien: creator of the impossible', *Focus on Film* 16 (1973), pp. 18–48.

Smith, Steven C., *A Heart at Fire's Center*, Berkeley and London: University of California Press, 2002.

Solomon, Aubrey, *Twentieth Century-Fox*, Metuchen, New Jersey: Scarecrow, 1980.

Solomon, Jon, *The Ancient World in the Cinema*, New Haven and London: Yale University Press, 2001.

Spoto, Donald, *Otherwise Engaged*, London: Hutchinson, 2007.

Spraos, John, *The Decline of the Cinema*, London: Allen and Unwin, 1962.

Stephens, John Russell, *The Censorship of English Drama 1824–1901*, Cambridge: Cambridge University Press, 1981.

Sternberg, Josef von, *Fun in a Chinese Laundry*, San Francisco: Mercury House, 1988.

Swanson, Vern G., *Sir Lawrence Alma-Tadema*, London: Ash and Grant, 1977.

Tanitch, Robert, *Oscar Wilde on Stage and Screen*, London: Methuen, 1999.

Thomas, Tony, *Ustinov in Focus*, London: Zwemmer, 1971.

Turner, Frank M., *The Greek Heritage in Victorian Britain*, New Haven and London: Yale University Press, 1981.

Ustinov, Peter, *Dear Me*, Harmondsworth: Penguin, 1978.

Vance, Norman, *The Victorians and Ancient Rome*, Oxford: Blackwell, 1997.

Vance, William, *America's Rome*, 2 volumes, New Haven and London: Yale University Press, 1989.

Wagenknecht, Edward and Slide, Anthony, *The Films of D.W. Griffith*, New York: Crown, 1975.

Walker, Alexander, *Vivien*, London: Weidenfeld and Nicolson, 1987.

Wansell, Geoffrey, *Terence Rattigan*, London: Fourth Estate, 1995.

Wentworth, Michael, *James Tissot*, Oxford: Clarendon Press, 1984.

Whitfield, Stephen, *The Culture of the Cold War*, Baltimore: Johns Hopkins University Press, 1996.

Wilcoxon, Henry, with Orrison, Katherine, *Lionheart in Hollywood*, Metuchen, New Jersey and London: Scarecrow, 1991.

Wilding, Michael and Wilcox, Pamela, *Apple Sauce*, London: Allen and Unwin, 1982.

Williams, Tony, *Body and Soul: The Cinematic Vision of Robert Aldrich*, Lanham, Maryland: Scarecrow, 2004.

Winkler, Martin M. (ed.), *Gladiator: Film and History*, Oxford: Blackwell, 2004.

Winkler, Martin M. (ed.), *Troy: from Homer's 'Iliad' to Hollywood Epic*, Oxford: Blackwell, 2007.

Wood, Alan, *Mr Rank*, London: Hodder and Stoughton, 1952.

Wood, Christopher, *Olympian Dreamers*, London: Constable, 1983.

Wood, Michael, *America in the Movies*, London: Secker and Warburg, 1975.

Wood, Michael, *In Search of the Trojan War*, London: BBC Books, 2005.

Wood, Robin, *Howard Hawks*, London: Secker and Warburg, 1968.

Wyke, Maria, *Projecting the Past: Ancient Rome, Cinema and History*, London: Routledge, 1997.

Wyke, Maria and Biddiss, Michael (eds), *The Uses and Abuses of Antiquity*, Bern: Peter Lang, 1999.

Young, B.A., *The Rattigan Version*, London: Hamish Hamilton, 1986.

Young, Freddie, *Seventy Light Years*, London: Faber, 1999.

Zeffirelli, Franco, *Zeffirelli*, London: Weidenfeld and Nicolson, 1986.

Index